THE UNGODLY

DONNER LAKE, CALIFORNIA

THE UNGODLY

A NOVEL OF THE DONNER PARTY

By RICHARD RHODES

STANFORD GENERAL BOOKS
An imprint of Stanford University Press
Stanford, California

Stanford University Press
Stanford, California

Library of Congress Catalog Card Number: 72-95170
Printed in the United States of America on acid-free, archival-quality paper.

The Ungodly was originally published in 1973 by Charterhouse Press.

For John Cushman and Richard Kluger

Virile to risk and find;
kindly withal and a ready help.
Facing the brunt of fate;
indomitable,—unafraid.

This novel was written in part under a grant
from the Kansas City Association of Trusts
and Foundations, for which I here offer my thanks.

Excellent histories of the Donner Party exist. George R. Stewart's *Ordeal by Hunger* and Bernard DeVoto's *The Year of Decision: 1846* are two of the best. The story that follows is not a history. It is a work of fiction, written to other ends.

Yet I have attempted to include, and nowhere to violate, every known historical fact. Names, places, dates, events, letters, diaries and a few speeches are authentic. Because the characters in the story bear real peoples' names, I have taken care to attribute to them only those acts of note that are revealed in, or implied by, the record.

History enlivens what is known, fiction what might have been and still might be. Neither is adequate without the other. Mercifully, both concern matters of the heart.

Richard Rhodes

15 Continued in the afternoon   we crossed great Blue river and camp^d. on the East Bank

This stream affords some rich vallies of cultivateable land and the Bluffs are made of a fine lime rock with some good timber and numerous springs of clear cool water   here I observed the grave of Mrs. Sarak Keys agead 70 yares who departed this life in may last   at her feet stands the stone that gives us this information   This stone shews us that all ages and all sects are found to undertake this long tedious and even dangerous Journy for some unknown object never to be realized even by those the most fortunate and why because the human mind can never be satisfied never at rest allways on the strech for something new some strange novelty

James Clyman's Diary
July 15, 1846

ONE

THE TRAIL

1846

In the year 1846 men took their families west to California and a new life. The families of the Donner party went among them.

George Donner's advertisement for teamsters appeared twice in the *Sangamo Journal* of Springfield, Illinois. Once on March 26 and once on April 12, just three days before the Donners expected to leave.

WESTWARD HO!

For Oregon and California. Who wants to go to California without costing them anything? As many as eight young men, of good character, who can drive an ox team, will be accommodated by gentlemen who will leave this vicinity about the middle of April. Come on Boys. You can have as much land as you want without costing you anything. The Government of California gives large tracts of land to persons who move there. The first suitable persons who apply will be engaged.

George Donner and others.

April 15

Sangamon County, Illinois. Two Germans named Reinhardt and Spitzer signed on. Three local boys, Noah James and Sam Shoemaker and Hiram Miller. An Englishman, John Denton, a gunsmith from Sheffield. George Donner and his brother Jacob figured they could find more help in Independence. George could handle some of the work in the meantime. He was a big man who still at 62 had all his strength. Jacob was 65 and ailing but he'd get along. They were each taking 3 wagons and goodly herds of cattle and kine. They had money. George made $10,000 selling a piece of land he owned in Chicago. He sold one of his farms too and left the others to his grown sons who were staying behind. George was a traveled man. He'd even been to Texas once.

Moving west was nothing new. Most folks had moved before. It was something in the blood. Their pappies had done it. They could do it too. California seemed like a good place to go. Colonel Fremont commended it in his *Report,* just published. The traveler Lansford W. Hastings claimed in his new book *The Emigrant's Guide to Oregon and California* that December in California was as pleasant as May. California needed Americans. Drive the goddamned English out of Oregon and the goddamned Mexicans out of California. God's country and the rightful property of the U.S. of A. But that wasn't the all of it. A man got old just sitting around. The old folks'd had land no white man had ever turned before. Sycamore trees big as barns and deer thick as rich men's droves and corn taller than the cabin. Nothing else but new land was good enough for them and what was good enough for them was damned well good enough for you. In America a man could have just as much as he had guts enough to take and California was there for the taking. He'd better take it, too, before the lawyers and the politicians had time to flock around and peck the life away.

George was working on his third wife. The best catch of

them all. Tamsen Eustis had been her name. She was originally from Newburyport, Massachusetts. She'd been married once to a man named Tully Dozier down in North Carolina where she'd taught school. Bore him 2 children but lost children, husband and all to the cholera within the space of 3 weeks at Christmastime of 1831. She went back to Massachusetts for a time but then she came on out to Illinois to make a home for her brother's motherless children. Not many people anywhere in the States untouched by sickness. Life was precarious at best. That was a big reason for Oregon and California. Tamsen caught George Donner's fancy. She was tiny. Didn't even weigh 100 lb. 45 years old. Dignified as a Senator's wife but she had a twinkle in her eye.

Leaving the homestead brought a few tears to family and friends. It looked like a parade with the 6 wagons and dogs and horses and children and teamsters and loose stock. All the Donner boys came over with their wives to see their fathers off. The oxen didn't act like they were much interested in the journey but the teamsters cracked their bullwhips and started them on. They were only going to Springfield the first day.

With Tamsen and George Donner went

Elitha, 14

Leanna, 12

George Donner's children by his second wife

and

Frances, 6

Georgia, 4

Eliza, 3

children of Tamsen and George.

With Betsy and Jacob Donner went

Solomon Hook, 14

Will Hook, 12

Betsy Donner's children by her first husband

and

George Jr., 9

Mary, 7
Isaac, 5
Sam, 4
Lewis, 3
children of Betsy and Jacob.

Arrived Springfield late afternoon. Distance 2½ miles.

James Frazier Reed and his family were waiting for them. Jim Reed was 46. He also had outfitted 3 wagons for the journey, one of them a giant wagon with a stovepipe sticking out the top and stairs letting down from the sides. He had a bed made up inside for his mother-in-law, Mrs. Sarah Keyes, aged 70 years. The others all set up tents on the Springfield common.

Reed came originally from Ireland. Was said to have the blood of Polish noblemen in him. Neighbors in Illinois named a town after him before he was 25. He'd sold a prosperous cabinet factory to get ready for the California emigration. Asked Senator Stephen A. Douglas to get him commissioned Agent to all the Indians west of the Rocky Mountains but the Little Giant couldn't bring it off. The Governor gave Reed a fine letter of recommendation though.

Reed was a handsome man with a craggy face framed by a well-trimmed beard and curly black hair. He had considerable taste and expected to travel in style. His daughter Patty had named the giant wagon the Pioneer Palace Car. The inside of the Car was lined with cabinets and drawers put in by the men at the factory. Reed stocked whiskey and fine cigars in those compartments, spices and smoked meats and cheese and a store of powder and balls for hunting. He rode a thoroughbred gray, a mare he'd named Glaucus. She was a match for any horse at the Springfield track.

What a crowd on the common. People were itching to move west. Not all that many had gone overland to California yet. The South Pass of the Rockies had been opened up to wagons only 5 years before and the pass through the California mountains only 2. Oregon was the more frequent destination but Lansford Hastings didn't speak well of Oregon. Rained a lot up there. California always had the sun.

Margaret Reed was 32. Small and pretty. She wore her brown hair in braids down her back. Reed had married her a widow. Everyone who knew her liked her for her intelligence and her kindness. She suffered from painful migraines. Mrs. Keyes was her mother. Mrs. Keyes knew she wouldn't live to see California but she thought she might make it to Fort Hall on the other side of the Continental Divide. If the Lord was with her. Her son Caden might be at Fort Hall on his way back from Oregon.

Virginia Reed was 13. She was Margaret Reed's daughter by her first husband, Mr. Backenstoe. Virginia adored her stepfather Reed and took on his name. She rode with him on her pony Billy. She was the only girl in the train to have a mount of her own.

Reed had recruited his teamsters from among the boys at the factory. Milt Elliott had been a foreman and was head teamster now. Walt Herron drove the two regular wagons. Baylis Williams herded the cattle. He was a strange-looking boy, part albino. He couldn't see too well by day but he could see like an owl at night. His sister Eliza came along to cook and do. She was slow-headed and deaf as a post.

Besides Virginia, the Reeds brought their three younger children

Patty, 8

Jimmy, 5

Tommy, 3.

Congressman Lincoln's wife was among those who came over during the evening to say goodbye to the Reeds and the Donners. The Springfield men gave Reed a bottle of brandy and told him to save it for the 4th of July. He was supposed to open it on the trail just at noon and look back toward Springfield. Think of old friends and cherished memories and drink a toast.

April 16

The three families left Springfield for Independence, Missouri, on the old Berlin Road. Patty Reed sang as the wagons rolled out. Gramma Keyes smiled. Patty sang on in a pretty voice. Gramma Keyes first saw the light the same year they got up the Declaration of Independence.

April 17–May 10

Followed the Berlin Road due west from Springfield. Crossed the Mississippi by ferry at Quincy, Illinois. Went down past Hannibal to St. Louis, then up the valley of the Missouri to Independence 6 miles south of the river.

May 11

Independence Mo. May 11th 1846

To Mrs. Poor from Mrs. George Donner.

My dear sister

I commenced writing to you some months ago but the letter was laid aside to be finished the next day & was never touched. A nice sheet of pink letter paper was taken out & has got so much soiled that it cannot be written upon & now in the midst of preparation for starting across the mountains I am seated on the grass in the midst of the tent to say a few words to my dearest only sister. One would suppose that I loved her but little or I should have not neglected her so long, but I have heard from you by Mr. Greenleaf & every month have intended to write. My three daughters are round me one at my side trying to sew, Georgia Anna fixing herself up in an old indiarubber cap & Eliza Poor knocking on my paper & asking me ever so many questions. They often talk to me of Aunty Poor. I can give you no idea of the hurry of the place at this time. It is supposed there will be 7000 wagons start from this place this year. We go to California, to the bay of Francisco. It is a four months trip. We have three waggons furnished with food & clothing &c. drawn by three yoke of oxen each. We take cows along & milk & have some butter though not as much as we would like. I am willing to go & have no doubt it will be an advantage to our children & to us. I came here last evening & start tomorrow morning on the long journey. Wm's family was well when I left Springfield a month ago. He will write to you soon as he finds another home. He says he has received no answer to his last two letters, is about to start to Wisconsin as he considers Illinois unhealthy.

Farewell, my sister, you shall hear from me as soon as I have an opportunity. Love to Mr. Poor, the children & all friends. Farewell.

T. E. Donner

Reed and the Donners didn't see any point in hanging around Independence in the mud the spring rains churned up. Mexicans and Indians roamed the streets. Santa Fe traders. Ox teams sold for $21.67 a yoke green broke just barely. The saloons were full of drunks and pissers. The main party for Oregon and California was already gone. The later you started the worse the grass.

George Donner took on a man named Antoine to herd the loose cattle.

May 12

The Donners and Reeds started for California in the early morning. They followed the Santa Fe trail southwest onto the Blue prairie. Rattlesnake-master and coneflower grew young and succulent. The lupine was in bloom and Indian paintbrush. The main party was said to be camped several days ahead waiting for the grass to get up.

May 13

Prairie travel. 9 wagons. A drenching thunderstorm.

May 14

Prairie travel.

May 15

Prairie travel. Margaret Reed suffered one of her frequent migraines.

May 16

Prairie travel.

May 17

Sunday. Traveled nonetheless.

May 18

Prairie travel.

May 19

The Donners and Reeds pulled up to the main party of Oregon and California emigrants encamped on Soldier's Creek, a tributary of the Kansas River. Colonel William H. "Owl" Russell captained the main party. It included former Governor Lilburn Boggs of Missouri, the man who had driven the Mormons out of Missouri just the year before. Edwin Bryant, a man with medical training much in demand among the wagons. Jesse Quinn Thornton, a journalist for Horace Greeley bound for Oregon with his invalid wife. A number of foreigners, mostly from Germany and Ireland.

The men got together after supper and unanimously voted the Donners and the Reeds into the train. Jim Reed delivered the acceptance speech for them all.

May 20

A drenching thunderstorm began at the nooning and forced an early encampment. Indians followed the train all day. Came begging into camp.

Distance 8 miles.

May 21

A glorious sunrise through clouds scudding low on the horizon. The train was blocked by a deep ravine. The men lowered the wagons into it and out of it with ropes. Another storm blew over in the afternoon. Lightning and thunder but little rain. Target-shooting after supper.

May 22

Prairie travel.

May 23

Prairie travel.

May 24

Sunday. The Reverend Mr. Cornwall protested travel on the Sabbath. Jesse Thornton argued that the oxen would be better for a day of rest. The others disagreed.

Prairie travel.

May 25

A storm in midafternoon but the people anticipated it and had their tents up. A flood of rain and after the rain a matchless rainbow reaching unbroken from the southern to the northern horizon. Mercury at sunset 73° with an east wind.

May 26

The party reached the bluff overlooking the junction of the Kansas and the Big Blue and found the Blue up 20 feet from spring flooding. The water at the ford ran 200 yards wide. No way to wheel across. The men voted to construct a raft. Thunderstorm at night.

May 27

The Big Blue ran so turbulent still that Colonel Russell postponed work on the raft.

Washing day in camp. Two men found a bee tree along the river and brought three buckets of wild honey into camp. Edwin Bryant picked wild peas and distributed them for canning.

Mrs. Keyes failing. Unable to speak.

Singing in camp. Pat Dolan, a bachelor Irishman traveling with the Patrick Breen family, got out his fiddle after supper and played some lively tunes.

May 28

River fell 15 feet and Russell ordered work resumed on the raft.

May 29

Mrs. Keyes died during the night with her daughter and her son-in-law and the 2 girls at her side. Everyone stopped work for the day in tribute. Some of the men made a cottonwood coffin and Margaret Reed and Tamsen Donner laid Mrs. Keyes in it gently in her best dress. She looked frail, her hair white as the tufts of cottonwood seed blown on the spring wind. Jim Smith and Walt Herron dug a grave at the foot of a majestic oak beside the trail. At 2 o'clock nearly everyone joined the funeral procession and the men carried the coffin to the grave. The Reverend Mr. Cornwall offered a prayer and after everyone sang a hymn he delivered the funeral sermon. He said Mrs. Keyes' death should remind them that they were put on earth to seek a better world beyond. Not Oregon or California he said but Paradise. After the sermon the men closed the grave and covered it carefully with the thick prairie sod. Wildflowers still bloomed from the sod. The women added more.

The Englishman John Denton had cut a stone at Jim Reed's request. The men set the stone securely in place at the head of the grave.

> Mrs. Sarah Keyes
> DIED
> May 29, 1846
> *Aged* 70

May 30

Finished the raft, two cottonwood canoes hooked together with planks. They christened her the *Blue River Rover*. Men on horseback fixed lines on the near shore and swam across and fixed them on the far shore. She was a jolly craft. Ferried 9 wagons across the river before dark. Nearly lost one though.

May 31

Sunday. Men in the water all day ferrying the wagons over the Big Blue. Made some of them sick. They were about ready to listen to the Reverend Mr. Cornwall. 2 men took to fighting, fists first but then they drew knives and their friends had to break them up. Mercury at sunset 44°. They got all the wagons across by 9 P.M.

Distance 1 mile.

June 1

The same men that fought yesterday fought again today. They disagreed about the ownership of a wagon and team. One owned the oxen, the other owned the wagon. The one that owned the oxen claimed the right to remove them from the wagon since he and its owner couldn't get along. The one that owned the wagon said the oxen were *inalienable*.

A dead ox lying near the trail, left behind by one of the wagons ahead. Near the camp the graves of 2 children only 4 days buried.

Distance 14 miles.

June 2

The arguing got out of hand so the leaders called a camp meeting first thing in the morning. Since the men who were fighting over the oxen and wagon were going to Oregon, Colonel Russell proposed that all the Oregon people separate from the main train and form a train of their own. Then they could go on as they wanted and deal with the men however they thought best. The Oregon people took the challenge in good spirits and the motion carried by a unanimous vote.

Not everyone was happy to see the parties separate. Many

of the women cried. Some of the young girls too, seeing their beaux going away.

Distance 12 miles.

June 3

A cold day, wind from the northeast.

A wagon turned over today. It belonged to a man named Lewis Keseberg. A tall blond German. Keseberg's oxen took it too sharp up a bluff and it spilled. Keseberg yelled. His wife was thrown into the creek with their little girl. Keseberg ignored the wagon itself and jumped down to help his wife. She was obviously in a delicate condition and he may have had a mind to that. The girl scrambled out of the creek. Keseberg helped his wife up. She looked to be all right if very shaken. Her silk dress was covered with mud. Most of the supplies had spilled out of the wagon and were covered with mud. The tongue broke too which was a good thing or the oxen would have been thrown over into the creek and might have broken their legs. Keseberg found occasion to swear in 2 or 3 languages at his teamster Karl Burger, who was on Keseberg's second wagon and had nothing to do with the accident. The whole family stayed behind to make a new wagon tongue and clean up the supplies.

Distance, except for the Kesebergs, 18 miles.

June 4

Antelope in large numbers now but fleet as the wind. The men chased them until their horses were exhausted. The antelope rewarded them from time to time by stopping and resting and waiting for them to catch up. A man brought a doe into camp, the first large game so far. All the hunters were having buffalo dreams but none were yet seen.

The Kesebergs caught up late in the evening.

Distance 22 miles.

June 5

Prairie travel.

Distance 21 miles.

June 6

Illness in camp. Chills, fever and diarrhea. Probably adjustment to the water and the wet weather. The leaders decided to stop corraling the oxen now that the train neared buffalo country. With buffalo plentiful it was said that the Indians wouldn't bother to steal the less appetizing oxen. The party still corraled the horses however.

Distance 20 miles.

June 7

The party left the Little Blue to cross to the Platte River. The drive was said to be dry but late in the afternoon Colonel Russell reported the discovery of a chain of pools of good water left over from the rains.

An axletree broke on one of Edwin Bryant's wagons. Bryant allowed the rest of the train to go by and then sought out William Eddy, a carriagemaker from Belleville, Illinois, to fit a new axletree he had brought along from Independence. Eddy was a man of average height but stocky and strong. Bryant had the necessary tools and the carriagemaker made quick work of the assignment. The wagon rolled toward camp before sunset. Eddy was bound for California with his wife Eleanor and their 2 young children, a boy and a baby girl. Seemed to be reliable.

Distance 16 miles.

June 8

The party reached the bluffs above the Platte or Nebraska River at 3 in the afternoon. Got to the river itself an hour later. They camped in the river bottoms opposite the Grand Island, which ran up and down the river out of sight in both directions.

Distance 25 miles.

June 9

The train traveled up the Platte River bottoms on the river's south shore. The river in places ran more than a mile wide but so shallow that a man could walk across it without ever getting water above his knees. The wagons rolled through thick dust now. The dust had enough alkali in it to burn the eyes.

Up the Platte River bending like a great bow around from the Rocky Mountains. Up the river toward the Continental Divide.

Distance 18 miles.

June 10

Travel up the Platte. The train passed a prairie dog village with a good 500 mounds. The men shot some of the animals for supper. Water bad and mosquitoes worse.

Distance 18 miles.

June 11

The train encountered a party of mountain men attempting to bring out a shipment of hides and furs on bull boats. They were hauling the boats over sandbars more often than they were floating them in the shallow river. They said they'd come from Fort Bernard, a little trading post a few miles below Fort Laramie on the Laramie River near the North Platte. They needed flour, bacon, sugar and coffee. Some of the people traded with them for buffalo robes at the rate of sugar and coffee @$1/lb, flour @50¢/lb and buffalo robes @$3 each.

Distance 17 miles.

June 12

The Donners and the Reeds left Independence 1 month ago this day. Jim Reed shot an elk. Travel up the Platte. Good spirits in camp. Mercury at sunrise 50°, sunset 65°.

Distance 16 miles.

June 13

Governor Boggs and Mr. Grayson shot the first 2 buffalo taken by the train, 2 choice cows. Everyone crowded round and congratulated the men. For their part, they generously shared the meat.

The only fuel available for cooking since coming upon the Platte was the dried manure of the buffalo, which the women and children collected in gunny sacks. To make a fire the men cut up a slab of sod about 1 foot wide, 3 feet long and 8 inches deep. The women put dry grass and the buffalo "chips" into the trench and kindled them. After awhile the chips burned with an almost smokeless flame and the women could set their skillets on the trench supported by the sides or sink their Dutch ovens directly into the coals. No skillets or ovens for the buffalo meat however. Those who received portions broiled them on sticks directly in the flames.

Distance 18 miles.

June 14

Sunday. Edwin Bryant was called forward to attend to a boy in another train who had broken his leg. When he got to the boy, Bryant was told that the break had occurred 9 days previous. The wound was crawling with maggots and gangrene had set in. Bryant told the mother he could do nothing for the boy but she wouldn't listen. A halfbreed Frenchman in the party claimed he'd been a hospital orderly and the mother agreed to let him amputate the leg. He commenced to cut the boy's leg off at the calf. The boy was awake but didn't cry out. Someone held a cloth with camphor in it to his nose. The halfbreed drew pus from his incision and decided to amputate the leg higher up. The child was obviously dying. Frenchie was too busy to notice. He looped a cord around the leg and drew it so tight it cut into the flesh. He circled the leg with his butcher knife cutting down to the bone. Then he sawed through the bone. The boy died under the saw. They laid his severed leg to rest beside him.

There was a wedding that night in the same company at the same time as the funeral. In another company a baby was born.

Distance 20 miles.

June 15

Travel up the Platte. Colonel Russell took sick with chills and fever. He said it was an old malaria. Some of the boys were out hunting buffalo. Jim Reed made his first kill today and brought back enough meat to feed most of the camp.
Distance 18 miles.

June 16

South Fork of the Nebraska,
Ten Miles from the Crossings.
Tuesday, June 16, 1846

To Jas. W. Keys, Esq. from James F. Reed

Today, at nooning, there passed, going to the States, seven men from Oregon, who went out last year. One of them was well acquainted with Messrs. Ide, and Caden Keys—the latter of whom he says went to California. They met the advanced Oregon caravan about 150 miles west of Ft. Larimere, and counted in all for California and Oregon (excepting ours) four hundred and seventy-eight waggons. There is in our train 40 waggons, which makes 518 in all; and there is said to be twenty yet behind.

Tomorrow we cross the river, and by our reckoning will be 200 miles from Fort Larimere, where we intend to stop and repair our waggon wheels; they are nearly all loose and I am afraid we will have to stop sooner if there can be found wood suitable to heat the tires. There is no wood here, and our women and children are now out gathering "Buffalo chips" to burn in order to do the cooking. These "chips" burn well.

So far as I am concerned, my family affairs go on smoothly, and I have nothing to do but hunt, which I have done with great success. My first appearance on the wilds of the Nebraska as a hunter, was on the 12 inst., when I returned to camp with a splendid two year old Elk, the first and only one killed by the caravan as yet. I picked the Elk I killed, out of eight of the largest I

ever beheld, and I do really believe there was one in the
gang as large as the horse I rode. We have had two Buffalo killed. The men that killed them are considered the
best buffalo hunters on the road—perfect ''stars.''
Knowing that Glaucus could beat any horse on the
Nebraska, I came to the conclusion that as far as buffalo killing was concerned, I could beat them. Accord-
ingly yesterday I thought to try my luck. The old buffalo hunters and as many others as they would permit
to be in their company, having left the camp for a hunt,
Hiram Miller, myself and two others, after due preparation, took up the line of march. Before we left, every
thing in camp was talking that Mr. so and so, had
gone hunting, and we would have some choice buffalo
meat. No one thought or spoke of the two Sucker hunters, and none but the two asked to go with us. Going
one or two miles west of the old hunters on the bluffs,
and after riding about four miles, we saw a large herd
of buffalo bulls. I went for choice young meat, which is
the hardest to get, being fleeter and better wind. On we
went towards them as coolly and calmly as the nature
of the case would permit. And now, as perfectly green
as I was I had to compete with old experienced hunters,
and remove the stars from their brows, which was my
greatest ambition, and in order too, that they might see
that a Sucker had the best horse in the company, and
the best and most daring horseman in the caravan.
Closing upon a gang of ten or twelve bulls, the word
was given, and I was soon in their midst, but among
them there was none young enough for my taste to
shoot, and upon seeing a drove on my right I dashed
among them with Craddock's pistol in hand—(a fine
instrument for Buffalo hunters on the plains)—selected
my victim and brought him tumbling to the ground,
leaving my companion far behind. Advancing a little
further, the plains appeared to be one living, moving
mass of bulls, cows and calves. The latter took my eye,

and I again put spur to Glaucus and soon found myself among them, and for the time being defied by the
bulls, who protected the cows and calves. Now I thought
the time had arrived to make one desperate effort,
which I did by reining short up and dashing into them
at right angles. With me it was an exciting time, being
in the midst of a herd of upwards of a hundred head of
buffalo alone, entirely out of sight of my companions.
At last I succeeded in separating a calf from the drove,
but soon there accompanied him three large bulls, and
in a few minutes I separated two of them. Now having
a bull that would weigh about 1200 lbs., and a fine large
calf at full speed, I endeavored to part the calf from
the bull without giving him Paddy's hint, but could
not accomplish it. When I would rein to the right where
the calf was, the bull would immediately put himself
between us. Finding I could not separate on decent
terms, I gave him one of Craddock's which sent him
reeling. And now for the calf without pistol being
loaded. Time now was important—and I had to run up
and down hill at full speed loading one of my pistols.
At last I loaded, and soon the chase ended. Now I had
two dead and a third mortally wounded and dying.
After I had disposed of my calf I rode to a small mound
a short distance off to see if Hiram and the others
were in sight. I sat down, and while sitting I counted
597 buffalo within sight. After a while Miller and one
of the others came up. We then got some water from
a pond near by, which was thick with mud from the
buffaloes tramping in it. Resting awhile the boys then
wanted to kill a buffalo themselves. I pointed out to
them a few old bulls about a mile distant. It was understood that I was not to join in the chase, and after
accompanying the boys to the heights where I could
witness the sport, they put out at full speed. They
soon singled out a large bull, and I do not recollect of
ever having laughed more than I did at the hunt the

boys made. Their horses would chase well at a proper distance from the bull. As they approached he would come to a stand and turn for battle. The horses would then come to a halt, at a distance between the boys and the buffalo of about 40 yards. They would thus fire away at him, but to no effect. Seeing that they were getting tired of the sport and the bull again going away, I rode up and got permission to stop him if I could. I put spurs to Glaucus and after him I went at full speed. As I approached the bull turned around to the charge. Falling back and dashing towards him with a continued yell at the top of my lungs I got near enough to let drive one of my pistols. The ball took effect, having entered behind the shoulders and lodged in his lungs. I turned in my saddle as soon as I could to see if he had pursued me, as is often the case after being wounded. He was standing nearly in the place where he received the shot, bleeding at the nostrils, and in a few seconds dropped dead. I alighted and looped my bridle over one of his horns. This Glaucus objected to a little, but a few gentle words with a pat of my hand she stood quiet and smelled him until the boys came up. Their horses could not be got near him. Having rested, we commenced returning to the place where I killed the last calf. A short distance off we saw another drove of calves. Again the chase was renewed, and soon I laid out another fine calf upon the plains. Securing as much of the meat of the calves as we could carry, we took up the line of march for the camp, leaving the balance for the wolves, which are very numerous. An hour or two's ride found us safely among our friends, the acknowledged hero of the day, and the most successful buffalo hunter on the route. Glaucus was closely examined by many today, and pronounced the finest nag in the caravan. Mrs. R. will accompany me in my next buffalo hunt, which is to come off in a few days.

The face of the country here is very hilly, although it has the name of "plains." The weather rather warm—thermometer ranging in the middle of the day at about 90, and at night 45.

The Oregon people tell me that they have made their claims at the head of Puget Sound, and say that the late exploration has made the northeast, or British side of the Columbia, far superior to the Willamette valley, in quality and extent of territory.

Our teams are getting on fine so far. Most of the emigrants ahead have reduced their teams. The grass is much better this year throughout the whole route than the last.

Respectfully your brother,
James F. Reed

Near the Junction of the North
and South Platte, June 16, 1846

To the Editor of the Springfield *Journal* from Mrs. George Donner
My Old Friend,
We are now on the Platte, two hundred miles from Fort Laramie. Our journey so far has been pleasant, the roads have been good, and food plentiful. The water for part of the way has been indifferent, but at no time have our cattle suffered for it. Wood is now very scarce, but "buffalo chips" are excellent; they kindle quickly and retain heat surprisingly. We had this morning buffalo steaks broiled upon them that had the same flavor they would have had upon hickory coals.

We feel no fear of Indians, our cattle graze quietly around the encampment unmolested.

Two or three men will go hunting twenty miles from camp; and last night two of our men lay out in the wilderness rather than ride their horses after a hard chase.

Indeed, if I do not experience far worse than I have yet done, I shall say the trouble is all in getting started. Our wagons have not needed much repair, and I can not yet tell in what respects they could be improved. Certain it is, they can not be too strong. Our preparations for the journey might have been in some respects bettered.

Bread has been the principal article of food in our camp. We laid in 150 pounds of flour and 75 pounds of meat for each individual, and I fear bread will be scarce. Meat is abundant. Rice and beans are good articles on the road; cornmeal, too, is acceptable. Linsey dresses are the most suitable for children. Indeed, if I had one, it would be acceptable. There is so cool a breeze at all times on the plains that the sun does not feel so hot as one would suppose.

We are now four hundred and fifty miles from Independence. Our route at first was rough, and through a timbered country, which appeared to be fertile. After striking the prairie, we found a first-rate road, and the only difficulty we have had, has been in crossing the creeks. In that, however, there has been no danger.

I never could have believed we could have traveled so far with so little difficulty. The prairie between the Blue and the Platte rivers is beautiful beyond description. Never have I seen so varied a country, so suitable for cultivation. Everything was new and pleasing; the Indians frequently come to see us, and the chiefs of a tribe breakfasted at our tent this morning. All are so friendly that I can not help feeling sympathy and friendship for them. But on one sheet what can I say?

Since we have been on the Platte, we have had the river on one side and the ever varying mounds on the other, and have traveled through the bottom lands from one to two miles wide, with little or no timber. The soil is sandy, and last year, on account of the dry season, the emigrants found grass here scarce. Our cattle are in good order, and when proper care has been taken, none have been lost. Our milch cows have been of great service, indeed. They have been of more advantage than our meat. We have plenty of butter and milk.

We are commanded by Captain Russell, an amiable man. George Donner is himself yet. He crows in the morning and shouts out, "Chain up, boys—chain up," with as much authority as though he was "something in particular." John Denton is still with us. We find him useful in the camp. Hiram Miller and Noah James are in good health and doing well. We have of the best people in our company, and some, too, that are not so good.

Buffalo show themselves frequently.

We have found the wild tulip, the primrose, the lupine, the eardrop, the larkspur, and creeping hollyhock, and a beautiful flower resembling the bloom of the beech tree, but in bunches as large as a small sugarloaf, and of every variety of shade, to red and green.

I botanize, and read some, but cook "heaps" more. There are four hundred and twenty wagons, as far as we have heard, on the road between here and Oregon and California.

Give our love to all inquiring friends. God bless them.

Yours, truly,

Mrs. George Donner

Distance 17 miles.

June 17

Wagons crossed the South Platte at the lower crossing. All made it safely across. The herd cattle didn't much want to go. Little ones jolly in the splashing after the afternoon heat. Water on the river rising fast. With the crossing the people in the train truly felt started on their way to California.

Distance 17 miles.

June 18

Trail followed the north bank of the South Platte. Angry arguments in camp over whose turn it was to camp nearer the river. Some claimed the rotation related to the directions north and south and not to the location of the river. They'd camped on the north side of the circular corral (nearer the river before crossing it) the night before and asserted it was now their turn to camp on the south side of the corral (still nearer the river now that it had been forded). The arguments all settled down around Owl Russell's head and at last he blew and shouted that he had a fever and tendered his resignation. The other officers resigned too, Mr. Kirkendall, Mr. George Donner, Mr. Jacob and Mr. West.

Mr. West was appointed temporary captain by a voice vote of the assembled.

Distance 17 miles.

June 19

The train made the dry drive 22 miles across from the South Platte to the North Platte over rolling prairie blue with lupine.

The German, Keseberg, walked off during the nooning and came back with a buffalo robe. When the men asked him where he got it he said he'd taken it off a dead Indian. The Indians in the region wrapped their dead in buffalo robes and laid them out on scaffolds to dry for a year or more before burial. They were of the fierce Sioux tribe and dangerous to the train.

The men found James Reed. He listened to the tale and went over and told Keseberg to take the robe back before it got the entire party in trouble. Keseberg held out against Reed but Reed had the men behind him and at length prevailed.

The train hauled up a bluff and then down Ash Hollow, so named for the ash trees that grow there. Down to the bottoms of the North Platte in the late afternoon. Found a spring of pure cold water in the dry ravine, also a small log cabin used by emigrants to post letters and notices. Interesting reading.

In camp that night Reed got feeling going against Keseberg and the men voted to banish the German from the train. They told him to pitch his tents somewhere else. They said if he waited he could join up with the wagons supposed to be a few days behind. He refused to answer them but took his wagons out of the corral.

Distance 22 miles.

June 20

Toiling up the valley of the North Platte.

June 21

Sunday. No more thought of stopping for the Sabbath. Everyone was concerned to get to Fort Laramie before the tires fell off.

June 22

Approached Chimney Rock, an unusual formation shaped like an inverted funnel standing isolated on a barren plain. Beyond it stood Courthouse Rock. It looked like an ancient ruin. Remarkable regularity for a natural formation but in this dry region many of the bluffs threw back images borrowed from ancient architecture to tease the civilized eye.

June 23

The dust was alkaline and terrible. It caused the eyes to suppurate. A few of the people had thought to buy goggles in Independence and wore them all day. Many used salves around the eyes. All were coated with dust from head to toe. They might have just come from sacking at a flour mill except that flour would have been bliss after the bitter dust.

June 24

Hauled up through Scott's Bluff. It was named for a man

left there for dead by his companions. He crawled far enough away to convict them of fatal dereliction. Fantastic forms in the badlands around.

Keseberg quietly rejoined the train. He followed along behind for a few days after his banishment and then started coming into camp at night. Nobody wanted his avarice taken out on his wife. She was due to deliver any day.

June 25

Civilization approached. Will Eddy said it had better because the wagonwheels needed fixing.

June 26

Forded the Laramie River and camped at little Fort Bernard. The Laramie was named after a trapper, Jacques La Ramie, who built a cabin where Fort Bernard now stood. Had his throat cut by the Sioux. Bernard was just a two-room log cabin chinked with mud. Plenty of Sioux camped around it but nothing like the number said to be camped at Laramie.

Owl Russell and some of the boys got drunk with Richard, the Fort Bernard *bourgeois*. Said they were using up their whiskey to lighten the load on their oxen. A buckskinned gentleman from Boston named Francis Parkman visited the fort. Russell clamped onto his fringes and blew clouds of tales about how he'd been deposed as captain of the train.

Moved on to Fort Laramie. Governor Boggs had taken command of the train some days previous, by general consent.

June 27

Thousands of Sioux at Fort Laramie, invited there by the American Fur Company to trade. A tall sturdy tribe. Graceful belles in creamy buckskin with open faces and small lovely feet. They sprawled when they were drunk however. The American Fur Company owned the fort.

Owl Russell, Edwin Bryant and several other unattached men traded their wagons for mules and mounts and went on for California on horseback after a pitiful morning learning to pack the mules.

A mountain man by the name of James Clyman passed Russell and Bryant on the trail and came into camp in the midafternoon. He turned out to be a friend of Jim Reed's. Fought beside Reed in the Black Hawk War. He'd traveled for years all over the West. Boggs said he was one of the men who discovered the South Pass through the Rocky Mountains.

Clyman had just come from California with Lansford Hastings. He'd left Hastings back at Fort Bridger on the other side of the Continental Divide. He didn't have one good word for Hasting's "Cut-off" that many had been talking about all winter and spring.

Hastings described the Cut-off in his book. Jacob Donner had a copy. Hastings said

The most direct route for the California emigrants, would be to leave the Oregon route, about two hundred miles east from Fort Hall; thence bearing west southwest, to the Salt lake; and thence continuing down to the bay of St. Francisco.

The route would save the California people several hundred miles of trail but Clyman said it was too dangerous. Reed asked him how he knew and he said he'd just come across it on horseback and he'd only barely made it through. Reed said if Clyman could get through then so could he. Clyman disagreed.

—Take the regular wagon track said Clyman and never leave it. It's barely possible to get through if you follow it and it may be impossible if you don't.

—There's a nearer route said Reed and it's of no use to take so much of a roundabout course.

Clyman told Reed he'd always known him to be a stubborn man but he'd never thought he was foolhardy. Reed said he didn't mean to question Clyman's judgment but he couldn't imagine a man like Hastings signing his name to a book that was full of misinformation. Clyman said Hastings had never traveled his Cut-off before he wrote about it.

—Hell, he come over it the first time just last month with me.

Reed looked at Clyman as if he were lying and Clyman shrugged.

—It's true Reed. I ain't makin it up.

—Okay Clyman said Reed I heard you but I'll wait to talk to Hastings before I make up my mind.

—Bull said Clyman you've already got your mind made up.

They went on that way through the evening. The Donners sided with Reed and Clyman finally gave up arguing. He convinced Governor Boggs to try for Oregon, however. The different parties wouldn't have to separate until after they got over the Divide.

June 28

Bourdeau, the *bourgeois* at Fort Laramie, warned Boggs that the Sioux were on the warpath and didn't want the white-tops around. He said the chiefs would give them safe conduct if they would leave immediately. No one wanted to mess with the Sioux. Their tents covered the plain around the Fort. Looked like shocks of corn crowded in a winter field. They had thousands of horses that had eaten down the grass all over the plain. They could put 5 arrows into a target in the time it took a white man to get powder and ball loaded into his gun.

The wagons pulled out before noon and rolled past the fort. People looking down by the river could see the Sioux dead spread out on scaffolds all over the place.

In the late afternoon a crowd of Sioux warriors rode up behind the train. There must have been 300 of them all on horseback and fiercely painted. The women leaned to panic but Governor Boggs told everyone to hold steady. Instead of causing trouble the warriors rode in two lines on either side of the wagons and turned the lines in to face the wagons and sat at ease. They had green twigs in their mouths and as the wagons rolled by none too slowly they cast the twigs on the ground in a peace offering. It looked as if they feared the train would give up going to California and take the side of the Crows, the Sioux's intended opponents in the war to come.

June 29

Travel up the Platte.

June 30

Travel up the Platte. Mrs. Keseberg was delivered of a baby boy during the night. Keseberg named the child Lewis Sutter. Some speculated the German knew the famous Colonel of the California fort but it was just as likely he had the fort in mind as a goal and stuck the child with the name the way some men stick their pocket with a rabbit's foot.

July 1

Argument today among the Murphy contingent. The widow Murphy piloted one of the largest families in the train. Besides her 5 dependent children she traveled with her 2 sons-in-law, Bill Foster and his wife Sarah and Bill Pike and his wife Harriet. The Fosters had 1 child, the Pikes 2. All told, the Murphys totaled 13 with 2 men and a 15-year-old boy, John Landrum Murphy, among them. Seemed to be decent folks. A little coarse. Came out from Missouri and before then from Tennessee.

Travel up the Platte.

July 2

Edwin Bryant rode back today from the mule train he and Owl Russell drove ahead. One of his bachelors had let himself get spooked by Jim Clyman's evil reports of California and left the mule train to join an Oregon party further up the trail. That only left 5 men in the mule train and Bryant didn't think 5 men was enough. He talked to the single men and eventually swayed George Donner's teamster Hiram Miller. George Donner sold Miller one of his saddle horses. Bryant helped to foot the bill. Then Miller rode on ahead to join the mule train. Bryant agreed to hold up his train long enough for both parties to celebrate the Day of Independence together.

July 3

Travel up the Platte.

July 4

Celebrated the 4th of July on Beaver Creek. Blasted awake at dawn by the trumpet playing an off-key rendition of "Star-Spangled Banner." After breakfast and morning duties the men got some trunks together and Owl Russell climbed up and delivered himself of a long oration on the subject of Manifest Destiny. Said this whole vast land from ocean to ocean ought by rights to belong to Americans. Said the people going to California were traveling according to God's Divine Plan. Ought to be some special credit in that but it doesn't stop the alkali dust from smarting the eyes and the alkali water from sickening the oxen.

At noon Jim Reed shared his Springfield brandy and Mrs. Reed served lemonade. The men shot off their guns in lieu of fireworks at intervals throughout the day. Pat Breen and his family celebrated as enthusiastically as any. Breen came from Keokuk, Iowa. Had only recently gotten his U.S. citizenship. Had lived in Keokuk some time before deciding for California. He was a dark, thin man with a spindly voice. His wife Peggy was plain as a mud fence. Big and rawboned. The Germans stayed discreetly in the background. America had been 70 years a nation. When Jim Reed said that, Milt Elliott grinned and said may she be a nation 700 years more.

July 5

Heavy heads in the morning but the train left in good time. Travel up the Platte.

July 6

Travel up the Platte. The people were leaving the buffalo country behind. The beasts would be devoutly missed. Some of the old trappers at Fort Laramie had said they could live out their lives on buffalo alone and never know a day of sickness.

July 7

Travel up the Platte. It was becoming a more constricted and clearer stream.

July 8

The river reached its northernmost point and curved southwest. The point was 3 miles due north of a long, flat-topped mountain that ran east and west instead of north and south. The people were weary of the Platte. It seemed to run on forever through countryside of no special distinction.

July 9

A difficult route through low hills to the west of the flat-topped mountain.

July 10

Near the end of the day's march the train crossed to the Sweetwater River, a clear mountain stream that flowed down from near the Continental Divide at South Pass. Everyone was cheered to leave the Platte, Nature's dullest river. The water tasted a damned sight better in the new river too.

July 11

Followed along the Sweetwater. The men brought the ladies saleratus for biscuit-making spooned up from the bed of a dry lake. The sage smelled like camphor. After awhile the smell got hard to take.

July 12

The train nooned at Independence Rock, a dome of red granite protruding up isolated on the plain. Thousands of travelers had carved and painted their names on the rock. It seemed a hotel register of the western emigration. Jim Reed found time to carve his name and John Denton and many of the boys. The train halted for the nooning on the sandy ground beyond the rock just this side of a ford of the Sweetwater. Before dinner was over a lone rider came into camp with a letter from Lansford Hastings addressed "From the Headwaters of the Sweetwater." The letter offered Hastings' services as a guide across his Cut-off. Reed said that did it he was going the Cut-off. George Donner agreed. Some of the others said they'd wait and talk to the forward emigrants.

The lone rider was a man from Oregon named Truman Bonney. He agreed to carry back any letters the people had. Virginia Reed gave him a letter she had been chewing away on since the starting of the journey.

Independence rock Julyth 12 1846

To Mary C. Keyes from Virginia E. B. Reed

My Dear Couzin I take this oppertuny to Write to you to let you know that I am well at present and hope that you are well. We have all had good health—we came to the Blue—the water was so hye we had to stay there 4 days—in the mean time gramma died, she became spechless the day before she died. We buried her verry decent We made a nete coffin and buried her under a tree we had a head stone and had her name cutonit and the date and yere verry nice and at the head of the grave was a tree we cut some letters on it the young men soded it all ofer and put Flores on it We missed her verry much every time we come into the Wagon we look at the bed for her. We have come throw severel tribes of Indians the Kaw Indians the soux the shawnies, at the Kaw viliage paw counted 250 Indians We diden see no Indians from the time we lefe the Kaw viliage till we come to fort Laramy the soux Indians are going to War with the crows we have to pass throw ther Fiting ground, the Soux Indians are the pretest drest Indians thare is, paw goes bufalo hunting most every day and kils 2 or 3 buffalo every day paw shot an elk some of our compian saw a grisly bear We have the thermometer 102°—average for the last 6 days We celebrated the 4 of July on Plat at Bever crik, severel of the gentmen in Springfield gave paw a botel of licker and said it shoulden be opend till the 4 of July and paw was to look to the east and drink it and thay was to look to the West and drink it at 12 o clock paw treted the compiany and we all had some lemminade, maw and paw is Well and sends their best love to you all. I send my best love to you all. We have hard from uncle Cad severl times he went to california and now is gone to oregon he is well. I am going to send this letter by a man coming from oregon by hisself. He is going to take his family to Oregon We are all doing well and in hye sperits so I must close your leter, you are for ever my affectionate couzen

Virginia E. B. Reed

In the afternoon the train passed to the south of Devil's Gate, an extraordinary rock formation. A cleft in a foothill of the Sweetwater Mountains only about 30 feet wide but 150 feet or more high. The Sweetwater ran right through it with its water whitened into rapids on the gravel bed. Huge boulders lay in the stream of the river as if flung down by a giant hand. The Devil could have made such a rare formation in that barren land. Many of the men rode through it though the trail went around the hill. Keseberg told another German in the party, Mr. Wolfinger, that he felt the chill of the mountains in the shadows inside the Gate despite the excessive heat of the day.

July 13

Toiled up the Sweetwater. Except for the grassy margins of the river the land was dry and desolate. The oxen suffered from a shortage of grass. Earlier parties had cropped it close. Sometimes the animals sickened from drinking alkali water. The remedy was to dose them with a mass of tallow or other grease shoved down their unwilling throats with a stick. If they survived the treatment they usually got well.

July 14

The nights became colder as the train struggled ever upward toward the Continental Divide. By day the heat was unmitigated. A study in harsh contrasts in a harsh land. The Sweetwater no longer seemed a pleasant river but only another intolerably long pull. The men counted the days and found themselves far behind the best time recorded in the guidebooks.

July 15

The train encountered on this day a slough of grass-covered mud that proved to shelter a thick layer of ice. Jim Reed, his black beard never looking nobler despite the clinging dust of the trail, contrived to chip out some of the July ice and make himself and his friends a round of cold drinks.

July 16

Toiled up the Sweetwater. Some of the oxen died. Some of the people suffered from severe headaches. Boggs named the condition mountain fever and said it was caused by the thinner air of those altitudes.

July 17

The train passed an oil spring that oozed a black, pitch-like oil onto a slough. It stank of sulfur.

July 18

The train left the Sweetwater in the morning and toiled up the broad divide of barren land called the South Pass. The people seemed confused in a mood of elation mixed with dread. Elation that they had achieved nearly half their journey. Dread that they had somewhat more than half their journey yet to go. The season was late and more than once in the preceding days they had waked to frost and a pane of ice on the water buckets. A storm blew up as they hauled up the South Pass and a cold rain fell to increase their discomfort. The snow billowed fog-like clouds on the high peaks of the mountains to the north, the Wind River chain of the Rocky Mountains. Much talk among the wagons of the need for all possible determination and speed to achieve the distant California mountains before the winter should set in in earnest. It seemed to the people ridiculous to fear for winter in the midst of July but they had found that nothing of the natural laws they learned in Illinois and Missouri obtained in that desolate and inhuman land.

Imperceptibly the train crossed the Continental Divide. Will Eddy told Bill Foster that he proposed to piss in both oceans. He chose a spot away from the wagons that he said certainly marked the actual line of the Divide and pissed to the east and pissed to the west and declared himself master of the continental waters.

Despite Eddy's bluster of humor the train featured mostly long faces. It was as if the sight of those forbidding mountains to the north banished all feeling of goodwill. From that day forward the people expected to see fewer smiling faces and to feel the strength of fewer helping hands. There bent the mighty continent's back. There the train crossed the spine of North America and approached the unknown region on its other side. There stretched for 1000 miles a region inhabited by no white man alive. While the oxen coughed and the wagons creaked.

The train camped for the night at the headwaters of

Pacific Creek, the first water encountered on the journey that flowed west to the great ocean at the continent's distant end.

July 19

At the end of the day the train rolled into the bottoms of Little Sandy Creek and a great encampment of emigrants bound for Oregon and California. It had stopped in the good grass there to recruit the oxen and cattle. There the discussion went on about the various routes the parties could take. Greenwood's Cut-off for Fort Hall turned aside from the main road just a little way to the southwest. It required a 40-mile dry drive but was the most direct route to Fort Hall. It avoided Bridger's Fort or Fort Bridger a week farther to the south. Hastings' new Cut-off departed from Bridger's Fort and went through the Wahsatch Mountains down into the valley of the Great Salt Lake and around the south shore of the lake. It was said to be a far shorter route. Reed was disappointed not to find Hastings himself waiting at the Little Sandy camp. The open letter that Bonney had shown them at Independence Rock (and proposed to read to the assembled that day but Reed insisted he would read it and he did) indicated that Hastings would wait for them at the head of the Sweetwater on the other side of the Divide but he hadn't been there. Now Reed got the news that Hastings had gone on to Bridger's Fort with a party of emigrants more advanced than Boggs! Reed wasn't happy about Hastings' elusive behavior but he still thought the new Cut-off the best route.

George Donner agreed but Tamsen Donner had serious doubts. She confided in Jesse Thornton, whom she found with an Oregon outfit at the big encampment, that she was sick at heart for the men following a man who was probably no better than an adventurer. She said she had been taken with the testimony of Colonel Clyman back at Fort Laramie. There was nothing for it but that she must go with her husband.

In the evening Mrs. Donner was approached by a pale young man named Luke Halloran. He said he had been directed to her by mutual friends. He looked ill. He said he was consumptive and was going to California for his health but was no longer able to ride his horse as he had been formerly. He needed a place to lie down during the day when the coughing came on. Here he burst into tears. No one would take him in he said and he feared he would be left to die in that godforsaken wilderness. He had heard that she was a good woman. Would she take him in?

Mrs. Donner knew at once that she would but she sought her husband's permission before agreeing to the arrangement. She immediately set out to make the young man comfortable. It might be a comfort for him. It was also a distraction for her from the question of the better road. Halloran had only a small trunk which had been carried in another wagon. Noah James retrieved it and loaded it aboard the Donner family wagon.

A chill day. Mercury at sunrise 46°, sunset 52°.

July 20

The group for Hastings' Cut-off set out for Bridger's Fort at dawn. About 20 wagons in all.

July 21

On the Big Sandy River the group for Hastings' Cut-off met in camp. It consisted of 8 families and a number of individuals as follows.

George and Tamsen Donner and their children, 5 girls

Jacob and Elizabeth Donner, 7 children

James Reed and his wife Margaret, Virginia and Patty Reed, 2 boys

Will and Eleanor Eddy, 2 children ages 3 and 1

Pat and Margaret Breen, 7 children including 1 nursing babe

Lavina Murphy family, 5 Murphy children, Bill and

Sarah Foster and 1 child, Bill and Harriet Pike, 2 children
Lewis and Phillipine Keseberg, 1 child, 1 babe
Mr. and Mrs. Wolfinger
Charles Stanton, 35, a Chicago businessman traveling in his own wagon unattached
Pat Dolan, a bachelor Irishman with his own wagon, a friend of the Breens
Luke Halloran
Mr. Hardkoop, a Belgian from Cincinnati traveling with the Kesebergs
The Donner teamsters
The Reed teamsters and help
Dutch Charley Burger, Lewis Keseberg's teamster.

George Donner hoped that Jim Reed would be elected captain of the party, but a little conversation among the foreigners convinced him that Reed wasn't their man. They said he carried himself too fancy. He was stuck up. Thought he was better than the rest of them.

At the morning camp the men of property got themselves together and voted George Donner their captain. A steady and sober man. Thereafter the train was called the Donner party.

July 22

The Donner party proceeded down the Big Sandy through a barren land.

July 23

Across the Green River sweet with grass.

July 24

Down the Green swinging back somewhat eastward.

July 25

A long day's dry drive across from the Green River to Black's Fork.

July 26

Up Black's Fork toward Bridger's Fort. The quaking aspen clothed the green valley around the Fork.

July 27

Up Black's Fork.

July 28

The Donner party arrived at Bridger's Fort late in the day and found Lansford Hastings already gone on the Cut-off with a party of some 60 wagons led by Mr. Harlan and Mr. Young. George Donner conferred with Jim Reed and announced that the party would camp 2 days at the Fort to recruit the teams. The Fort was as rude as Fort Bernard had been. 2 log cabins connected by a lashed-pole corral. After the drive down from the South Pass even that much civilization looked good. The women used the occasion to do their considerable backlog of washing. Reed and the Donner brothers talked to Jim Bridger and his partner Louis Vasquez. Both men praised the new Cut-off. Reed wrote home later in the day praising the Cut-off—

The new road, or Hastings' Cut-off, leaves the Fort Hall road here, and is said to be a saving of 350 or 400 miles in going to California, and a better route. There is, however, or thought to be, one stretch of 40 miles without water; but Hastings and his party are out ahead examining for water, or for a route to avoid this stretch. I think that they cannot avoid it, for it crosses an arm of the Eutaw Lake, now dry. There is plenty of grass which we can cut and put into the waggons for our cattle while crossing it. We are now only 100 miles from the Great Salt Lake by the new route—in all 250 miles from California; while by way of Fort Hall it is 650 or 700 miles—making a great saving in favor of jaded oxen and dust. On the new route we will not have dust as there are but 60 waggons ahead of us. Mr. Bridger informs me that the route we design to take is a fine level road, with plenty of water and grass, with the exception before stated.

Bridger lied cleverly. If the new Cut-off became popular his Fort would prosper in preference to Fort Hall far to the northwest. Edwin Bryant had even left a letter with Vasquez warning Reed not to take the new route but Vasquez hid the letter away.

July 29

The party recruited its strength at Bridger's Fort. A giant of a man walked up to George Donner in the middle of the day and asked if he might join the party. He said his name was William McCutchen. He had teams and a wagon and a wife and baby daughter. He stood 6'6" and came from Missouri and Kentucky before that. He said he'd been taken sick with a recurring fever and had to stay behind when the Harlan-Young party went on. George Donner shook hands and Will McCutchen joined the Donner party. He was fond of quoting Shakespeare.

July 30

George Donner signed on a French-Mexican blend named Jean Baptiste Trubode to replace Hiram Miller. Trubode said he knew something of the way and could talk to the Indians. He was a little man with a big belly and a banty rooster's strut. He wore a drooping moustache that seemed too large for his round face with its small features crowded together in the center like a bullseye.

July 31

The Donner party left Bridger's Fort early in the morning and rolled west. Followed the trail of the Harlan-Young party that Lansford Hastings was guiding.

August 1

Sunday. The party rolled southwest over rough mountainous terrain. Crossed a creek thick with mud. Camped nearby.

August 2

Followed Hastings' trail, such as it was. Bad traveling.

August 3

Reached the valley of the Bear River. Lush with grass. It appeared Hastings entered a canyon over a ridge from there. The canyon was aimed like a rifle into the heart of the Wahsatch Mountains.

August 4

Mastered the ridge and entered the canyon. It was steep. Walls towered up 200 or 300 feet. A somber red. Every grinding wagon wheel set up echoes fired back to the listening ear by the canyon walls. The creek bed was a fierce tangle of trees and brush but Hastings' party had cut some of it away.

August 5

Pushed on through the echoing canyon.

August 6

The trail debouched into the valley of the Weber River and turned northwest, following the river downstream. 4 miles downstream the party located the campsite of the Harlan-Young party. Prominent on a cleft stick in the open area where that train had camped Jim Reed found a letter from Hastings. He read it to the assembled laced with anger. It said that emigrants should not attempt to follow the route the Hastings train had taken from that point on but should send forward to fetch Hastings and he would return and guide them according to another and better route he knew. Reed said instantly that he would go forward to confer with Hastings. He asked for 2 volunteers. The foreigners looked at him sceptically but little Charlie Stanton stood forward and then big Will McCutchen unwound himself from where he was sitting and allowed that if someone would loan him a horse he would be glad to serve as scout. George Donner made the loan and the 3 men went off immediately after the nooning. They followed the Weber River as Hastings' train had done.

August 7

Resting in camp.

August 8

Resting in camp. Reed & company were expected to return today but they never showed.

August 9

Considerable concern among the people of the party over the continued absence of the men sent out to find Lansford Hastings.

August 10

Some of the people talked of going on without the scouting party but cooler heads prevailed and they agreed to wait. The nights were cold and the Donner party was just about the last party on the trail and no one breathed very easy about it.

August 11

At evening when most had given up on the scouting party a haggard Jim Reed rode a stumbling horse into the Weber River camp. He hadn't eaten in 48 hours and while he chewed venison and gulped coffee thick with brown sugar he told a bitter story. It had taken him and Stanton and McCutchen 2 days to get out of the Wahsatch and on their way they saw why Hastings warned them against the Weber River route. Its canyons narrowed so badly that wagons could hardly be driven through. One wagon had crashed down a mountainside and smashed up on the bottom. All the oxen were killed. The wolves had already stripped their bones. Once on the plain below the 3 men quickly found the Harlan-Young camp some miles over near a black rock. Hastings refused to ride all the way back with them. He claimed he had to stay with his party and guide them across the dry drive (and probably knew he would be scalped if any of the Donner people laid eyes on him). He agreed to ride part way with Reed and sketch the alternate route he had in mind. Reed said it was the route Hastings had come eastward with Clyman on. Stanton's and McCutchen's horses had given out and they stayed in the camp to recruit them. Reed traded his horse (it was not his precious Glaucus but one of his spares) for another and set out with Hastings. —He was a dynamic man said Reed but I had the feeling we were all of us doing his exploring for him. He rode me up to the top of a shoulder of hills down there in the valley and pointed out the way from there. I tried to travel it coming back and I think I got it right. I marked the way with blazes.

Reed said Stanton and McCutchen would follow along shortly. No one was happy with his story and Tamsen Donner was fit to be tied but no one had any better idea than to follow the route Hastings had promised. How this man who had crossed the mountains 3 times and written a book about his experiences could be so confused no one understood. His name had achieved the reputation of a sovereign curse among the emigrants of the Donner party.

August 12

Roadmaking in the Wahsatch. In the morning the party turned up a canyon running into the Weber River canyon from the southwest. The going was hard, cutting through a tangle of aspen and willow and serviceberry brush. Only 2 miles in, the canyon narrowed until it was no longer passable. An Indian trail led up and over the ridge. By evening the men were exhausted. Many had blistered hands. Reed worked as hard as the best of them but he was not the most popular man in camp that night.

August 13

More roadmaking. The work hurt. Despite the size of the party it had too few able-bodied men. The women and children did what they could but some of the men worked with bloody hands. At the end of the day they camped beside a spring in a pleasant hollow but the hollow butted against another ridge and the next day they would somehow have to contrive to get the wagons over it.

August 14

With windlasses and doubled teams the men hauled the wagons up another Indian trail over the dividing ridge. It was a burden but at least from the ridge the people could see the sky instead of the narrow gloom of the canyon floor. The ridge led to a ledge above the canyon of Bossman Creek and the party descended to the creek through a draw. This creek was worse than the last. Its bottoms were crowded impassably with serviceberry and poplar. Nothing for it but to continue roadmaking. The boulders were as terrible as the brush. Some were too large to be moved. The men had to pile up fills of gravel and brush on either side of them to make a road the wagons might go over. People cursed whenever someone got in their way. Every able-bodied man was averaging roadmaking to the extent of 2 chains a day.

August 15

Sunday. A mile at a time and less than a mile the men cut the road. They left stumps that reached up almost to the bottoms of the wagonbeds. The road crossed and recrossed the bed of the creek through which ran cold mountain water. They were making only a mile or 2 a day. The men crawled into their blankets at night almost as soon as supper was done. Some of the poorer families discovered their provisions getting low. Before long they would have to count on the more prosperous families for food. That didn't settle their sleep much.

August 16

The party turned from the canyon of Bossman Creek and headed up a side canyon. It looked no better than the creek canyon and very possibly worse but it followed the route Reed had marked.

August 17

Crossed a swamp by riprapping it with loose stones. There seemed no end to roadmaking. Men worked black with anger but they had plenty of timber to take out their anger on. By the end of the day they shuffled with exhaustion like the living dead.

Late in the afternoon 3 wagons and a passle of cattle, dogs and children descended to the canyon floor. They might have descended from the blue sky itself, so surprising was their appearance in those godforsaken mountains. This was the family of a Vermonter named Franklin Ward Graves, called Uncle Billy, a man near 60 years traveling with his large family from Illinois. His wife Elizabeth carried a nursing babe that bore her name, Elizabeth Graves Jr. Her other unmarried children spanned the years up to 20-year-old Mary Graves. Mary was a pretty girl. A sight for sore eyes. 8 children in all not counting the oldest girl Sarah, married to a Jay Fosdick. Counting Snyder, Fosdick and 18-year-old Billy Graves, the family added 3 strong men to the task of roadmaking. The Graves were roundly welcomed to the party.

August 18

Heavier timber and the road ran steeper upward as the canyon ascended a big mountain. The party scratched its way to the top. From the peak the people could see in the distance the hazy valley of the Great Salt Lake. It was harder getting down the mountain than getting up. The wheels had to be locked and a ravine filled in. They descended to an open canyon and camped. Before the day was out a search party brought Stanton and McCutchen into camp half-starved and miserable-looking. They had been lost in the mountains and despaired of ever finding the train. They were ready to eat their horses when they were found.

When they could speak they blurted out their terrible news. It was not yet enough to have crossed the big mountain. The wagons could not yet merely descend downstream. The road would have to be cut farther upstream to encounter another canyon. The canyon the party was camped in ran down to nowhere.

That news set the camp buzzing. People gathered among the wagons. The foreigners seemed to cluster in one knot and the plainer people in another and the Donners and Reeds with Stanton and McCutchen in another. No question but that many of the people were blaming Reed for the disaster of the Wahsatch passage. Someone speculated that the Weber River route would have been better than the one they had taken even if it was hard because at least the Hastings party would have done some road clearing along the way. It was too late for speculations however. Eventually everyone simmered down and organized the coming work.

August 19

Roadmaking up a traverse canyon. No one said a kind word to anyone. The oxen looked poorly. There wasn't that much besides browse to eat. At sunset the sky glowed red. The smell of smoke from mountain fires hung in the air.

August 20

The party broke today into a likely-looking canyon but the men forward said it narrowed and filled until it looked completely impassable. The arguments came thick and fast but at last the men agreed that they would have to back-track. They were near to tears for the wasted effort. Some of them took it out on their oxen. They hated to go back up the timber and brush that they had blistered and sweated to clear. The Germans were in the lead after the turnaround and when they came to a slight decline in the west ridge they announced that they would not retrace their steps any farther and began chaining their oxen in double teams. Reed and George Donner came forward and argued with them but they were stubborn. Eventually the 2 leaders withdrew. One by one the wagons followed the German example and were dragged and wedged and pushed and pulled over the ridge. The act was foolhardy in the extreme but the Providence that had previously toyed with them decided now to give them the benefit of the doubt and nothing was lost and nothing hurt excepting the whipsore oxen.

August 21

Descended down a respectable canyon with what seemed like breakneck speed after the crawl of the previous weeks.

August 22

Debouched onto the glorious green plain of the Great Salt Lake valley. After the mountains the valley seemed a paradise capable of sustaining and sweetening the human spirit.

The Donner party had occupied most of a month traveling no more than 40 miles however. They were dangerously behind the season and they knew it.

August 23

A fine sunny morning. They traced the trail of Hastings' party to the other side of the river that connected the Utah lake with the Great Salt Lake. Crossed the valley and camped at springs east of the first small range of hills or mountains.

August 24

Commenced passing the point of the mountain that ran
down to the shore of the salt lake about 9 A.M. A rough
passage through the marshy sand and mud of the lake
sloughs. The lake soured the people. Dead water no good to
man or beast. Dead fish lay on its shore and it smelled like
no water they had ever known. They thought it a poor omen.
During the day's passage around the point of the mountain
the George Donner wagons fell behind. Luke Halloran had
been steadily weakening in the crossing of the Wahsatch and
now was not long for the world. Tamsen Donner had nursed
him as best she could but for 2 days he had been coughing
blood. In the afternoon he hemorrhaged and choked with
Tamsen kneeling beside him firm-featured and dry-eyed.
He drowned in his own blood about 4 P.M.

Jim Reed's supply wagon broke an axletree coming down
off a rock. The teamsters had to ride back to the Wahsatch
to find timber. Will Eddy went to work on a new axletree
as soon as the timber arrived.

At 8 P.M. the Donner wagons came up to the camp at the
big black rock on the other side of the point. No one wanted
to take much time burying the consumptive from St. Joe
until George Donner examined the effects in Halloran's
trunk and found the apron and regalia of a Master Mason.
He also found $1500 in gold coin but only told his wife to
avoid exciting jealousy in the badly-provided. Reed was also
a Master Mason and gathered together the other Masons in
the party and proposed they take a day of rest and convene
a lodge and provide for Halloran's proper burial. The men
agreed.

August 25

After moving camp up from the sloughs to a spring on
better ground the Masons convened a lodge and proceded
to bury Halloran in a makeshift coffin assembled from some
wagon boards. They had dug a resting place beside the

[49]

grave of one of Hastings' party, a man named John Hargrave. Reed said the traditional words and threw in an evergreen branch left over from the trimming of his axletree.

August 26

Followed the shoreline of an old lake around south from the sloughs of the salt lake. The salt lake appeared to be the dried-up remains of a giant lake that was probably fresh at one time. The old shoreline and sandy beaches curved away from the salt lake south for some miles. Sometimes the old shoreline ran along high on the hills. It was that shoreline that the Donner party followed. They came to a place of natural wells in the early afternoon and decided to camp for the day. The oxen were still recruiting from the Wahsatch and all knew they faced a dry drive ahead. Reed named the place "Twenty Wells" for the number of curious wells there. They varied in diameter from 6 inches to 9 feet. When the women took water from them they immediately refilled just to the brim and no more. The earth around them was grassy and firm. Will McCutchen lowered a rope weighted with a rock into one and payed it out 70 feet without sounding bottom. Curious that all should run with fresh water when the lake nearby was salt. A curious land.

August 27

Traveling back toward the salt lake the party passed another point of land but this one was not so crowded up against the water. They found a big spring on the other side of the point but it ran cold salt water. 15 miles down in the valley beyond the point the party halted at a pleasant spring in a fine meadow. A board had been hammered into the ground at the spring and a message nailed onto the board. The message was torn and scattered however by the Indians or the birds. Tamsen Donner asked the children standing nearby to gather up the scraps of paper. She got her sketch board from her wagon and rested it on her lap and proceeded to assemble the scraps. Some of the illiterate among the people marveled. The scraps proved to be the remains of a message from Lansford Hastings. It started a plenty of cursing. Hastings had lied again. He had said the dry drive was a hard crossing of a day and a night. The note said "2 days—2 nights—hard driving—cross desert—reach water." Hastings couldn't have come back across to leave the note so he must have known the extent of the crossing before he left which would have meant that he knew when he informed the parties of his Cut-off. He was a plain old lying bastard then said Pat Breen and the others agreed and vented their fury on the Donner brothers and Jim Reed as if all hadn't concurred in the decision of those 3 worthies.

August 28

Rested in camp in the meadow. The men cut grass and loaded it into the wagons for the oxen. There would be none in the desert. Everyone worked at filling every available jug and bucket and cask with water. They planned to begin the drive at dawn and not stop except for breath until they reached the other side. 2 days and 2 nights was hard but it could be done and there wasn't much choice after the Wahsatch but to do it. They couldn't go back and follow the Fort Hall trail now.

August 29

Sunday. Began at daylight following the Hastings trail across the valley a little north of west. Got to the foot of the mountains on the other side before noon. The pass was steep. The people hauled up the steep road all through the afternoon. The first wagon to the top was Will Eddy's. His eyes couldn't register what he saw. The sun glared from miles and miles of shimmering white salt broken in the foreground by low rocks and jagged hills. It looked like the plains of Hell. No one in his right mind would think the distance less than 70 or 80 miles. You could just catch the faintest notion of a mountain at the horizon like a puff of low clouds. The other wagons came up as Eddy's moved on.

Some of the women cried when they saw the hellish prospect before them. The wagons rolled down the steep trail on the other side. They crossed a sage plain. The dust was fine as ash and burned the eyes. They crossed a volcanic ridge sometime in the night.

August 30

They made temporary camp beyond the volcanic ridge. Built fires against the cold desert night and rested the oxen and nursed them with a little water and the cut grass. After the temporary camp the train rolled on up a steep ridge not unlike the previous one. It took some digging at the sides of the trail to keep the wagons upright. Then down among boulders rolling them aside. An ox broke a horn. One of the men fortified himself with a slug of whiskey and passed the bottle around and got it back empty and cast it aside. Water jugs began to line the trail as the people emptied them and threw them away to lighten the wagons. Eddy and Graves led the way and the Donners, Reed and Keseberg brought up the rear. Across a sage plain. Into sand dunes that cruelly strained the oxen. Their hooves sank into the sand and the wagon wheels dug in halfway to the hubs. Beyond the dunes the party halted again in the night to rest the oxen. That night the oxen got the last water that would be spared for animals.

August 31

The train entered the most barren stretch of desert just about at dawn. No sage grew nor any other plant, only the white crust of salt stretching away. As the sun heated the desert the wagons seemed to be surrounded by lakes of water. The heat pressed the people to the ground. Salt dust stung their eyes. Their lips cracked. Tamsen Donner gave the girls lumps of loaf sugar moistened with peppermint oil. At other times they sucked on bullets Noah James had flattened for them.

Will Eddy saw 20 men in the distance marching beside 20

wagons. He thought for a crazy moment that Hastings had come back to help them across but then he saw that the 20 moved as he moved. They were 20 men of a mirage. They were 20 Will Eddys 20 times determined to cross the salt hell. A desert like a skull under the Indian sun.

Another rest that night and more fires. The wagons were stringing out with the heavier ones falling behind. No one looked beyond the salvation of his own family now. That was proving to be chore enough.

September 1

In the middle of the desert the wagons fanned out to cross the sink. Under a thin crust of pure salt lay sandy slush oozing salt water. No wagon dared to follow in another's track for fear of becoming mired. The oxen cut through the crust with their hooves and the salt mud cruelly burned their sore feet. Some collapsed in their yokes and were unpinned and left to die. Salt blew as dust across the trails. Across the faces of the oxen and the women and the men. Young children rubbed their reddened eyes. The mountain that had guided the wagons was hidden by a low outcropping ahead marked with green. Some thought it might have water. The trail turned a little to the southwest to approach it.

September 2

During the night Eddy and the Graves passed the green outcropping or rock. It offered no water they could find. The green was only greasewood. On the other side of the rock, which rose out of the salt flats like an island, they rounded another island of rock and saw the salt stretching out miles more. They hauled on. Their oxen smelled water then and found fresh strength. Nearer the foot of the mountains Eddy released his oxen from their burden and let them move on in. Finally at 10 in the morning Eddy reached the spring just beyond the salt flat surrounded by willow trees.

Back on the other side of the islands Reed's oxen had

given out. The Pioneer Palace Car broke through the salt crust of the sink. The oxen could pull it no farther. Reed realized his desperate condition and proposed to ride ahead for help. He mounted Glaucus and spurred ahead having instructed his teamsters to haul on as far as the oxen could go with the 2 remaining wagons and then unyoke the animals and drive them on in and figure to return later for the wagons.

Reed hadn't slept since the first night out from the meadow. He rode through the day past the rock islands and arrived at the spring on the shoreline of the desert just at dusk. Graves agreed to rest Glaucus and loaned Reed another horse for the return trip. Reed filled the water jugs hung on his saddle. Eddy went partway back with him.

In the moonlight sometime before midnight Reed came upon Milt Elliott and Jim Smith driving forward his cattle and horses. He rode on and reached his wagons just before daylight. His family was safe but his wagons were the farthest back of any in the train. Walt Herron took the horse and turned it around and set out for the spring. No use to let the animal die.

Reed expected Milt and Jim or some other men to reach him during the day. He needed sleep desperately and proposed that the family rest in the wagons. He woke sweating in the shimmering heat of the late afternoon and immediately realized his predicament. The Reeds set out then on foot, Jim Reed carrying 3-year-old Tommy. Reed drove forward with fury at the treatment his men and the others in the party had accorded him. Night fell and the children became cold and exhausted. They lay down and Reed covered them with a blanket but still their teeth chattered. Reed then ordered the 5 family dogs to lie down on the blanket around the children, Tyler, Barney, Trailer, Tracker and Cash. Reed and his wife sat at the edge of the blanket facing the wind to screen the children. Soon they quieted down. Something loomed in the moonlight. The dogs were up and barking before anyone could see. Reed cried that an ox had gone mad. Dogs barked wildly. The children bounded out of the blanket and scattered in the night. The ox galloped by. Reed saw the froth at its mouth and realized it was crazed with thirst. The dogs had succeeded in turning it aside. After that the children wanted no more resting. Late at night the Reeds came up to the Jacob Donner family asleep in their wagon. Reed left his wife and children with them. They had some water left. He stumbled on toward the spring.

September 4

When Reed reached the shore of the salt flat he found most of the party out looking for animals. They hardly paid any attention to him when he stumbled in. He found Jacob Donner returning with 2 yoke of oxen to retrieve his wagon and told him about his family. Jacob brought in Reed's family during the day and Reed's teamsters retrieved one of their boss's wagons after transferring food from the second wagon. The second wagon they abandoned to the salt desert. Reed discovered worse news. About 10 miles from the spring Milt and Jim Smith had stopped to raise a fallen horse and when they turned back to the oxen they found the animals had disappeared. Most likely run off into the desert. James Frazier Reed, one of the wealthiest men in the party, now had 1 ox and 1 cow to pull his wagon with. People wouldn't even agree to carry his food unless he allowed them to use it as their own. Jacob Donner had lost 1 wagon. Keseberg had left 1 behind and had 1 left. 36 oxen had been lost, 18 of them Reed's. Rich in money but short of animals, Reed was suddenly a poor man. More than one of the men of the Donner party smiled at that. More than one of the women too.

September 5

Sunday but no day of thanks. Some of the men vowed to kill Lansford Hastings when they reached California.

Resting in camp at the spring.

September 6

Resting in camp at the spring. Many people were occupied in searching for missing animals. Cattle, oxen and horses. All the dogs came through.

September 7

Resting in camp.

September 8

Resting in camp.

September 9

Resting in camp. The party planned to leave the next day. Reed succeeded in borrowing an ox from Graves and 1 from Breen. With his ox and his cow that made 2 teams, enough to pull his wagon if he distributed most of his food. Reed held up his head during the distribution and got credit at least for that. No one ever had anything against Mrs. Reed.

September 10

Being recovered somewhat from the crossing of the desert the people of the Donner party left the spring camp. They were reduced from 23 to 19 wagons and those none too tight but no one had died in the desert and the oxen had recruited some for their 5 days of rest. The people might have been optimistic but before noon a snowstorm blew up and cut off their view and they suffered the lateness of the season once again. They camped after making only 6 miles south-southwest from the spring camp. About 3 P.M. Milt Elliott and young Billy Graves came back to them with another note from Hastings they had found while scouting cattle farther on the trail. The note announced yet another dry drive, this one supposedly of 40 miles. The men raged but this time they were practical enough to suggest sending a scouting party ahead on horseback. The snowstorm let up and 2 men were fitted out and sent on.

September 11

The party left at dawn with the 2 men not yet back. They had been told to meet the party on the way. The party followed Hastings' trail 10 miles across an open plain to a gap in a mountain range. Just beyond the pass the 2 men rejoined the train and announced that Hastings' trail veered off northwest and then veered back almost south but that the party could cut straight southwest and shave 10 or 15 miles off the Hastings route. This they did. Some of the oxen gave out during the long haul. The wagons rolled on through the night.

September 12

At dawn the party arrived at a small lake with green grass and many springs. The people rested all day in camp. Reed's teams were giving out. He cached his property in a trench his men dug for the purpose. Eddy put his team to Reed's wagon to spare the cow and 1 failing ox. Bill Pike accepted Eddy's wagon in place of his own, which had lost one of its tires.

Food was low. Some people didn't have enough to last the rest of the journey and knew it. By late afternoon the talk was such that George Donner decided to call a meeting. Everyone came. They had to send someone ahead to California to seek relief from Colonel Sutter. That would be their only chance to make the rest of the journey. No one much wanted to go. There was no guarantee that whoever went would come back. Why the hell should he once he was over the mountains. Little Charlie Stanton volunteered to go. Some of the men laughed bitterly. Stanton said he would give his word of honor to return for them with relief but some still laughed and shook their heads. Stanton said he'd returned in the Wahsatch hadn't he and someone said he didn't have much choice with the desert in front of him. Big Will McCutchen volunteered then and the people looked up. He'd have to leave his wife and baby girl behind.

They supposed he loved his wife and his baby enough to come back for them didn't he. Mac flushed and swore.

After more such talk it was decided and Mac took off on a horse and Charlie on a mule. Off for Sutter's Fort on the other side of the far California mountains. The hopes of all rode with them.

September 13

Rolled west a day's journey to a good valley.

September 14

West through another pass to another good valley. All the valleys had their springs on their western sides under the protection of the ranges of mountains that ran north and south. They called the valley the Valley of the 50 Springs. Some were hot, some warm, some cool, some slightly acid. One had a cone of mineral deposits to a height of 10 feet around it. Indians in large numbers wandered in the valley but they showed no signs of hostility. The men shot antelope and bighorn sheep in abundance for meat.

The scouts came into camp from following Hastings' trail and reported it turned due south. Everyone knew California was west. What could Hastings have been up to now. The men talked it over and decided they had to follow the trail. When the women got the word they were mad as hell. Were the men just cowards that they followed that adventurer wherever he chose to go? Couldn't they see that a trail heading south wasn't going to get them closer to their destination? Did they want to spend the winter out in those mountains? The men figured that Hastings had veered south to find a pass through the mountains. None was in sight to the west. There was nothing for it but to follow the trail of the Hastings party. South it was down the Valley of the 50 Springs. Reed called the camp the Mad Woman Camp.

September 15

Traveling down the valley due south. Snow on the mountains to the west as there had been snow on the mountain beyond the salt desert.

September 16

Traveling down the valley. No sign of a passage west.

September 17

Traveling down the valley. Still no pass. The grass was good and the weather pleasant but all felt as if they were walking in a dream. They knew they were making no progress toward California and they knew the lateness of the day. They should have been cabin-building somewhere off from Sutter's Fort by then.

September 18

The trail turned at last to the west and up a mountain pass. They crossed the ridge of mountains during the day and camped at a creek in the valley on the other side. The creek ran due north and likely ran into Mary's River. The passage across the mountain they reckoned at 15 or 20 miles. That was as much west as they had traveled in 3 days.

September 19

North up the western valley.

September 20

North up the valley.

September 21

North. No progress west. Hastings must have had the world's worst judgment. God's own fool or the Devil's.

September 22

The trail turned northwest.

September 23

The trail continued northwest and the creek ran into another larger stream.

September 24

The party camped at the head of a narrow canyon into which flowed the creek or fork they had been following. They saw large numbers of Indians naked as jaybirds.

September 25

The party entered the canyon in the morning. Spent much of their time in the water itself so narrow was the canyon. They made 8 miles and halted at 11 A.M. to take advantage of a campsite large enough to give them all space out of the water.

September 26

Made only 8 miles down the torturous canyon but emerged in the evening in the valley of Mary's River or the Humboldt. Forded the river at night and struck the California road. Camped on the north bank. Indians came into camp and indicated with signs that the party was still far from the place where the river sank into the sands of the desert. It had begun to seem to the people of the party that their journey would never end. That night some of the women wept without consolation.

September 27

The trail going west crossed the north fork of Mary's River where that stream ran into the river itself. Later the trail approached a creek with banks whitened by an encrustation of salt. The oxen broke the crust and set up a cloud of dust that choked them and made people cough fearfully. A barren land.

September 28

Down Mary's River. Grass was so poor that the party

agreed to break up into 2 sections. The Donners with 5 wagons made up the forward section. Reed's teamsters went with them except for Milt Elliott. The others took up the rear. Uncle Billy Graves immediately claimed the part of leader in directing who would break trail &etc. He was rich with oxen and horses.

September 29

Down Mary's River. Both sections camped together at the site of several hot springs at the foot of a mountain range. The springs boiled and frothed like cooking pots. They drained their boiling water into the river. The water was brackish but acceptable when cooled.

September 30

The forward section leaving early passed first over the mountain range at a gap above the hot springs camp. About 11 A.M. an Indian joined the second section. Eddy named him Thursday in honor of Robinson Crusoe's Friday, Thursday being the day of the week and the land about being duly barren and the people of the party feeling almost as long abroad as that English worthy. Another Indian came into camp about 4 P.M. who knew the words *gee* and *haw* and *whoa* by which communication he appeared to believe he had exhausted the resources of the American tongue.

Camped at a spring halfway down the side of the mountain. One campfire started a blaze in the greasewood that grew on the mountainside and would have burned a wagon but for the quick intervention of the Indians who saw the danger and pointed it out. They got a fair supper for their pains such as supper was.

October 1

The Indians stole away during the night taking with them one of Uncle Billy's shirts and what was worse an entire yoke of oxen. Uncle Billy muttered and fumed and at last sent young Billy Graves out to look for the oxen but they didn't turn up and there wasn't any help for it. Graves had more than enough oxen to go on ahead anyway. Jim Reed said privately that it looked as if *Thursday* just wasn't Uncle Billy's day.

October 2

Down Mary's River.

October 3

Sunday. The ashen dust and foul water preached a notable sermon in humility.

October 4

Down Mary's River. Passed a beautiful clear-running stream that drained into the river. Down a ways several warm springs bubbled on the other bank.

October 5

Uncle Billy Graves had a horse stolen in the night. It put him in a foul mood. Will Eddy went out during the morning to hunt antelope and was shot at by the Indians. He said the arrows would come whistling down from nowhere without enough force to do him much harm even if they had hit him. He returned to the second section of the party during the nooning and found them camped below a long sandhill. After the nooning they began hauling up the hill. All the wagons got over easily except Reed's, Pike's and one of Uncle Billy's. Milt Elliott unchained one team from Reed's wagon and moved it up to help haul Pike's when the team got tangled with Uncle Billy's teams. They were being driven by Uncle Billy's teamster John Snyder. Snyder was hot and tired and sick of the whole journey. The mixup of the animals got him pissed. He started to argue with Elliott and they were about to come to blows when Jim Reed ran up and called Snyder down. Snyder told him damn you you're the cause of all this trouble in the first place. I've half a mind to whip your ass Snyder said. He brandished his bullwhip in Reed's face. Reed said you just try it Mister and pulled a goodsized knife from his belt. The knife didn't faze Snyder. He hit Reed across the head with the handle of his bullwhip and opened up a gash. Snyder's arm came up to lay on another blow and Reed's arm came up at the same time with the knife and Reed's arm came down first and the knife went into Snyder's chest like a sticking knife into a pig's throat and then Snyder hit Reed again and the blood poured from Reed's head. Mrs. Reed ran up and tried to pull the men apart. She didn't realize Reed had stabbed Snyder but neither did Snyder yet. His arm came up again and he hit Mrs. Reed across the head and started her bleeding too. Then Snyder felt the knife and dropped to his knees with a look of terror on his face as if he never expected the matter to come so serious. Reed in the meantime had realized where his knife was and he was looking around as if the man who had done the deed might be trying to get away. He pulled the knife from Snyder's chest as Snyder went to his knees and when he saw that he held the knife he threw it away the way a man would throw away a rat or a snake. Oh my God Reed said. Oh my God. By then Milt was helping Mrs. Reed and Virginia Reed was on her way to her father. Reed dropped beside Snyder who had now fallen backward to the ground. Blood was foaming from his mouth. The knife had pierced the lung and probably the heart too. He said something to Reed and then danced the death dance and died away.

The section halted right there with Reed and his family drawing a ways apart. Reed was distracted. He found his knife and threw it into the river as if the river could wash it clean. Virginia bathed her parents' gashed heads and dressed the wounds. The body lay where it had fallen on the ground while the men of the party convened a meeting. Reed was not invited. The men took depositions with a mind to a California prosecution. They argued over what should be done with Reed. Eddy and Milt Elliott stood up for Reed saying that Snyder had begun the fight and provoked the attack. No one else had a good word to say for Reed however. He was the author of their grief so far as many of them were concerned. They blamed him for their own ill decisions. Thus are heroes brought low who fail to tame the popular dragons.

In the evening Keseberg proceded from his supper to his wagon and silently propped the wagon tongue into the air. The gesture was unmistakable. Keseberg had devised a desert hanging tree. The men talked together and looked Reed's way. Eddy and Milt soon joined Reed and were seen to be supplied with considerable armament. Eddy had 2 six-shooters, 2 double-barreled pistols and a rifle. Milt had a rifle and a double-barreled shotgun. Reed himself had abandoned the role of penitent in favor of a more earthly salvation and armed himself with a six-shooter, 2 double-barreled pistols and a rifle. The men came over anyway but halted at a respectable distance and demanded Reed be turned over to them. Eddy told them that they were fools, that the fight had been fair. Keseberg swore at Eddy in German but Eddy didn't speak the language and the curse thundered on by. You can't guard him forever Graves said. No we can't said Eddy we had best come to a compromise. What kind of compromise you got in mind Graves said. Banish him from the train said Eddy. In this godforsaken wilderness that would be punishment enough. Keseberg disagreed violently but after they had considered the alternatives the men came back and said they would agree to a banishment without gun or water. Reed said they might as well hang him and get it over with. Eddy said the proposition wasn't acceptable. Graves said it would have to be. Reed said they could all go to hell he wasn't going to leave his wife and children behind at the hands of a pack of blood-thirsty wolves. Shut up someone said and Reed all but brandished his pistols their way.

There was nothing for it but that Reed must go. Milt and Eddy promised to take care of Reed's family.

October 6

Reed offered to help with the digging of the grave but was contemptuously turned away. Snyder was buried wrapped in a blanket with a sideboard below and a sideboard above. They hoped the boards would discourage the wolves.

Reed rode off on Glaucus at midmorning. They had not allowed him gun or powder. Not long after Reed's departure Eddy suddenly burst out angrily that they could all go to hell he was going to take Reed the bare means of survival among hostile Indians in an untracked wilderness. He took a spare gun and powder and ball and rode after Reed. Reed would have found succor with the Donners but only after a dangerous day's passage among the Indians alone. Will Eddy was a brave man to turn his back on a hanging jury of his peers.

October 7

Indians shot at Eddy and Bill Pike while they were out hunting. The wagons pulled through valleys of ashes amid hills of cinder and slag and there was no color on the land except the colors of mud and ash. No one could stomach the dust. It coated the skin and gritted the teeth. Everything tasted of it except the water. The water tasted of alkali and salt. Reed left behind a letter in a cleft stick marking the site of Indian depredations among an advance party. At the evening camp old man Hardkoop was missing. He was the Belgian who was traveling with Keseberg. Keseberg said he didn't know what had happened to him. Eddy insisted that someone should go looking for him and after some reluctance Uncle Billy Graves agreed to the use of one of his horses for the purpose and young Billy Graves rode out. He found Hardkoop about 5 miles back on the trail and helped him mount and rode him forward to camp. Hardkoop said that Keseberg had put him out of the wagon and told him to walk or die. Keseberg denied the charge but said he had to think of his oxen and his family's food.

October 8

To lighten the load on the oxen Eddy cached some of his clothing and tools. He abandoned Reed's wagon and borrowed a lighter wagon from Uncle Billy Graves. Uncle Billy insisted on a considerable payment for the loan when they reached California. About half an hour after the party started on the trail Hardkoop came up to Eddy and said that Keseberg had put him out of the wagon again. Eddy could see that the old man was weak. His feet were so swollen he could hardly walk. He had cut gashes in the sides of his shoes to ease the swelling. Hardkoop begged Eddy to take him into his wagon. Eddy was anguished. He wanted to help the old man but his oxen could barely pull the light wagon through the sandy barrens on the trail. Their bones poked out their hides like tentpoles supporting slack tents. Half the time they had to be beaten to make them move at all. Eddy told Hardkoop that if the old man could make it across the stretch of sand ahead of them that he would do what he could. Hardkoop looked crestfallen but said he would try.

Eddy was so preoccupied with the oxen he forgot about the old man until he got into camp that night. Some of the boys said they had seen Hardkoop sitting under a sagebush about half alive. They said you could see blood on his shoes. The gashes in the shoes looked like wounds they said. Eddy had the first watch that night. He built a bonfire with greasewood on the side of a hill to help guide Hardkoop into camp if the old man was coming. It was a cold night. Eddy fretted through his watch and when Milt came on to take over he asked him to keep up the watchfire and Milt agreed.

October 9

Margaret Reed, Milt and Eddy went to Keseberg as soon as they saw that Hardkoop hadn't come up during the night. They asked him to go back and look for the old man. It was his responsibility they said because he had brought

Hardkoop along so far and the old man was of his nationality. Keseberg flushed. Hardkoop was a Belgian not a German he said and anyone who couldn't stand the journey should not have started. Hardkoop could keep up or he could die said Keseberg it mattered not to him. Should he sacrifice his wife and his little girl and his baby boy for an old man who never had a kind word for anyone? The German was angry but his anger covered a considerable shame or so Margaret Reed thought. Eddy only thought of his own forgetfulness.

The 3 benefactors then went to Pat Breen to see if they could borrow a horse to ride back and look for the old man. Breen was harsh as Keseberg had been and refused to loan the horse and said if Hardkoop couldn't keep up then he could damned well die behind.

Then the 3 went to Uncle Billy Graves and he was the angriest of all. He said bluntly that he would not kill one of his horses to save the life of a worthless foreigner who probably never did anyone any good. Graves flailed his arms and seemed almost ready to attack the delegation. Leave me alone he shouted I don't want to be bothered about the old bastard again. Then Milt and Bill Pike and Eddy proposed going back on foot to look for Hardkoop but the other men swore and said they wouldn't wait for any stragglers they would just go on and leave them. Eddy was furious but there was nothing for it but that he must go on. Even 3 men together in that Indian country wouldn't stand a chance and 2 of them had families and Milt was looking after the Reeds. They thus went on leaving Hardkoop behind.

At about 11 A.M. the section arrived at a place where a trail cut off to the north probably for Oregon. The section halted there for the nooning and the benefactors again tried to convince Breen or Graves to make them the loan of a horse but neither patriarch would be moved. Eddy accused them of playing God but both men only cursed him in return.

God was playing to be sure. About 4 P.M. the section encountered a slough of loose sand which occupied their suffering oxen until 4 A.M. the next morning.

October 10

The section camped beyond the sand at the place where a Mr. Salle of an earlier party had been killed by the Indians. The Indians had dug up the body and robbed it and the wolves had stripped the flesh from the unfortunate bones. They lay scattered about the gravesite. The desecration made the widow Murphy cry but her daughters comforted her. All were exhausted from the long haul and lay down to sleep through the morning. They awoke to find Graves' horses run off by the Indians. Graves was fit to be tied but Eddy told him he'd got no more than he deserved. At 10 A.M. they cached one of Graves' wagons and went on. That night there was hardly any grass for their animals and hardly any water in the river. The river had gotten smaller as they hauled down it instead of larger as a river ought. Before long it would sink into the desert with hardly a trace. Such were the peculiarities of that hellish land through which they traveled. Having gone astray before from the straight road.

October 11

A day of dust and ugliness. Graves had a cow stolen during the night. The section camped at the day's end at a place with poor grass and poorer water. Pat Breen's best mare got herself mired in a slough of mud in the bed of the river and couldn't get out. All else failing, Breen begged Eddy for help. Eddy coldly reminded the Irishman of Hardkoop. The mare perished. Indians shot arrows into some of the cattle but none died. The point of the target practice was to weaken the animals so that they would fall behind and could then be dispatched for a savage feast. Nor were the Indians' small bows likely to kill such large animals. They were bows meant to persuade creatures no larger than jackrabbits.

October 12

Traveled down Mary's River. One of Eddy's oxen collapsed and had to be left behind. All the oxen were poor. Desperate to complete this endless leg of their journey the people drove on until midnight before camping. At last they had reached the sink of Mary's River. Once it had been a large lake but at that late season it showed only mud and dust and a few pools of foul water. The whole area was covered with a fine choking clay thrown up from the earth below and salt mingled with that. The sink recalled the salt desert. In the moonlight it looked like the very barren plains of hell. For all their pains the Donner party had brought themselves to the brink of another desert. They would haul again across burning ground.

October 13

At daylight the boys drove the cattle to poor grass some distance from the encampment. Later the guard they had left there came in for breakfast. The sneaking Indians had been lying in wait. While the guard was gone they shot arrows into 21 animals. When the guard returned the animals lay crippled and suffering. The Indians had temporarily disappeared. That seemed to the people the final depredation. Eddy had lost all but 1 ox and the German Wolfinger similarly. Some of the party slaughtered out their animals and cut off hunks of loin to carry along for food. Eddy cached all his possessions in his worthless wagon. He and Ellie would have to walk. He would carry little Jimmy and Ellie would carry baby Margaret. He took nothing from his wagon but about 3 lb. of loaf sugar, some bullets and his powder horn. He left his rifle behind because a broken lock rendered it useless. Wolfinger insisted on burying his possessions in the hope of returning for them from California. The party was ready to go on. No one proposed to wait for the German. Then Reinhardt and Spitzer agreed to stay with Wolfinger and help him make his cache if he would pay them for the work.

It was 40 miles or more across the sink according to the

guidebooks. The families no longer traveled as a party. Every family looked out for itself and damn all stragglers. Eddy walked in soft-soled moccasins across broken rocks and cactus, carrying a child and cursing a misbegotten Providence. Even those who still had oxen and wagons knew that everyone who was able must walk and the wagons be lightened almost to emptiness. One of the Murphy boys carried a copper kettle on his head like a helmet rather than burden the oxen with its load. All walked beside the wagons except the sick and the infants. Walked through choking dust across a landscape empty of life or so it seemed to them. The Indians knew otherwise. They could make a fine feast of grasshoppers or white grubs. Oxen would do however. Eddy imagined the Indians watching them from the ridge of every hill. Laughing at their civilized incompetence in the desert where the Indians made their home. He wasn't wrong.

October 14

Staggering through the night the people came in the hours before dawn to a spring that jetted a geyser of steam high into the air. 2 pools boiled nearby. The region appeared to have been a center of volcanic activity once. Vast quantities of mud now dried to dust filled the plain around. Will Eddy saw his family's exhaustion and applied to Tamsen Donner for coffee. Tamsen consented and Eddy contrived to boil the coffee in one of the boiling pools. He gave it to his wife and children to drink saving none for himself. He revived by watching them revive.

Families started straggling away again about 9 A.M. Eddy and his family staggered on through the day without water until sunset when Eddy realized his children must have water or collapse. He had helped Breen fill his water casks at the sink. He went to the Irishman and asked him for a cup of water for each of his children. I can't do it man said Breen. I don't know but that I'll need it for me own. Eddy usually kept himself level but now he exploded with anger.

You son of a bitch said Eddy you give me some water for my kids or I'll cut your goddamned throat. Breen paled and started backward at Eddy's fury. Eddy leaned to Breen with knotted fists. He moved left and right looking for a foothold. Then he broke and turned from Breen and stomped furiously to the water cask on Breen's wagon and tore loose the cup that hung there and filled it with water and stared at Breen and drank it down. Breen was still done in by Eddy's anger and only stared nervously back. Eddy held Breen's eye and called his wife and she came over with the children and they had a good drink. By then Breen had recovered and was sputtering and gesturing in Eddy's direction. Eddy resisted the urge to spit and gathered his family and walked away.

He walked on as they all walked on through the dry drive where other emigrants had discarded every kind of possession from chests to jugs to guns to family portraits. The Donners cached their store of books along the way. 3 yoke of oxen collapsed in the last 10 miles of loose sand and were left to die. The moon lit the lurid plain as if the ground had been rubbed slick with mercury gone black with corrosion in the shadows and at the edges. They staggered on. They could do nothing else but lie down and die or stagger on.

October 15

In the morning at dawn trees poked up over a ridge ahead. Real trees for the first time in weeks of wandering. Cottonwoods and aspen. The oxen smelled water and perked up. Men and women and children who were dragging their feet found their strength again. Over the ridge they saw the green grass and the tall trees of a river bottom. The Truckee River. It cut through the ash-gray hills green with life. The River of Eden. The River of Heaven. The water blue in the distance. The juicy grass and wet trees green. They had never seen anything so lush in all their lives. Paradise had sent out its welcome into the sere barrens of hell.

They ran as they reached the bottom of the hill. Ran through the grass. Ran past the trees. Ran to the cool sweet ribbon of water. Jumped in and splashed each other. Ducked under. Drank the water through their ears and their eyes and their mouths and their noses. Through their skin. Through the palms of their hands and their elbows and their feet. Laughed and cried and mingled their tears with the waters of the river. The oxen dragged the wagons half into the river and sucked up the water in great gouts. Animals nor men has tasted such water since the far side of the South Pass. When they were full and fresh the people looked up the river and saw it silver in the morning light. A silver latchstring hung out all the way from the California mountains.

Eddy applied to Mrs. Breen and then to Mrs. Graves for a little meat. His children and his wife hadn't eaten for 2 days and nights except for the loaf sugar. Nor had he. Those worthy mothers found they could spare nothing. Eddy did succeed elsewhere in borrowing a gun and went off hunting. It was the season of migration for ducks and geese and Eddy killed 9 geese in 2 hours. He dragged them back to camp and found himself at the center of a circle of admirers, Mrs. Breen and Mrs. Graves among them. They said the geese looked excellent and Eddy contemptuously told them they ought to help themselves and watched dumbstruck as each of them took 2. He gave 1 to Keseberg and roasted the other 4 and saw to his family's providing for that day and the next and shared his feast then with whoever was in need.

October 16

Rested in camp. Considerable hilarity over the appearance of the oxen. They had eaten so much grass they bulged like cows about to freshen.

October 17

Traveled up the Truckee River. Reinhardt and Spitzer came up during the day without Wolfinger. Mrs. Wolfinger was beside herself with grief. The Germans said Wolfinger had been killed by the Indians and his wagon burned. They said they barely escaped with their lives. They looked none the worse for their experience however. No one trusted their story but no one proposed to do anything about it either. Tamsen Donner took Mrs. Wolfinger in.

October 19

Traveled up the Truckee. In midafternoon the families forward in the train saw a string of mules progressing down the canyon of the river. Closer they realized it was Stanton. The little gentleman had kept his word. He came up to the first wagons riding a mule with great dignity. He said McCutchen had been taken sick with an old malaria and was forced to stay behind at Sutter's Fort. He had 7 pack mules loaded with flour and jerked beef. 2 Indians from Sutter's named Luis and Salvador accompanied him. The Indians had been trained by Sutter. They wore shirts and trousers of homespun.

Stanton left a mule's-worth of supplies with the forward wagons and rode on back to those in the rear. He came up to Mrs. Reed and was able to inform her that her husband had gotten through along with Walt Herron who had accompanied Reed from the Donner section forward. They had barely survived and were reduced one day to eating rancid tallow from a tar bucket they found along the trail but they got through finally in good order and Glaucus too though Stanton said you could play a tune on that fine mare's ribs. Margaret Reed and the girls cried with joy.

October 20

Stanton took on the Reeds. They didn't have to walk any more. Margaret and Tommy rode pack mules. Patty and Jimmy rode behind Luis and Salvador. Virginia rode behind Stanton.

The brothers-in-law Bill Pike and Bill Foster of the big Murphy family resolved during the nooning to make their own attempt at relief. They planned to go to Sutter's and bring back more food. Stanton's supplies wouldn't be enough to see the whole party through. They commenced to pack their equipment. In the course of packing, Pike handed Foster a loaded pepper-box pistol. Hardly had Pike turned around when the thing went off in Foster's hands and fired a ball through Pike's back. He slumped to the ground and shortly was dead with his wife Harriet screaming at his side. She beat on Foster but there was nothing on earth anyone could do. The widow Murphy finally pulled her away. Foster sat and stared into the cooking fire. Could anything else happen to them. Could they suffer any more than they already had.

The party buried William Pike wrapped in a blanket without board or coffin. A light snow fell in lieu of flowers on the grave.

October 21

The last stragglers reached the broad meadows below the first foothills of the mountains late in the day. For all the fine pasturage of the Truckee River bottoms the necessity to haul on up the canyons of the river had not relieved the oxen much of their long strain. The people resolved to camp in the Truckee meadows long enough to strengthen the oxen for the grueling climb over the mountains. Stanton affirmed that the big snows never came to the mountains until the middle of November. Sutter told him so. They would have a few days grace to recruit the oxen. There was nothing else to do in any case. The animals weren't strong enough as they stood to take the wagons over the pass.

October 22

Resting in Truckee meadows.

October 23

Some of the people wanted to continue in the meadows but others were for moving on. The Breens, Pat Dolan, the Kesebergs and the Eddys started out early in the day to follow the trail up over the mountains. The Breens were the best-supplied of all the families in the train. Dolan was their friend. Keseberg was impatient of delay and so was Eddy. By late afternoon they had forded the river 49 times and camped where the trail swung off to the right to avoid a narrow canyon. Eddy caught an Indian shooting arrows into the oxen. That was as much as Eddy could take and he put a ball in the bastard's back. The ball went right through the lung and came out in front. The Indian leaped into the air with a scream and fell down a bank into a grove of willows. Eddy slid down the bank and looked the Indian over. He was no more than 15.

October 24

Stanton left the meadows with his Indians and the Reeds, the Graves and the Murphys. The Donners and their teamsters and the people they were helping still stayed on in the meadows.

In the first easy mountains the advance party traveled through light snow.

October 25

The Donners left the meadows. The other sections toiled upward. The river was cold and the air colder. No one loved the Truckee any more.

Keseberg stepped on a stob during the afternoon and severely punctured his foot. Breen grudgingly loaned the German a horse and Phillipine Keseberg rigged a sling.

October 26

The 3 sections hauled up the California mountains each at its own pace.

October 27

Cloudy day. Late in the morning George Donner's family wagon dropped off a ledge of rock and broke an axle and turned over. Father and mother escaped injury but the girls

Georgia and Eliza were caught inside the wagon. Georgia yelled and they sought her and pulled her free. Eliza made not a sound. They dug frantically among the bedding and turned her up. She was half-smothered. They soon revived her and found her none the worse for wear. George and Jacob proposed to repair the axletree. The teamsters cut down a choice pine and the 2 farmers began the work of trimming and shaping. While carving away at one end George lost control of his chisel. It slipped from the resiny wood and came down and gashed the back of his hand. He dropped the chisel and held the hand up in the air. Dark blood streamed from the gash. George clamped his other hand around his wrist and staunched the flow of blood. Tamsen bandaged the wound and back to work he went. Completed the axletree by the end of the day.

October 28

Hauling up the mountains. These were lesser mountains. The main range lay several days ahead. On this day it began to rain and sleet.

October 29

Hauling up the mountains. Very little for the oxen to eat since snow covered up the grass. They bellowed at night something pitiful. Rain and sleet miserable.

October 30

Hauling up the mountains. Still raining.

October 31

The Breens rounded the pine-covered hills first and rejoined the Truckee River in its upper canyon. To the west, hooded with clouds, they could see the high mountains that barricaded their way. With Dolan and the Kesebergs and the Eddys they followed the Truckee to where a lesser stream branched off due west. Rain begrimed their passage. An inch of snow lay on the ground. Half a mile from the fork they halted and made camp. As the sun set the rain turned to snow.

Riding through the warm rain in the Sacramento Valley, James Frazier Reed reached Sutter's Fort after resting up at Johnson's ranch on the Bear River. He found his old friend Edwin Bryant at the Fort and presented to Colonel Sutter his letter of good character from the Governor of Illinois.

November 1

Snow in the lead camp lay a foot deep but now rain fell again. The 3 families and Pat Dolan set out for the pass. A mile forward they found a rough cabin made of saplings roofed with dead pine branches. Beyond the cabin they followed a precarious trail along the shores of a narrow lake. Truckee Lake. It was gray and almost transparently clear. A mountain lake deep and cold. At the head of the lake they fought through the wet snow. Above them rose the pass. The farther up they climbed the deeper the snow. The oxen had little strength to haul the wagons. The men couldn't even find the trail. Ahead of them the wall of the pass still showed bare rock but all its pockets and crevasses were full of snow. The pass rose up 1000 feet above the lake. Late afternoon they turned around. They would have to wait for Stanton to guide them across. Breen reached the cabin first. The roof leaked so badly the dirt floor had turned to cold mud. They slept in their wagons that night. Rain turned back into snow in the night cold.

November 2

Rained all day. The forward section stayed in camp waiting for Stanton. At dark the second section came up to the camp with Stanton and his Indians in the lead. They could get through if anyone could. No sign of the Donners.

November 3

The oxen had to be whipped into their yokes. They had

[77]

starved for days on nothing but browse. They looked as if they would slip their yokes they'd gotten so thin. They were starved and half-dead.

—Ho there Josie! Chester! Gi on there!

Some talk about the Donners. People said they should have come on when they had the chance. It was their lookout if they didn't make it over the pass. No one could do them any good waiting in camp.

Stanton led the way with his mules along the north shore of the lake. Snow still lay in patches on the ground. The lake was open yet. A swath of cloudy ice curved out from the near shore marking an edge of thaw and freeze. It looked like a highroad laid out at the edge of the water. Tall pines grew near the lake shore with reddish-yellow bark and prickled cones big as a man's hand. Gray dead pines lay scattered on the slope of the ridge beyond the southern shore of the lake in the debris of gray rock where no grass grew. Clouds piled heavily over the peaks ahead. No sun cast shadows. No shadows marked the passing of the wagons over the patchy snow.

Beyond the lake the snow deepened as the trail bent upward. Soft power blew in the contrary wind. Knobs and shoulders stuck out bare above the snow. The sandy lake shore gave way to rock. The wagon wheels cut into the powder until the axles were buried and the wagon beds skidded along the surface of the snow.

They saw they must abandon the wagons. They pulled their belongings out of the wagons and spread them on the snowy ground. Few agreed on what to pack. Some spoke for tobacco while others spoke for calico. Keseberg sat his borrowed horse like a lord. He shouted at them to quit bickering over what they would take and pack up and start on. They listened to him no more than they listened to the wind. The rain wet everything through. The oxen didn't like the unfamiliar packs the men put on them. They bellowed and bawled and tried to buck them off or roll them off in the snow. Everyone fell to laughing at the antics of the oxen. It was the funniest thing they'd ever seen in their lives. Children and parents rolled in the snow along with the oxen.

Stanton got them up and calmed them down. They set out ahead driving their oxen. Stanton and the Indians broke trail with their mules. The families stumbled on in the sleeting rain of late afternoon.

The lead mule had lost the trail and was burying itself in snow-filled gullies. Stanton forced his mule ahead with Luis behind him and struggled for the road and found it. The families hung back while he worked toward the summit on his mule. The wind gusted down the trough of the pass and whipped the sleety rain into their faces. They could tell the wind was coming by the way the heads in front of them turned aside. Then the wind hit and they turned aside too. They might have been trees climbing the rocks the way they turned aside in the wind.

Stanton called back down Come on! come on! we've made a trail for you! but the light was fading as the sun set beyond the mountain pass and beyond the pall of clouds and no one came on. No one said stop either but they stopped at a patch of pines below the blunt cliff that marked the pass itself. They were almost to the pass but they stopped in the thickening dark. They said Can't climb no mountains in the dark. Women and children got to have a rest. Can't just go on and on. Keseberg rode among them scolding them in a bitter voice. Someone told him to go back to Germany or go on to Hell.

Stanton returned from the summit tight with anger that they hadn't come on while they might have. The Indians didn't say a word.

Milt Elliott set fire to a dead pine. It caught with a whoosh! and crackled and roared to a torch bright as daylight. The people around it moved back. Their long shadows burst behind them edged with red and black on the snow. Children crowded the burning tree and held out their hands and shoved each other and grinned. No one watched the oxen. They rolled in the snow and wallowed off their packs. Clambered up and shook themselves and stood chewing their cuds in the firelight.

Keseberg rode over to a cluster of men, Eddy, Stanton, Fosdick, Graves.

—What can this mean? Keseberg said. If we do not cross the pass now we never cross it.

The men looked up with distaste to the German on the horse.

—There'll be rescue parties soon enough said Stanton. Colonel Reed will see to that.

—Colonel *Reed* said Keseberg.

No one noticed the shift of rain to snow. The rain fell with sleet and then as if a barrier had been drawn away only large flakes of snow fell. With the snow came a silence soft as eiderdown. Sounds no longer carried beyond the circle of speech. Light no longer carried beyond the circle of fire. People found the packs of the oxen and removed food and ate in silence staring at the burning tree. The snow enclosed them in light. They lay shawls and blankets on the snow and put their children down to sleep and then lay down themselves or sat against trees with their knees drawn up. They forgot the day before and the day after in the shelter of the snow. No one contended. The tree burned low fading to orange and then to red. Glistening on the snow.

Phillipine Keseberg had helped her husband off his horse and tethered it to a pine tree. She had seen him comfortably wrapped in a quilt and had wrapped her little girl Ada next to him and then wrapped the baby Luis Sutter in with her and rolled onto her back and freed her breast and nursed the baby there in the snow feeling the hard gums on her nipple as she watched the snow fall into the light. After awhile she turned on her side and cradled the baby in her arm. She pulled the blanket to cover her head and stared fading into sleep at the snow fading red in the firelight.

Keseberg dreamed his torn foot was nailed to the earth. He woke up kicking and the kicking sent up a flare of pain.

He couldn't see. He was buried alive. He flailed his arms and pulled them free and sat up. False dawn lit the snow around him a faint blue. The trees rent the blue, black as crevices in a stone wall. Where people had lain down the night before Keseberg could now see only soft contours of snow. They had all run away and left him. They had all died. Keseberg screamed.

Around him heads popping up from the snow. Faces pulling up through the snow. The snow falling away from the features, the nose first, then the forehead and the eyes, the cheeks, the ears. The faces turned to him empty of expression. Shocked awake and not yet composed. He could see nothing of their eyes. The eyelids were drawn back and the eyes empty bare sockets. Empty and black and bottomless. The mouths open too and black and bottomless as the eyes. The cheeks drawn back in a grimace. His own mouth was open the same way. They were seeing him just as he was seeing them. Souls imprisoned behind the flesh they lived in. Souls black as night behind the holes of eyes and mouths. This is how the earth will be on the day of reckoning. Bodies sitting up in graves. The dirt falling away from their faces. Their hollow mouths and empty staring eyes.

Keseberg screamed again.

—Jesus Christ Keseberg! said Will Eddy what the hell's the matter?

A child cried and a mother smacked it and it cried louder.

—We were all buried under the snow said Keseberg I had to warn you to wake up.

—You was screaming like a stuck pig said Jay Fosdick.

—Ja said Keseberg better I should scream than you should smother.

Disinterred from the snow they stumbled to the edge of the pines and stared up at the pass. It rose unmarked before them. From summit to summit the trail was blocked by a solid wall of snow.

TWO

THE CAMP

November 4

At the old cabin below the lake the Breens had only to patch the roof to make themselves a shelter. Pat Breen and Pat Dolan cut brush and pine branches for the cabin roof. John and Edward Breen spelled the men. Pat Jr. and Simon and Peter carried and little Jimmy played at hand. Over the roof of brush the men and big Peggy Breen threw slickers. Old clothes and hides.

—It's a terrible place yiv brought me to Pat said Peggy as they worked.

—It's the Lord's will said Breen.

—It's not the Lord's will at all it's men's foolishness.

—Ah Peggy said Pat Dolan yi be too hard on us.

—Yir both fools said Peggy and what a terrible place yiv brought us to.

Crying. Twisting her coarse face, her shoulders shaking. Crying against the knuckles of her powerful hands. She blew her nose between her fingers to clear it and the men moved off sheepishly to cut firewood.

Lewis Keseberg hobbled to build a leanto against the west wall of the Breen cabin sheltered a little from the incessant wind. He squatted on the slushy ground with most of his weight on his right foot, the healthy one. He chopped down pine saplings thick as his wrist and threw them into a pile that Phillipine and Dutch Charley carried to the cabin site. Phillipine's face was flushed from the cold and the work. A buxom comely woman, honey-haired and tanned by the trail sun.

Will Eddy and Bill Foster searched for a cabin site in the woods around the old cabin clearing. They found a rock round as a cannonball and larger than a wagon. Farther on they saw another rock shaped like a fist but with one end split flat. They hiked over. The rock rose up 12 feet high. Little Georgie Foster tried to climb it but Lem Murphy pulled him off and set him crying.

—This'd make a fine firewall said Foster.

—Sure as hell would said Eddy. Save us building one whole wall.

They walked around the rock.

—Must of fallen down the mountain said Eddy.

—Glad I wasn't around when it come said Foster shaking his head.

They ran their hands down the cold granite.

—Let's get started said Eddy.

With broadhead axes they cut a stout pine. Dropped it crashing to the ground while the Murphy children squealed. Skinned off its branches and told the children to pull them aside and pile them up. They sawed the trunk into 2 long logs for the sides of the cabin and a shorter log for the front. They chained up Eddy's single remaining ox and dragged the logs into place one by one to form the foundations for the walls. They butted the side logs against the big rock. It would serve for a back wall. The children climbed the rock while the men worked. The men slapped it with their gloved hands whenever they got near it the way they would slap a prize bull.

After they had notched and laid the foundation logs they cut smaller logs and saplings. They sharpened the logs into posts and dug holes on each side of the foundation logs at the ends and halfway between and set the posts, then stacked the saplings into the slots between the posts to make sapling walls. They fitted the ends of the saplings back against the big rock matching its contours.

Before the walls were even done Lavina Murphy had built a fire against the rock. The smoke sooted a path up the granite. The children leaped back and forth over the foundation logs and then over the sapling walls as the sides went higher. For the first time in 6 months they had a house to live in.

The Graves and the Reeds chose to camp in the abandoned wagons. Stanton advised them not to bother building a cabin because they would soon cross the mountains.

6 miles from the lake camp at a meadow on a feeder creek the Donners had halted the night before in the heavy snow. During the day they started to cut logs for cabins but realized they had neither time nor manpower and decided to put up their tents while they still could. George Donner worked with his bandaged hand setting up the family tent and cutting saplings to make an extension from the tent to a big pine tree behind it. The tree had a fork of roots growing out of one side that formed a natural hearth. George cut the saplings and the girls and the teamsters leaned them against the tent and the tree at Tamsen Donner's direction and tied them together to make a brush house with an opening in the top against the tree for a smokehole. Mrs. Wolfinger would live with them but they could hang blankets inside to make a little privacy. Jacob Donner was ailing. The teamsters helped Uncle Jacob build a tent-and-brush house like his brother's against a tree. The teamsters bent a grove of saplings over on itself and lapped the crowns of the young trees and tied them together to make a brush shelter. Bolts of cloth and clothing and robes came out of the wagons to cover the brush shelters and exclude the snow. Tamsen bundled Georgia and Eliza in buffalo robes and set them leaning against a log to watch the work. They laughed at the swirling snow that filled the folds of the warm robes. They couldn't even see their Uncle Jacob's house across the creek for the falling snow.

James Frazier Reed and Will McCutchen rode out from

Johnson's ranch in the Sacramento Valley just beyond the western foothills of the mountains with a relief train of 30 pack and saddle horses and a mule. 2 of Sutter's Indians rode with them to work the horses. The animals were packed with jerked beef and beans and with flour the Indians at the ranch had ground by hand in stone mortars. They followed the Bear River to the mountain foothills and then took the trail that paralleled the river a few miles to the north. The rain soaked them through and the water chilled them in the swollen streams they were forced to ford. Reed was keen with the excitement of setting out. The party would need the relief by now. It ought to be over the pass. Hauling down toward Bear Valley. They'd be damned sick of poor beef and no flour and mountain snow. Reed was already sick of the goddamned rain. It wasn't going to do Mac's ague any good. Folks at camp ought to be glad to see their *banished* foe, even old Graves.

November 5

With a flap of canvas cut from a wagon top to make a door cover Peggy Breen put the finishing touch to her cabin. Breen and Pat Dolan cut firewood and the boys stacked it against the wall inside the door. The men had made bed frames of staked and lashed poles laid over with planking from the wagon. Peggy assembled quilts and blankets and made up beds. The weather was still gray and the snow falling. She could hear the Kesebergs working on their leanto beyond the wall. On the bed the baby Isabella began crying and Peggy gave up her work and sat down and unbuttoned her dress and lifted one pendulous breast free and set the baby to nurse.

The Englishman John Denton and young Solomon Hook hiked into camp along about noon. They sought out Will Eddy in the nearly completed cabin at the big rock.

—We've settled in beyond the ridge Denton told Eddy.

—How are the Donners taking it? said Eddy. He was sharpening a bed stake.

—Cheery enough wouldn't you say Solomon?

—Yes sir.

—It looks like we'll be stuck here awhile said Eddy. He picked up another stake. Some of the men think we can push on through when the snow stops.

—Is it likely to melt? said Denton.

—Don't nobody know. I don't see as it can melt up there in the pass. It's five feet deep or more. But maybe it'll melt on the trail.

—Well said Denton there's no reason for our party to move up here with yours. If the snow melts then the extra miles won't matter.

—Yeah said Eddy you might as well stay on down the trail there. Anyway, Reed and Mac is likely on their way up the trail right now.

—I suppose they are said Denton. He pulled on the blond beard that masked his freckled jaw. I suppose they are.

The oxen crowded under the trees beyond the cabins. With their long tongues they caught low branches and pulled them into their mouths. Clamped them between their front teeth and tossed their heads aside and stripped them of their needles and bark. They worked the needles out the sides of their mouths with their tongues but salvaged the bark and chewed it to sweetness and swallowed it. It served hardly at all to satisfy their hunger. They bellowed and bawled until Breen sent his boys to the creek to cut rushes. Back with the oxen the boys amused themselves lifting great fistfuls of loose hide from their backs.

—They got their own handles said John.

—Pitiful lookin things ain't they said Edward. All hide and clackety bones. We oughta just butcher them out and get it over with.

—Stupid. Butcher them now and they'd putrify.

—They're going to die anyway.

—It gets colder though and they'll freeze and keep said John.

—Yeah that's so I guess said Edward kicking the pile of rushes closer to the herd.

Still riding through the foothills of the mountains Reed

and McClutchen found a spring beside the trail and set their animals to feed and camped for the night.

November 6

Continued snowing. Some of the men went fishing. They could see the fish swimming deep in the clear lake but nothing they tried would bring them up to bite. Bill Foster loaned Eddy his gun and Eddy went hunting. Between the Murphys and the Eddys there was only 1 ox left and Eddy was keeping it alive to save it from spoiling if the weather warmed up. Eddy followed along the creek that led east from the lake. A mile from camp he halted in a clump of rushes at a place where the grass around the creek was beaten down. With his gun on his knee he waited in silence as the snow fell. A buff head with a black nose popped out of the grass and looked around out of mad yellow eyes. It might have been the head of a fox swollen with greed. Eddy brought the gun to his shoulder and drew a bead on the head. The coyote stepped forward to drink and Eddy tracked it in his sights. He squeezed the trigger and the gun went off and the animal jerked and fell and the creek momentarily ran red.

It stank in the cooking like skunk. The women and children could hardly choke it down. There was nothing else for dinner.

—The Breens and the Graves got plenty said Bill Foster. I don't see why they don't share some of their meat.

—They got mouths to feed themselves said Sarah Foster.

—Give me another try at hunting said Eddy chewing coyote meat. If I don't do no better tomorrow I'll go ahead and slaughter out that ox.

On the ridge above Mule Springs Reed and McCutchen at last came to snow. They were 40 miles out from Johnson's ranch and 30 miles from the lake camp. Not their skills nor the Indians' could prevail over the rain-soaked wood on the trail. Except for the cold jerked beef they chewed they went supperless.

November 7

Reed sat his horse on the ridge above Bear Valley. He studied the valley covered with snow unbroken by any trail. If the party had made it beyond the pass they would have made it there. There or maybe the summit valley but they couldn't stay up that high in bad weather. Yuba bottoms maybe.

—Goddammit Mac they've got to be along here somewhere.

McCutchen on horseback towered beside the six-foot Reed. He stretched his shoulders forward to ease his back.

—Hell. I know it. We ought to of seen some sign of them by now. He straightened on his horse. Listen to this Jim. This's old Lear. *Poor naked wretches* he boomed *wheresoe'er you are, that bide the pelting of this pitiless storm, how shall your houseless heads and unfed sides, your looped and windowed raggedness, defend you from seasons such as these?*

—That's about the size of it said Reed drily. Let's get on. Maybe they're up the valley a piece.

A morning's hunting bagged Will Eddy only an owl and during the afternoon he and Bill Foster butchered the remaining Eddy ox. Graves, Dolan and the Breens were also slaughtering cattle. The camp dogs feasted on the blood and scraps. The meat was shiny and blue and entirely without fat. They stacked the quarters beside the cabins like cordwood.

At the Donner camp Tamsen Donner supervised the butchering. With the possibility of a winter encampment at hand she directed the teamsters to cut away the guts and set her girls to washing them in the creek. She let nothing be wasted except the blood. The tripe and sweetbreads and liver and kidneys she planned to cook up first and set the rest of the meat aside to freeze. The hides went onto the roof of the shelter once they were scraped reasonably clean. In the midst of the work of butchering she remembered her mood back at the Little Sandy and thought again of Lansford Hastings and clenched her small fists in fury.

Pushing to the upper end of Bear Valley, Reed and McCutchen saw smoke blowing from a mound of snow. Closer the mound resolved itself into a shelter, a pen roofed with a tent piled with snow. Snow water dripped from the edges of the tent. A smell of roasting meat warmed the cold mountain air.

Both men called. A grizzled man and a woman in a man's coat and hat popped out of the shelter waving their arms.

—Saved! We're saved!

—Oh heavenly days they've rescued us!

Inside the shelter Reed and McCutchen and the Indians warmed themselves at the cooking fire. A Dutch oven sat among the coals, steam whisping from the margins of its lid. Spit filled McCutchen's mouth.

When Reed had thawed he looked the couple over.

—What in God's name are you people doing out here?

The man smiled a crooked smile.

—We got fed up with the folks we was travelin with. They didn't live by the Book. We figured we'd camp up here for the season.

—Didn't you know about the snow in these parts? said Reed.

—It were the prettiest fall in this valley you ever seed said the man. Look here he added my name's Jot Curtis.

He extended his hand and Reed shook it.

—I'm James Reed. This is Will McCutchen.

—Pleased to meet you Mr. Reed. Mr. McCutchen. Look here we want to get down out of here. We just about run out of food. Our cattle done took off for the mountains.

The woman nervously watched the men. She shied from the Indians who stood silently by the fire.

—Sure we'll help you said Reed. We're on our way up the trail to relieve our party but as soon as we get them we'll pick you up on the way back down. We expect they're caught in the snow just like yourselves.

—We ain't seed nobody said Curtis. Don't think they ever got this far along. Curtis's hands plucked at his pants. A whine edged his voice. I don't see how you're goin to make it any futher along than here. That there snow just gets deeper the futher up you go. It's sure five or six feet deep above the valley. Might just as well go on back down from here.

—How'd you know how deep the snow is? said McCutchen.

—Why I walked it tryin to scout up my cattle said Curtis.

—We've got family up ahead Mr. Curtis said Reed. No question but that we got to get through to them first. Reed noticed the Indians. You boys better get on out there and take care of the horses. See they get to that browse over at the edge of the valley. You might bring in a pack of flour first for Mrs. Curtis here.

The woman moved to the fire.

—You men is welcome to eat with us she said. All· we got is dog though. Had to kill our dog after we ran out of beef. Don't taste half bad.

Reed and McCuchen looked at each other.

—Thank you ma'am said Reed. Maybe you can make up some bread with this flour of ours. The boys'll bring some in for you in a spell here.

—That'd be right nice said Mrs. Curtis. You'll help us get down from here won't you?

Ready to cry.

—We'll do whatever we can ma'am said Reed kindly. We've got to go on to our own party first but we'll be sure and pick you up on the way back.

The woman's lip quivered.

—How long'll that be? I don't think I can stand it here much longer.

—We can't stay here a-waitin said Curtis. You got to help us get on down right away. Resentment in his voice. Ain't no tellin how much more snow we're goin to get up here.

—Look here Curtis said McCutchen. We said we'd help you and we mean to help you but our first duty's to help our own. There's eighty, ninety people up there and they ain't got enough food to last them even if they had anyplace decent to hole up in.

—How come you boys got over the mountains okay? said Curtis. You take the back trail out of camp did you?

—Goddammit man.

—*Mac* said Reed. Simmer down. These folks are just upset. He turned to Curtis. We'll see that you get rescued Mr. Curtis if you'll just hang on here a few days. We'll even leave one of the Indian boys with a few of the pack horses. They're about give out anyway. We'll get you out of the mountains on our way back down.

—That's white of you Mr. Reed said Curtis. I just don't think you're goin to git much futher east of here.

One of the Indians brought in the flour and went back out. The woman set to making bread. Reed and McCutchen felt their clothes drying out in the heat of the fire. Curtis began a long tale about the mistakes and meannesses of the party he had come west with. Reed kept the conversation going more from courtesy than from interest. McCutchen brooded over Curtis's insinuations. His stomach rumbled with hunger.

—I think the bread's ready now said Mrs. Curtis eventually. You boys want to taste this here roast afore you try it? Don't suppose you get dog every day.

—I'll have a taste said Reed.

The woman cut a corner off the roast and forked it up from the pot and handed the fork to Reed. He sniffed the unfamiliar meat and found nothing unusual in the smell. He blew on it to cool it and brought it to his mouth and nibbled off a bite and chewed it.

—That's fine said Reed. To McCutchen he pretended a face. I think you better taste it before you eat it Mac. You may not like it.

Reed passed the fork to McCutchen who eyed it sceptically. He sniffed it. Sniffed it again. Sniffed it again. Took a bite. Rolled it around his mouth. Chewed it up then and swallowed it and nodded his head gravely to Mrs. Curtis.

—Very good dog ma'am.

Reed burst out laughing.

November 8

Eddy had no luck at hunting. Returning to camp he passed a dead ox that belonged to Graves. After he had put away Foster's gun he hiked over to the Graves wagons. The old man stood at the campfire holding a tin cup of hot tea.

—What you want Will? he said.

—That dead ox of yours Uncle Billy said Eddy.

Graves squinted.

—What about it?

—If you ain't got no use for it I sure as hell do said Eddy.

—It's kinda high said Graves. Don't have much palate for a old ox.

—How about if I haul it away for you?

—Ayeah said Graves. He looked into his cup. Well. What's it worth to you?

—You want to sell it? said Eddy. But you said you wasn't going to use it.

—Ayeah said Graves I wasn't but I don't see just givin it away.

—I got fifteen mouths to feed beside my own.

—That's you lookout ain't it Will?

Eddy's face reddened with anger.

—I ain't got no money.

—You're likely good for it ain't you? Graves grinned.

—I'm good for it Eddy said. He spat. How much you got in mind?

—Seems to me that old ox oughta be worth a pretty up here said Graves. I'd say twenty-five dollars.

Eddy exploded. His hands came up in fists and then he checked them.

—Twenty-five dollars! That's goddamned robbery!

Graves sucked his teeth.

—Spect Mrs. Reed'd be glad to buy it at that price.

—She ain't got no money neither said Eddy calming down.

—Her man does though if he ever gets back here to collect up his family. Graves squinted at Eddy and sucked his teeth again. Take it or leave it son. I don't give a fart in Hell.

—Twenty-five dollars for a rotten ox said Eddy. You must figure to get your reward in Heaven.

—Ayeah said Graves shifting under Eddy's stare. Nobody never done me no favors. Don't see why I should do none. I got me a big family to settle. Ain't as young as I used to be neither.

—I'll buy it said Eddy cutting Graves short.

—We'd best write out a paper then said Graves.

Reed and McCutchen set out from Curtis's camp at first light. They left one of the Indians and 9 jaded horses behind. They had wrestled the string of horses and the 1 mule into line before dawn. Curtis offered no help at all. They drove through the deepening snow up the steep wall of the mountain to the southeast of the valley aiming for the gap where emigrant parties lowered their wagons down into the valley with ropes. Across the gap the snow no longer lay packed down by the rain but piled up dry and powdery. They struggled on through the day making only 3 miles and camped in 3 feet of snow.

While they were making camp Reed and McCutchen discovered that their other Indian had deserted them. Both went for the horses but Mac mounted his first and rode off down the trail they had made during the day's march. Reed stood and watched him go and turned back to setting up camp.

McCutchen chased the Indian all the way to Curtis's place. When he got there he realized both Indians had lit out and taken the horses with them. He dismounted and advanced on Curtis in his pen.

—Where'd my Indians go Curtis? said McCutchen.

The old man sat on a trunk huddled near the fire. He poked at the fire with a stick.

—Don't rightly know he said. They was whispering and then they just disappeared.

—Just disappeared said McCutchen. Couldn't be you had

something to do with their disappearing could it? He jerked
Curtis's stick out of his hands. *Could* it?

—By Jesus McCutchen said Curtis you just watch who
you're pullin on. You ain't got no cause to spect me of
nothin. I ain't done you no wrong. He cringed farther back
on the trunk.

—Where's my Indians Curtis? McCutchen poked the stick
in Curtis's direction. Tell me where my Indians is before I
find some new use for you.

Curtis stared at the dirt floor of the pen.

—They done gone on down the mountain same as all of us
ought to.

—They done gone on down the mountain did they said Mc-
Cutchen. I wonder who put them up to that.

He jammed the stick into the fire sending up a flare of
sparks and turned and left the shelter. In the snow he
mounted his horse and headed for the mountain gap. Plunging through the pitch dark.

His horse staggered into camp at midnight. Reed had
kept the fire going and some hot meat in the pan. McCutchen
ate it with his fingers and licked them clean and rolled up in
his blankets and immediately fell asleep. Reed sat awake a
little longer listening to the blind wind force its way from
the canyons where it had strayed.

November 9

Uncle Billy Graves had had enough of living in wagons
while others sat by comfortable fires. Despite Stanton's ad-
vice he decided to go ahead and build himself a cabin.
Young Bill and Jay Fosdick could help and the women and
girls could fetch and carry. Graves told Stanton and Mrs.
Reed of his plan and Stanton hemmed and hawed but then
proposed that they build a common wall with the Graves
and extend a cabin of their own out to the east. Margaret
Reed sent Virginia to find Will Eddy and ask for his help.
The long-haired girl ran over the snow to the cabin by the
big rock and found Eddy not yet gone hunting and dis-

couraged of going at all. He agreed readily to help in the cabin raising and got his ax and followed Virginia over the mile to the cabin site Graves had picked downstream.

Eddy was reluctant to work with Uncle Billy but gave up his reluctance as a favor to Mrs. Reed. Stanton and the Indians helped and Milt Elliott. Patty Reed and Nancy Graves tended the campfire and kept water hot. The Graves even shared their coffee with the Reed contingent.

The supplies Stanton had brought from Sutter's were exhausted. All the jerked beef and flour had been distributed and eaten. As she worked on the cabin Margaret Reed framed a plan in her mind and when they halted for dinner she approached Uncle Billy.

—It's going to be a brave cabin she said standing above him by the fire.

He looked up at her sceptically.

—It'll do Miz Reed he said. I'd a sight rather be down in California though.

—We all would Mr. Graves Margaret Reed said. She accepted his remark as an invitation and sat down beside him on a log. But it looks as if we're here for awhile, doesn't it.

—It does said Graves. He blew on his coffee. Looks as how we might be here all winter.

—Mr. Graves said Margaret Reed. My family will need food. I wonder if you would consent to sell us two yoke of your oxen.

Graves was careful not to look at her. He let the silence go on.

—Can't sell two he said finally. Wouldn't have enough to feed my own.

Margaret Reed straightened her back and took a deep breath.

—Then sell us one. I'll pledge to pay you whatever you want to charge.

Graves stirred.

—Tain't that Miz Reed it's just I have to think of my own.

Margaret Reed smiled and brushed back her hair.

—Of course. I understand completely. But surely you can see your way to sell me a yoke of your oxen.

Graves going canny.

—Suppose I could. I'll have to ask you to pledge two yoke for it though. Down in California.

—That would be fine Mr. Graves. I'm sure Mr. Reed would see to that.

Graves frowned.

—I ain't talking about him. I'm talking about you.

—Then you have my word. She stood. Would you be so kind as to point out the animals you had in mind?

Later she bought another yoke from Pat Breen. He exacted a similar price.

Reed and McCutchen ate a hasty breakfast of boiled jerky and assembled the horses and drove up to the ridge between the Bear and Yuba rivers. They pushed on 3 miles in the crackling cold through the white powder that made the horses stumble and plunge. The snow deepened as they went until the horses buried themselves to their necks with every plunge. Their eyes bulged and they snorted in the unfamiliar snow. At the summit of the ridge Reed estimated the snow to be 4½ feet deep. There the horses found themselves buried in drifts until only their packs showed above the snow and then in a frenzy they would buck and kick themselves halfway free. The men looked at the horses with pity. There was nothing for it but to leave them where they were and reconnoiter forward on their saddle horses. The pack horses couldn't go much farther. If the families were camped in Yuba bottoms the men could find their way back and relieve the horses of their packs. The bottoms were obscured by the trees on the ridge. Reed and McCutchen left the pack horses and rode on. Heading down the ridge. Even the saddle horses could make little progress. They bucked and plunged while their riders struggled to stay on. After another mile and the snow deepening the horses were frothing at the mouth. The men dismounted into the powder sinking up to their waists. They stretched out their hands ahead of them above the snow and kicked their feet like swimmers and pushed on down the hill. The powder blew into their eyes and stung their faces. Snow was still falling but only lightly now.

Gasping for breath they pushed free of the trees onto a ledge where they could look down into the bottoms. The snow stretched unbroken out of sight to the east. The river itself was frozen over and bridged with snow. No smoke rose from any campfire. Only the wind blew the pines and swirled the snow into white whirlwinds that roamed up and down the empty valley.

—They ain't there said McCutchen.

—No said Reed they ain't there. Looks like the end of the road Mac.

McCutchen flailed the snow in a sudden fit of anger.

—Jesus Christ sweet son-of-a-bitch! he yelled. I didn't come all this way just to *fail them* Jim. He pulled back. I could go on. I could get to that camp even if it was all the way down the other side of these bastard mountains if I wanted to.

Reed took McCutchen's arm.

—I know Mac but it wouldn't do them or us any good. They don't need another mouth to feed and we couldn't pack enough over to them on our backs to make much difference.

McCutchen jerked loose from Reed's grip and kicked the snow.

—Oh hell I know they don't need another mouth to feed. They don't need my big mouth to feed.

—They'll have a hard winter Mac but they've got enough beef to see them through. When these winter snows get over we'll come back and relieve them. Sutter'll help. There's men back there who'll help.

McCutchen looked at Reed with pain in his face.

—We're so close. They got to be over to the lake. Truckee Lake.

—We'll be a lot more use to them if we go on back and

cache all that food we brought up. Keep it away from scavengers. Mark it so they'll find it if they try to hike on through.

McCutchen's shoulders sagged.

—I guess we would. Goddamn it to goddamned hell though.

At the crest of the ridge they dug out the pack horses that had buried themselves in the snow. They got back to Curtis's camp just after dark staggering with exhaustion. They felt their weakness the more for having fulfilled Curtis's prediction.

Mrs. Curtis was sick. She lay on the floor of the shelter wrapped in blankets, her face pale in the firelight. McCutchen and Reed stood for a time in silence before the fire warming their hands. They swayed with the effort of standing. They hadn't eaten since morning. After warming himself McCutchen went out to the pack horses and brought back some beef. He scooped the Dutch oven full of snow and set it to the fire. When the snow melted he added more until the pot was half full of water and then he dropped in the jerky. He sat down to warm his feet and stir the water as it boiled.

Curtis moved from the trunk where he had been sitting to the floor beside his wife.

—You're just good for nothin woman he said.

Silence. Reed and McCutchen stared into the fire.

—I knowed you took a likin to that one fella in the train said Curtis a little louder.

—Jotham said Mrs. Curtis I never did.

—I sawed you talkin to him ever chance you got. You recollect your Commandments woman?

—I never did Jotham.

—I've a mind to give you a lickin. You ain't no better than a Jezebel. He hissed. These two is lost in sin. They'd as soon leave us die as look at us.

—They ain't done you nothin but good Jotham said Mrs. Curtis. They're cookin your supper right this minute.

—Ain't likely cookin nothin for us woman. You just think any man you meet is goin t' do for you don't you. I kin see I'm goin to have to kick some of the onryness outa you.

McCutchen sat up straight and glared at Curtis.

—Look here you little canker he said. You shut that stuff up or I'll peel that meanness off of you and broil it right here on the fire.

Curtis shuffled himself back from McCutchen's reach. His wife sat up on one elbow.

—Mr. McCutchen she said Jotham didn't mean nothin. He's just cranky from bein up here and all.

McCutchen smiled warmly at the woman.

—I'm glad he didn't mean nothing ma'am because I'd hate to have to take him up on his meanness. I'd have to tear off those puny sticks of arms and beat him around the head with the bloody ends.

When the food was cooked McCutchen served Reed's plate and gestured him close and stage-whispered.

—Jim, that little puke-guts over there looks right hungry. He's a villain and a rogue and for all his religion he's probably a whoreson too but him and his wife got to eat and I cain't bring myself to ask them. She looks like she needs a little food for sure. Jim, I'd ask the Devil himself to eat with me before I'd admit a Kentuckian ever turned anyone away from his board so why don't you ask that little bull's-pizzle and his wife to eat with us.

Reed laughed.

—I don't know as I'd eat with the Devil Mac said Reed but I think I can stand Curtis. He raised his voice. You folks come on over here and eat now.

Mrs. Curtis pushed her blankets aside and came to the fire. McCutchen spooned her up a plate of his stew. Curtis drew up his knees where he sat and glared at the two men with his lower lip stuck out.

—What's the matter with you, man? said McCutchen.

Curtis scuffed his feet and tossed his head.

—I ain't hungry.

McCutchen stood up until his head bumped the tent and then he bent over toward Curtis until his knees were straight.

—Why goddamn you I know better you villainous lack-brain you rotten sausage you knotty-pated fool. Curtis cowered under the onslaught. You can't sit over there and not eat this good supper when there's people in them mountains tonight that might be starving to death. You little dwarf if you don't get over here and eat this supper I fixed I'll shake you right out of your clothes.

Curtis scuttled on his hands and knees to the fire and McCutchen slopped a plate full of food and shoved it into the man's hands.

—Never knowed such an ingrate said McCutchen.

—There's a first time for everything said Reed grinning.

November 10

The building of the Graves-Reed cabin continued. Now there were three separate buildings at the lake camp. Farthest down the creek toward the Truckee was the double cabin with the Graves in the west end and the Reeds in the east. Upstream a mile and about a half mile from the lake the Breens occupied the old cabin they had repaired. Leaning up against the Breen cabin was Keseberg's brush hut. About 800 yards south of the Breen cabin Eddy and the Murphys had built one large undivided cabin against the big rock. The Donners and their teamsters had finished setting up their tents and brush shelters in the creek valley 6 or 7 miles northeast down the trail. The snow lay a foot deep in both camps now. Deeper in the pass. The higher mountains were almost bare but the clouds boiled through the low pass and dumped their snow on the upper trail. The landscape seemed to the people depressingly plain yet somehow not so bleak as winters had been in Illinois. Eddy studied the problem on one of his hunting trips and concluded that the evergreens made the difference. In Illinois the trees shed their leaves. Here the trees stayed green and took on an icing of snow. It seemed to Eddy a good omen.

Lewis Keseberg made himself comfortable in his hut. He had oxen enough and with the help of his teamster he had seen them butchered out and stacked. But his foot throbbed continually. He didn't know what to do with it. It was swollen and red and a boil of pus had formed over the instep. Phillipine had relieved it before with soaking.

—Phillipine! he called from his cot. She was outside but she heard his call and came to the door and raised the flap and looked in. My foot must be soaked he said.

—*Ja* I will get water. She entered the hut and checked her sleeping baby before picking up a pot and carrying it out to fill it with snow. The toddler Ada followed her in and out. She returned with the pot and set it on the fire. Is it much worse today? she asked her husband.

—The boil seems ready to break he said. He sat up on his cot and examined his foot again. There is something inside I think.

Phillipine came over.

—Let me see.

Keseberg shoved her aside.

—You do not need to see. See to the water and I will see to my foot. His wife timidly returned to the fire. Always you would treat me like a child. I am your husband. You should be respectful of me.

—I mean to be respectful said Phillipine.

—Then accept my judgment without question said Keseberg. Ada came toward him and he moved his foot onto the cot so that she would not bump it. She smiled at her bearded father. He cupped her chin in his hand. Little love he said. What do you do today?

The girl wiggled her head in his hand.

—Eat snow she said. Eat snow. *Cold* Papa. Snow *cold*.

Keseberg's smile faded and he released his daughter's chin.

—*Also* he said. Go and play then. The child turned and ran out of the shelter. Keseberg stared into the fire. They are

such fools he said. If they had listened to me we would be
over the mountains now.

—*Ja* said Phillipine. You told them to go on.

—I told them to go on but they think they know better. They
are Americans and they are better than others. They said
Reed would come back for us. Where is he then? Have you
seen the murderer Reed? Phillipine smiled nervously. *Nein*
said Keseberg. Reed has not returned for us. Reed will not
return to rescue the men who witnessed his crime. He
would be a fool to return. We will stay here and rot if we
wait for Reed to return. The only way from this trap must
be on foot over the mountains. Keseberg pointed to the
steaming pot. It is ready. Would you scald me?

Phillipine lifted the heavy pot off the fire and westled it
over to the floor beside her husband's cot. He carefully
swung his leg to the floor.

—Test the water he said. I do not want to scald myself.

Phillipine put her wrist to the surface of the water and
held it briefly before jerking it away.

—It is hot but I think not too hot.

—You pulled away your arm said Keseberg.

—*Ja* said Phillipine but the wrist is more sensitive than
the foot.

—The water is too hot.

—The water must be as hot as possible she said. It will do
you no good unless it is hot.

Keseberg stuck a finger into the water and swirled it
around.

—It is too hot he said.

—If you would plunge the foot in it it would quickly accept
the heat said Phillipine.

—Be damned! said Keseberg glaring at his wife. Do not
argue with me! Go and get some snow.

He raised his hand to strike her and she flinched and got
up and left the hut. She came back with her hands cupped
full of snow and kneeled before her husband and dropped a
handful of snow into the pot.

—Try it now *bitte* she said.

—Test it first said Keseberg. You do not know if you have cooled it enough. She moved to drop the other handful of snow onto the dirt floor. Not on the floor! Keseberg shouted. Throw it outside.

She threw the snow outside and rubbed her hands and tested the water once again.

—It is perfect now she said.

Gingerly Keseberg eased his lame foot into the water. The toes went in first and then with considerable grimacing the instep and finally the heel. He squirmed on the cot and raised and lowered his foot but finally he sat still.

—Is it better now? asked Phillipine.

—*Ja.* Much better. I must soak it more often. We will only escape this place on foot.

With Curtis and his timid wife standing by, Reed and McCutchen cached their beef in the trees around the Curtis camp and their flour in the Curtis wagon and put the couple on horseback and headed off down Bear Valley. They led the string of horses but the mule had frozen to death during the night and they left it behind. The snow was deeper in the valley than when they came up and they decided to call a halt in the early afternoon at the lower end. Curtis found occasion to become abusive again and McCutchen no longer hesitated to give the man a shaking. Curtis promised to pay McCutchen back triple but the threat only amused the Kentuckian and he practiced all his Shakespearian curses on the skinny emigrant. Since most of them were originally designed with the bulk of Sir John Falstaff in mind they hardly fitted Curtis but they amused Reed and McCutchen and after their failure at relief they needed amusement. Curtis contented himself with lecturing his horse and with avoiding any semblance of labor in camp.

November 11

By midmorning the Graves and the Reeds had finished the big double cabin down the creek and stripped the wagons and moved in. Eddy had worked for 2 days side by side with the 2 families after coming in from early morning hunting. He accepted their hospitality for a sort of housewarming and brought his wife and children over to eat dinner with the Graves. After dinner the snow stopped. Everyone went outside to watch the last of the clouds roll away. The sky was a crisp blue. They cheered and pounded each other's backs, the women included. The sun glared on the snow. The peaks that guarded the pass glowed in the distance through the screen of trees.

Stanton, Eddy and Jay Fosdick immediately settled down to planning the next attempt at a crossing. It had snowed off and on for 2 weeks without the clouds even once breaking up. Now that the sky was clear the men could figure on at least a few days of good weather before some other storm came through.

—We got to *move* said Eddy. We got to get some food together and scratch up a party and *move*.

Jay Fosdick packed a snowball and threw it against the trunk of a pine.

—Every man and woman that gets across leaves that much for them as stays behind he said.

—I don't see any problem said Stanton. I do think we ought to send someone over to the Donners to let them know what we're planning. They may want to go with us.

—That's a fine idea said Eddy. Who can we get to go?

—Someone said Fosdick. Maybe one of the teamsters.

—We need to decide when we're leaving said Stanton.

Eddy stood up and stamped on the snow.

—Hell. Tomorrow morning right off.

—We've got to dry some meat said Stanton.

—We don't have to dry no meat said Eddy. Just whack off some hunks and pack them across. They'll stay mostly frozen.

—That's true said Stanton. He turned to Fosdick. Will you find someone to visit the Donners then Jay?

—Sure thing said Fosdick. Let's get moving. I want out of this godforsaken place so bad I can taste it.

Milt Elliott said he would go to the Donners.

November 12

Early in the morning a contingent from the Donner camp arrived prepared for the mountain crossing but none of the Donners came with them. Jim Smith, Dutch Charlie Burger, Antoine and Jean Baptiste and the German Gus Spitzer all came over with Milt Elliott. They milled outside the Graves cabin making small talk. They showed signs of wanting to go on but they were used to taking orders and they had no leader among them.

Eddy prepared to leave. Ellie and little Jimmy cried. Eddy wore a pack and a blanket roll on his back and a wool coat and 4 shirts. His pants were of homespun and over his moccasins he and Ellie had contrived boots made of the skin of the coyote he had killed.

When all were assembled they found themselves 15 strong including 2 women. Sarah Fosdick had decided to come along with her husband. She was 22 and had no children and saw no reason to stay behind. Mary Graves was 20 and single and thought to go with her sister Sarah. She had been engaged to marry John Snyder but he was buried in the alkali dust along Mary's River. Uncle Billy Graves would go. Milt Elliott. Stanton and his Indians Luis and Salvador.

Everyone except Keseberg came out to see them off but it was not a cheerful occasion. Husbands were leaving wives and fathers children. Even though all knew it was better that whoever could go should do so they felt the finality of the separation. Stanton reassured them but for all they knew the earth might drop off into darkness in the canyons beyond the pass. They might never see each other again.

The 15 hiked to the lake and followed the trail along its north shore. Luis and Salvador led along Sutter's pack mules. They were only lightly loaded with gear. They were thin by now and weak with hunger having lived on little more than pine browse.

Granite boulders lay scattered beside the trail. They reminded Stanton of some ancient race of Titans grown so old and wise that they no longer moved or breathed but only sat silently contemplating the passage of time. They knew what people hadn't learned. That all their struggle would take them nowhere except to that dark veil beyond which all troubles cease. They no more laughed at people than they pitied them. They didn't consider them at all. People moved by too fast for them. They had set their senses to a cut so coarse that men slipped between their teeth.

The 15 made no better progress that day through the snow than the entire party had made before. By nightfall they had struggled within 3 miles of the pass but knew they could not get over in the dark. Sarah Fosdick cried. The men set their faces and Mary Graves likewise. They turned around and stumbled back toward the lake cabins.

Reed and McCutchen arrived at Johnson's ranch after dark. They had delivered the Curtises to the snowline below Mule Springs and supplied them with beef and left them to their own devices. McCutchen decided to stay at the ranch and begin preparing for another relief. Reed said he would leave in the morning for Sutter's.

The 15 reached the cabins hungry and exhausted just at midnight.

November 13

Disgusted with himself, Eddy got up early despite his late return from the pass and borrowed Bill Foster's gun and went hunting. He had found a deep pool at a bend in the creek and before dawn he settled down there to wait for game. In the light of early morning he shot a duck and soaked his moccasins retrieving it and no more got himself settled and his gun reloaded than another flew in and he shot it too. Grinning he retrieved the second duck and shouldered his gun and paraded up the trail to the cabin. He gave Foster one of the ducks for the loan of the gun and presented the other to Ellie who took the duck in one hand and hugged her husband with the other.

Tamsen Donner wrapped her 3 little girls in warm cloaks and set them against a log outside the tent in the sun. Jean Baptiste had returned in the morning and now was cutting wood. The girls watched him work. He talked to himself and sometimes he talked to them. They played with the snow. Scooped it up and ate it and then rubbed their hands together to rub its coldness away.

George Donner's hand had become infected. Tamsen soaked it just as Phillipine Keseberg did her husband's foot except that George submitted willingly to the hot water. The infection only appeared along the edge of the deep wound and Tamsen wanted to keep it from spreading. It seemed to her that her husband showed more lassitude than was healthy.

—The sun would be good for you Mr. Donner said Tamsen as she put the soaking pan aside.

George looked over the wound as he might inspect a title deed.

—No Mother. I think I'll stay here and rest. Don't have much interest in seeing the sun. You go on out.

—It isn't I that need the sun it's you. She wrapped the hand in clean linen as she talked. I worry about you. You don't appear to be concerned about our condition.

He seemed far away.

—I'm concerned Mother but for the moment there's nothing to do.

—Jean Baptiste came back last night said Tamsen.

—Did he. Then they didn't make it across.

—He said the snow was too soft.

—I'm sure Jim Reed will find a way back said George. He's a resourceful man. Sutter's not likely to let us starve up here.

—There said Tamsen patting the bandage. But shouldn't we be active in our own behalf?

—I'm studying it Mother said George. We have enough for now. He lay back on his cot and turned his face to the wall.

Tamsen put away her scissors and the scraps of linen left

over from her work. She took up her coat and put it on and held aside the tent flap and went out blinking in the unfamiliar sun. The girls saw her coming and called to her. Jean Baptiste looked up from his work and ducked his head and then went on. It was a crisp clear day. The air was pure as the water in the meadow creek. Tamsen checked her children's cheeks and found them cold. The girls squealed as she touched them and she gave each a pinch and smiled at them and then stepped over the log and walked on preoccupied while their mittened hands reached back for her.

It was not the first time Mr. Donner refused to take the lead. It began the day he decided to leave his farms for a land of promises. People weren't meant to live where winter never came. They were meant to contend with the seasons. Perpetual summer below and in the mountains perpetual winter. Even the creatures went down from these heights. Tamsen greatly respected Mr. Reed but it was he after all who had committed them to Lansford Hastings. No. That wasn't fair. It was Mr. Donner too. They would suffer for that foolishness. He already bore the mark on his hand.

Remembering that her brother-in-law Jacob was ailing she changed the path of her walk to lead her to his tent.

November 14

Will Eddy went out hunting from the cabin by the big rock. He hiked cheerfully down the trail he'd made the day before along the creek running fast and cold between banks of snow. The ducks buoyed him. Ellie stewed theirs and they ate their fill for a change and the baby had some broth.

He came to the end of the duck trail and saw the drip of blood. Little holes like bullet holes in the snow. There was no taste like fresh duck when you'd been eating poor beef and lucky to get that. They had to get out of there. He had some living to do. Ellie was too pretty to be a widow.

Eddy broke a new trail in the snow along the creek. He wore his coyote-skin boots. His shoes were gone. He must have left a line of leather dust across the whole damned trail. Leather in the mountains. Leather in the salt desert. Leather along Mary's River. A devil could have followed that trail sniffing the ground with his pointy nose. Eddy had to get some meat to feed his family. What kind of a man didn't feed his family? Clyman had come over the pass in the dead of winter last year. Told them so himself. What would he say about their case? It was easier to do with just men but not so easy even then. They couldn't get those goddamned mules of Sutter's to go nowhere. The people were doing all right but the mules were breaking through. Clyman would of knowed what to do. He was the damndest figure of a man Eddy had ever seen. He told them. They were just too stupid to listen. He said don't take the Cut-off take the way by Fort Hall. They thought he was just bulling them. Reed thought he was testing his gall. Hell. He was just trying to save their skins was all. Eddy thought he should have spoken up. He did admire that man. Clyman looked like he knew what he was doing every little minute of the time. He's the one they should of trusted. Clyman and his greasy buckskins.

The sky beyond the dark pines was copper blue. The air still. No whisper of wind. The air thin. The air sharpened like a stake.

Jesus Christ there was a goddamned grizzly bear Jesus Christ.

Eddy stopped in his tracks trembling at the edge of a clearing where the grizzly foraged in the snow. He ducked behind a big pine. He had to be ready. No one he'd heard of had ever killed a grizzly in one shot. He had to be ready with his second shot or the goddamned grizzly'd kill him before he could get loaded again. If only it didn't see him. He uncorked his powder horn. Took a ball from his pocket and bit it between his teeth tasting the pale acid of the lead. He raised his gun. The grizzly bent over digging roots. It clawed away like a dog with both paws throwing the snow and dirt between its legs. Its stench hit Eddy, cabbage and rotten meat. It was a huge animal even bent over. Its humped back was turned toward Eddy. Its breath steamed out on both sides.

Eddy drew a bead holding his breath. He aimed for the back where the heart should be beating on the other side. He thought he could hit the spine or maybe break through and hit the heart. Hit the lungs anyway. Jesus what a stink.

Eddy squinted against the gold flash of the snow and squeezed the trigger.—*Crack!*

Oh Jesus I didn't kill him. He's coming after me oh Jesus looket him come got to get this powder poured oh Jesus.

The grizzly bolted on all fours its face twisted with rage its mouth open roaring. It broke through the trees at the edge of the clearing. Eddy had gotten his powder poured. The grizzly crashed like a boulder crashing down a mountain. Eddy ducked behind the tree. The bear swiped at him with one black paw and missed and fell over on its back addled by the wound. Eddy swung around the tree. He spat the wet ball into the barrel of the rifle and slammed it home against the tree. The grizzly stumbled up from where it fell and turned around the tree. Eddy stepped out behind it. He shouldered the rifle and fired at the brown blur in front of him. The ball tore into the grizzly's back and it slumped to the ground still roaring. It thrashed on the ground tearing away the snow making an angel in the snow. It clawed the bark off the pine at its feet revealing an underlayer pink as the ooze from a wound. Eddy backed up. He stumbled over a fallen pine. He dropped his gun to the ground and broke off a heavy branch and moved in. The grizzly watched him with narrowed eyes. Blood bubbling from its mouth. Dying and dead but not knowing that yet. Desperate to tear the thing that had pinned it to the ground. Eddy raised the club and bashed it across the grizzly's muzzle ripping away the black nose. Blood spurted from the mangled white bone where the nose had been. The club continuing downward broke away the bear's lower canines knocking them into its mouth. The club tore holes in the grizzly's tongue the grizzly screamed then like a screaming man. Eddy screamed like the grizzly and pumped the club up again and down across the grizzly's eyes. A stump of branch on the club punctured one eye. The club up and down again caved in the top of the grizzly's head and the skull oozed. The grizzly kicked spastically vomiting up roots and fur. The grizzly lay still an ear twitching. The grizzly lay still.

Jesus.

Jesus did I kill that?

—Oh Jesus Christ oh Jesus Christ goddamn!

Eddy swung the club around his head breaking off fresh branches around him. Their needles tore free and fluttered down lining green on the brown fur. The grizzly's mouth hung open and its torn tongue lolled to one side. One of its eyes was collapsed. The other stared open at the sky. Eddy flung the club away through the trees. It crashed through the trees like the grizzly.

—Oh goddamn goddamn!

He retrieved the gun and ran back along the trail heading for the cabin. He had to get somewhere out there with some oxen. Drag that big bastard back to camp. Jesus Christ they'd eat for a month. Jesus who'd ever of thought he'd of shot them a grizzly.

The Graves cabin was nearest. Eddy called to Graves as soon as the cabin came in sight. Graves stuck his head out the door.

—What're you hollering about? the old man called.

—I got me a grizzly Uncle Billy! Eddy came up to the clearing in front of the door. A grizzly bear! Knocked it down with two shots and finished it off with a club.

Other people appeared from both cabins.

—A grizzly is it said Graves. Tarnation.

—That's delightful Mr. Eddy said Margaret Reed.

Eddy smiled at her.

—You'll have some of it for your family.

—That's wonderful of you.

Eddy turned back to Graves. He was beginning to get his breath.

[114]

—Can you loan me a yoke of oxen to bring it in?

Graves looked pleased to be asked.

—Yeah. I kin do better than that. I'll help you with it for a share.

—What kind of share said Eddy frowning.

—Not much said Graves. Say whatever you share with Mrs. Reed.

Eddy grinned.

—Done then. Come on. Let's get out there before something drags it off.

—Ain't nothing likely to drag a grizzly off said Graves.

The 2 men yoked Graves' best oxen and set off down the creek driving the animals ahead of them. They were only a little way from the cabin when Graves began shivering. His body shook in spasms as he walked.

—I'm afeared Eddy he said poking one ox with his whip.

Eddy put aside his grin.

—What about?

—I'm afeared I'm goin to die up here. The old man looked around wildly. It's a judgment Eddy. I sinned not helpin old Hardkoop back there on the trail.

—Uncle Billy.

—No. I did. You tried to set me right and I was just too stubborn and afeared. I should of let you ride on back on my horse.

—It's done with now said Eddy. It doesn't look like Hardkoop would of made it anyhow.

—He would of if I'd of helped him. And Reed. We ought not have sent Reed forward. It's God's judgment I'm here in these mountains. I ain't never goin t' get free.

—Hell Uncle Billy said Eddy we're doing fine. You've got plenty to eat to last till relief comes.

—I'm goin to die. I can feel it. You don't get to be my age without knowin how it feels.

—I don't see talking about it said Eddy. It ain't right to just give up that way.

—I ain't said I was givin up. I just know what I feel.

—Well shut up about it! You just get the rest of us down when you talk like that. Eddy clamped his jaw and faced forward.

Graves' fit of shivering died away. They walked in silence to the clearing and chained the team to the bear's feet and began hauling the animal to the cabins. The weak oxen had trouble pulling. The bear's smell spooked them. Trees blocked their way. But eventually the men dragged the animal into the clearing outside the Murphy cabin. People from the other cabins came over to see. Eddy and Foster commenced butchering the animal out. Foster took half to pay for the loan of his gun. Eddy gave Graves and Mrs. Reed a hindquarter to divide and reserved a forequarter for himself. The dogs got the guts and fought for them in a snarling mass. It took the older boys a time to kick them apart. Eddy estimated the bear weighed 800 lb.

November 15

Flush with success and with his belly comfortably full for the first time in days Eddy went hunting again and bagged a duck and a gray squirrel. Foster accepted the squirrel as his share. He had a good supply of bear meat but his portion had to feed 12 people counting himself and Eddy's portion had to feed only 4.

Pat Breen was ill. He said he had the *gravel*. Diarrhea and nausea. He took to his bed and left the work to Peggy. Dolan helped where he could but Peggy couldn't boss him as she bossed her husband and he drew the line at hard labor. With her oldest sons Peggy took advantage of the clear days and cold nights to butcher out 2 yoke of oxen. The boys drove the animals one by one into the clearing outside the cabin. John drew a bead and shot them and Peggy cut their throats and all 3 boys did the work of skinning. The boys held their legs apart on the ground while their mother gutted them. Not much in the guts except pine needles and spit. They stripped them out at the edge of the clearing and piled them into the hide and dragged them to the creek and cleaned them. The Breens would have a stack of frozen quarters and innards to sustain them. Pat ate a mess of liver for supper and got gas pains and moaned all evening but then slept soundly through the night.

November 16

Patches of ground showed through the snow as the clear weather continued. Patty Reed and Nancy Graves played tea party outside their cabins. Patty had left her tea set with the Pioneer Palace Car in the salt desert but Nancy had most of one and Patty had her doll Penelope made of wood with jointed arms and legs and a china face. Penelope was only as tall as Patty's hand but she took tea too. Snow water was tea and snow was sugar.

—We haven't any salt Penelope said Patty. You'll have to do with beef.

—We had bear said Nancy.

—So did we. Mr. Eddy shot it and killed it with a club.

—I know. My Pappy says we'll never get to California.

—Is your pappy Uncle Billy? said Patty.

—Yes.

—He's so *old*.

—Anyway he's here said Nancy. He didn't get sent away.

—My Pappy got sent away but now he's in California. He's trying to find us.

—How come he hasn't brought us help like Mr. Stanton?

—He's trying isn't he Penelope but he can't get over the snow.

—Here's some more tea said Nancy do you want some?

—No thank you said Patty. She stood and brushed off her bottom. Her dog Cash jumped up and wagged its tail. Let's go for a walk Nancy.

—Huh-uh said Nancy what if there was bears.

—There isn't no more bears my Ma says said Patty. We're going to start eating hides soon.

—Ugh said Nancy we don't have to eat no hides.

November 17

James Reed ate chili beans and beef at the roughhewn common table at Sutter's Fort. Colonel Sutter commanded the table from the throne chair at the upper end. Reed had gotten used to the hot food they were served morning, noon and night. Sutter ate it with gusto whenever his Indians set a plate in front of him. The garlic and fire seemed out of character with a plump bespectacled European like Sutter. It amused Reed to imagine them all provided inside with blacksmith forges that burned beans and beef as a real forge burned coal. Certainly the smoke smelled the same. The fight was on for California. Reed would have to get into it with the Americans under Fremont. The war had drained the area of men just when he needed them. He'd work at recruiting for Fremont and maybe he could recruit for a relief party at the same time. At least the party in the mountains could hang on. He and Sutter had sat down the day he arrived from Curtis's Folly and added up the cattle and oxen the party had. Reed remembered the number from the count they had made at the spring beyond the salt desert. He and Sutter figured out numbers and weights and added up that they had enough poor beef to survive on through the winter. It wouldn't be much of a diet but it would keep them alive. Still they ought to be gotten out of the mountains as soon as was humanly possible.

November 18

It gnawed on Harriet Pike that she had to share the big rock cabin with Bill Foster. He was her brother-in-law and she tried to like him but he'd shot her husband and nothing anyone could say could change that. His hands were stained with blood. Men went through life making messes. Bill Foster sat over there whittling on a pine stick. It was Eddy who went out hunting. If none of them had come out from Missouri Bill would still be alive. She stared at the floor with her face in her hands.

—Harriet? said her mother. What's wrong Honey? You sure do look down in the mouth. Lavina Murphy held a wooden cooking spoon that dripped broth onto the dirt floor of the cabin. The dog came over to lick the drippings up.

Harriet burst into tears at her mother's words.

—It's Bill Momma I miss him.

Bill Foster stiffened at his place by the fire.

—I know Honey said Lavina Murphy I know. It's the Lord's will. You just got to bear it.

Something came loose in Harriet in the close cabin.

—I can't bear it Momma! I can't! Looking straight at Bill Foster. You *killed him*. You *killed* him. Sarah rushed to comfort her sister but Harriet shook her away. Leave me alone! Leave me alone. You've still got *him!*

The children in the cabin fell quiet. Bill Foster stood up.

—Harriet Honey he said it were a accident plain and simple.

—Shut up! Harriet screamed. Shut up! I can't stand to hear your voice!

—Listen *here* girl said Foster sternly you pull yourself together.

—Bill! said Sarah.

Foster jabbed his finger at his sister-in-law.

—I don't care. She's got no call to talk to me that way.

—She's just grieving Bill said Sarah leave her alone.

—Hell let her leave *me* alone. She's the one who's causin the trouble.

Harriet cried quietly now.

Eleanor Eddy tended the pot through the outburst in the Murphy family. She hunched her shoulders whenever someone yelled. How could they live with these people. They couldn't even get along in their own family. She'd never heard families before that yelled all the time.

Lavina Murphy came to Ellie's side.

—This here's ready Ellie she said. Where's your man?

—He's out hunting said Ellie. We can start if you want.

Bill Foster turned on her.

—He's out hunting is he. Don't he know when it's supper-time?

Ellie ignored him. She spoke to Lavina.

—The little ones look right hungry.

—The big ones is hungry too said Foster showing Ellie his teeth.

—My Will's probably starved out there hunting all day said Ellie.

Foster held out his plate. He spoke softly with an air of menace.

—Yeah. Good thing he's got my gun since he lost the hammer on his'n. Couldn't do much fancy hunting without a gun.

Ellie slopped the ladle of meat into Foster's plate splashing his hand with hot broth. Foster jerked his plate away and glared at her.

—I *beg* your pardon Mr. Foster she said.

Foster perched on his cot hunched over his plate. He watched Ellie and shoveled the bear meat in. He wiped his mouth with the back of his hand and made a face.

—I sure as Jesus Christ wish we had some salt.

Will Eddy threw open the blankets that served for a cabin door and kicked the snow off his boots and came in. His face glowed.

—Hell Bill he said I wish we had some salt too. I'd salt a duck's tail if I could find me a duck. He set the gun against the wall.

—Hunting bad today? said Foster.

—Hunting terrible today said Eddy advancing toward the fire.

November 19

A few people started feeling poorly from the short ration. Baylis Williams was sick. Margaret Reed took care of him as best she could but he needed food she didn't have. He lay on his cot drawn up and sore. His white hair and white eyebrows and pale eyes made him look like an old man. His cheeks were getting gaunt. He couldn't keep the meat down and even that was almost gone at the Reeds. The next thing they'd be eating was hides. Not much chance Baylis could thrive on those. Stanton went among the cabins drumming up interest in another attempt at crossing. This time not so many hung back. He signed up 6 women and 13 men plus himself and the Indians. They agreed to try the crossing 2 days hence. In the meantime they set to work drying their beef and arranging for their children. Some of the mothers would be leaving babies behind.

November 20

Pat Breen felt better. The diarrhea had quit and the nausea let up a little. He still got headaches if he tried to do much work but there wasn't much to do. The boys kept the woodpile up and Peggy had already butchered out most of the oxen. Still 3 left. Pat wondered if anyone else had ever gone through anything like what they were going through. He'd read Hastings' book and Colonel Fremont's report. It seemed to him someone ought to be keeping a record. You had to do things for yourself. He went to the big trunk and opened it up and dug around.

—What're you after Pat? asked Peggy from the hearth where she was sewing.

—Some o' that paper we've been saving said Pat.

—It's over on the left side at the bottom said Peggy. What be yi wanting it for? Expecting to write a letter are yi?

—Keep a journal said Pat.

—A journal is it. Have you secrets then?

—Let me be woman. I know what I'm doing. He found the paper.

—Will yi put down who did the slaughterin and who does the cookin and who cuts the wood?

—Leave off said Pat. I'd be dyin before you'd leave off leanin on me.

He returned to his bed with the paper and counted 8

sheets. Dug out his penknife and opened it and laid it on the blanket beside him. Folded the stack of paper from top to bottom and creased it. Folded the stack from side to side and creased it again and picked up the penknife and slit the 2 creases to make a quarto.

—Do yi want me to sew that for you then? asked Peggy.

—Aye woman I do said Pat. He carried the paper to his wife. She took up a fresh needle and threaded it and forced it through the fold of the quarto and down the length and out and in and down the length and out again where she brought the thread back to the middle and tied it to itself. Breen went to the trunk and took out a box of pens and a bottle of ink and closed the lid and set them down. He got the sewn quarto from his wife and drew a stool up to the trunk and sat down and after awhile he began to write.

Pat Breen wrote Friday Nov. 20th 1846 came to this place on the 31st of last month that it snowed we went on to the pass the snow so deep we were unable to find the road, when within 3 miles of the summit then turned back to this shanty on the Lake, Stanton came one day after we arrived here we again took our teams & waggons & made another unsuccessful attempt to cross in company with Stanton we returned to the shanty it continueing to snow all the time we were here we now have killed most part of our cattle having to stay here until next spring & live on poor beef without bread or salt it snowed during the space of eight days with little intermission, after our arrival here, the remainder of time up to this day was clear & pleasant frezeing at night the snow nearly gone from the valleys.

November 21

Pat Breen wrote fine morning wind N:W 22 of our company are about starting across the mountain this morning including Stanton & his indians

Stanton wanted to be the first man to cross the pass at the head of the company but he was stuck behind with Luis and

Salvador wrestling the mules up the slope. In the clear weather the snow had consolidated and formed a crust that held the people up but broke beneath the mules' sharp hooves. They scraped their legs on the ragged crust and plunged in the soft snow. Their troubles infuriated Stanton and he called forward for some of the men to help him but Eddy refused to take part. Eddy was the first to stand on the ledge of smooth wind-swept granite at the top of the pass. Like many of the others he was weak from short rations and had found the climb exhausting but now in midafternoon he stared back the way he had come while the line of men and women worked up through the snow below him with Stanton and his mules bringing up the rear. From the ledge he could see far off, across the snow and the snow-frosted pines, the hourglass-shaped lake spreading blue between the surrounding hills and beyond the lake columns of smoke from the chimneys of the cabins. The others came forward on the ledge after they hauled themselves up the last ramp of snow. Graves and Foster. The teamsters from the Donner camp. Mary Graves, her fresh face glowing from the exertion of the climb. Lavina Murphy and 3 of her children. Stanton struggled below. The mules slowed him down.

They took in the lake and the glowing snow. Urgently as they wanted to go on they were fixed by the sweep of the lake valley below them smoothed with snow. They looked from depth to depth in the distances defined before them by succeeding ranges of foothills until their eyes found the pale blue sky beyond them all. It was the sky over the long haul of Mary's River. Over the salt desert. Over the Wahsatch and Bridger's Fort. Over the South Pass. Over Fort Laramie. Over the Platte and Independence and what had once been home. They no longer thought home behind them. Home was in California before them and some of them flushed in fury to think that they were barred from that imagined valley of paradise by nothing more than snow when they had come so close. When they had come close enough to knock on the door. The Murphy children stood numbly staring and some of the women had tears in their eyes.

—Let's *go* said Eddy in a strangled voice.

The light faded as they made their way to the little valley beyond the pass. Nothing there but snow and half-buried pine trees blowing in the wind. They cut wood from the trees but had trouble starting a fire. Get the pine burning and it would melt the snow beneath it and hiss and smoke and then go out. While they struggled with the fire, Stanton and his mules came up with Luis and Salvador working behind them.

Guessing at the average height of the trees, Eddy calculated that the snow in the valley was 25 feet deep. That meant the fire would keep on melting down through the snow and going out. He saw Stanton come into the circle of shivering people around him at the fire and waved him over shouting into the wind.

—Charlie! Come here and give me a hand!

Stanton stepped up beside Eddy. His cheeks were marked with red splotches and he was breathing heavily. He was a short man but plump with jowls and large fleshy lips. His hands were pudgy. He seemed never to have lost his baby fat. His clear high voice added to the illusion that he was a small boy grown up unchanged.

—Having trouble with the fire? he asked Eddy.

—How the hell can we keep it going on this snow? said Eddy.

Stanton knelt down.

—I don't know. When we came over there wasn't this much snow on the ground. We just chose a bare spot. He pushed one of the branches into the sputtering fire.

—Can you ask your Indians? said Eddy.

—They don't know much about mountain lore said Stanton. They're valley Indians. Eddy abruptly stood up and jammed his hands into his hips.

—Well goddammit what're they good for then? He looked
around him. What the hell are you all standing around for?
Go cut some brush so you won't have to sleep on the snow.
Eddy waved his arms in the air. Go cut some wood! Go scout
some browse for these goddamned mules! Get busy! Get
something done! He turned back to Stanton as some of the
people moved off. Graves stayed and Foster. The Indians
came up. One of them began fiddling with the fire. What the
hell are we going to do about them mules? Eddy said.

What do you mean? said Stanton.

—I mean they ain't going to make it over the mountains.
You saw how they slowed us down today.

—They didn't slow us down much said Stanton. We made
it over the pass.

—In one day with a good crust of snow we made maybe six
miles said Eddy. He spat into the snow. We could of made
at least the other end of this valley.

Stanton flushed.

—What are you suggesting? That we abandon the mules?

—That's right said Eddy. We abandon the mules.

Milt Elliott joined the circle. Stanton stuffed his hands
into his pockets and rearranged himself.

—I can't do that.

—Why not?

—Because they belong to Colonel Sutter and I promised I'd
return them to him.

Eddy snorted.

—Jesus Christ. You mean to say you'd drag them mules
along even if it meant slowing us all down or maybe us not
getting over the mountains at all?

—I gave my word said Stanton.

—Oh my God said Eddy shaking his head. He looked at the
other men. Can you believe it? he asked them. Do you hear
this man? He says them mules is more important than us
people.

—I didn't say that said Stanton drawing himself up.

—You just as much as said it.

—I said I gave my word to Colonel Sutter that I would return these mules to him and I intend to keep that word.

As Eddy and Stanton argued the men and women who had left the circle returned. Luis and Salvador had succeeded in laying a flooring of green wood below the fire and it began to blaze.

—But you're our guide said Eddy. You ought to be at the head of the line finding us the way. Not back wetnursing them mules.

Stanton's eyes darted from Eddy's glare.

—You can argue all you like he said his voice squeaking but I have an obligation to return those mules.

—Goddamn you Stanton you got a obligation to guide us over these goddamned mountains! Eddy jerked on Stanton's coatsleeve and the small man pulled his arm away.

—Leave him alone said Graves. He stepped forward. He's right about them mules Eddy. If we leave them behind and they die up here we're goin to have to pay for them.

Eddy threw up his hands.

—My Jesus Christ do you people believe what you're hearing? He waved his arms in the air. Have you got any idea of the trouble we're in? This old man here is worried about money and this church usher here is worried about his good name. Why we're desperate. Did any of you know that? We're *desperate*. If we don't get over these here mountains we're all going to sit back in them cabins and starve to death. Do you know that? Do any of you care?

—Hell yes we care said Foster.

—Okay said Eddy. We got to get over the mountains. We got to relieve our people of feeding us so's they can hold out longer. So's we can bring back relief. Hell. We ought to eat them goddamned mules.

Stanton stiffened.

—No one touches those mules!

—Why by God if I was starving I would said Foster.

—No you wouldn't said Graves. Not without a fight.

—I wouldn't fight with you old man said Foster.

—You'd have to mister said Graves.

—Wait! Eddy yelled and got silence. He looked from face to face. It's this way. Either we leave the mules and go on or we go back and starve. Stanton knows the way. I don't know the way or Stanton could just stay here and nurse his mules and we could all go on. But Stanton knows the way so Stanton has to decide if we go on and live or go back and starve. What do you say Stanton? Which is it?

—You're building it up said Stanton. It's not that serious. I expect to see relief coming over any time now.

—*It is that serious.* Eddy's voice was barely under control. *It is that serious. It is live or die.* He pulled himself back. How can you expect relief he said to Stanton when your own goddamned mules can't make it six miles in a day? Nobody's going to come up here in twenty-five feet of snow. They don't even know we're short. For all they know we got enough beef to last the winter.

—Looky here said Foster. If this bastard don't want to guide us over the trail what about these Indians? They know the way, don't they?

Eddy grinned.

—They sure as hell do.

—They won't go unless I tell them to said Stanton.

—*Listen* Stanton said Eddy. You do whatever you need to do with them mules but don't stand in our way.

—I need Luis and Salvador to work the mules said Stanton.

—And we need Luis and Salvador to save our lives. Don't that mean anything to you?

Stanton grimaced.

—You keep making the situation worse than it is he said. We're in no great danger.

Eddy turned to the Indians. They had watched the argument without expression from their places on the other side of the fire.

—You Luis. You Salvador. You show us the way over the mountains? He pointed west. You guide us over the mountains?

—Luis! said Stanton. Salvador! You leave mules Sutter hang you dead! Stanton raised one arm as if holding a noose and bent his head over and stuck his tongue from the corner of his mouth and the Indians looked at him and vigorously nodded.

Eddy studied one and then the other and sighed. He seemed to shrink in the firelight.

—Well that's it then he said. He looked at Foster and then at Milt Elliott and then at the women standing silently by. Unless one of you can convince this hardheaded idiot. He shrugged. No? We might as well settle in then and crawl on back to camp tomorrow.

—Cain't we just go on? asked John Landrum Murphy. He was Lavina Murphy's 15-year-old son.

—Ain't no way across John Landrum unless somebody knows the trail said Eddy. He glared at Stanton one time more. Charlie Stanton he said I hope you burn in hell.

Pat Breen wrote thawed to day   wnd E

November 22

Pat Breen wrote froze hard last night   this a fine clear morning, wind E.S.E.   no account from those on the mountains

More than once during the night the fire had gone out at the camp in the valley beyond the pass. The cold wind blew up from the eastern desert dropping the temperature even as it cleared the sky of clouds. Shivering in their blankets on beds of pine boughs the people had watched the night sky wheeling above them. The air was clearer here than they had ever seen it in their lives. The clarity increased their sense of nakedness before the elements and secretly they craved the closeness of the crowded cabins by the lake.

Some got up before dawn and prepared to return. Lavina

Murphy roused her children and Sarah and Bill. They had slept a little apart from the others. The children shivered and rubbed their eyes. Lavina passed each of them a strip of dried beef to chew on. Bill and Sarah shook out the blankets and rolled them into packs. As they got them ready they tied them onto the children and each other. Lavina was lightheaded with hunger despite the meal of jerky. She was grateful for the help of her son-in-law. She had gotten used to doing without a man in the long years when her husband had drunk himself to death. They lost their cattle and then their farm. Finally he ruined his liver and turned yellow and died. Nothing left in Missouri and no reason to stay behind. Foster had a temper but he was good to Sarah. Lavina's favorite had been Bill Pike but he was dead. She gathered her children and started off up to the pass as the rest of the party began to stir. Harriet would be glad to see them.

They straggled into the lake camp throughout the late afternoon and evening. Eleanor Eddy cried with joy to see her husband but knew that he would soon have to go again and she would feel his loss all over. The teamsters from the Donner camp asked to stay at the lake until morning and were shared out to the several cabins. No one waited for Stanton and his Indians, not even Graves. The 3 guides straggled into camp near midnight. Stanton shivered with exhaustion but the Indians showed no outward sign of strain. They left the mules in the clearing beyond the Breen cabin and went directly to the Reed cabin and settled themselves in their blankets against the wall near the fire. They slept sitting up.

November 23

Pat Breen wrote Same weather wind W   the Expedition across the mountains returned after an unsuccsful attempt

The talk among the men was all for turning right around and trying again. Eddy said they could attempt to follow the trail themselves. He thought Stanton would be willing to describe the landmarks if somebody else asked him. Milt Elliott said he'd talk to Stanton since they shared space in the Reed cabin. With the chance that they might make another try right away, Milt decided not to report back to the Donners. So did the other teamsters. Milt had talked to George Donner when he went over to announce the previous crossing. Donner didn't trust any of his men to carry a message to Sutter for him. He didn't think they'd come back once they got to the fort. Milt told him he would do it because he was taking care of Ma Reed and the children. He'd be back for them he said. He owed Mr. Reed whatever he could do to make up losing his oxen in the salt desert.

The men had gathered in the big rock cabin. They sat on the edge of the cots in the firelit gloom. Eddy leaned up against the big rock on the north side of the fire where 2 scars in the granite angled above his back. The men had run the children outside to play in the sun. Eddy asked for a show of hands as to who would go the crossing without a guide. All the hands went up but Stanton and Graves weren't there.

—We'll need a couple days to get ready again said Eddy. Milt, you talk to Stanton. We ought all to pitch in and cut as much wood as we can for the families as stay behind.

That proposal brought grumbling. No one wanted to help anyone. It took too much strength. The teamsters were forced into it however to pay for their accommodations. Stanton made no friends with his hardnosed stand on the mules. The clear weather proved to them that they could have made the crossing if they hadn't turned back. There was still a chance. They got busy making ready. Trading with each other and the people they were leaving behind.

November 24

Mary Graves watched her baby sister nursing at her mother's heavy breast and her own breasts contracted in sympathy. Elizabeth Graves Jr. was the only member of the family who was getting enough to eat. They had more meat than any other family except the Breens but nothing else. They were just another family a few months ago and now they were the wealthy of the party. Her Pa could go easier on the others than he did. He was afraid they'd be poor in California but their riches there would only be in their friends anyway. Mary wished she were in California. She wanted to see the western ocean that she had heard of but could not imagine. Her Pa talked about the Atlantic but this ocean must surpass all belief. It would be lovely to be warm again.

With a pine branch she swept the rough stone hearth and laid the branch aside and pushed through the door flap to find the sky turned gray. She lifted 2 logs from the stack beside the door and returned inside and laid them carefully on the fire. Then she sat on the hearth and drew onto her lap the cutting board her brother Billy had made for her from wagon planking and began cutting thin slices of beef for drying before the fire. The clouds did not bode well for them. If they were to attempt the mountains again they'd have to do it when the weather was clear. They could not survive a storm in the mountains like the storm they passed through last week in camp.

She brushed back her hair with one hand without laying down her knife. She liked Mr. Eddy. He had courage enough to sustain them all. Already some were sick. They could not be suffering from lack of food. They may have lacked the variety. She could help most by going across the mountains. She would not have hesitated to go on. There would be nothing but suffering in the cabins.

She began to arrange the strips of meat on the rack of green pine branches her brother had built. Mr. Stanton was a pompous man. He was afraid to admit the severity of their condition. He was probably sorry today but he wasn't the kind of man to admit he was wrong. Many said he was heroic to return to the train after reaching California but his latest silliness only proved that he was a regular demon for following the rules. If you pledged him to jump off a cliff and he gave his word to it he would surely jump. That was not manliness. That was pomposity. Her John had been manly and so was Mr. Eddy.

The baby had fallen asleep in her mother's arms.

—Let me take her now Momma said Mary. You've held her till you're tired.

—Thank you Mary said Elizabeth Graves. Poor little thing. She does get heavy.

Pat Breen wrote fine in the morning   towards evening Cloudy & windy wind W   looks like snow   freezing hard

November 25

Milt Elliott was troubled by the face-off between Eddy and Stanton at the camp beyond the pass. Mr. Donner had told him Colonel Sutter was generous but Stanton's stubbornness about returning the mules argued otherwise. It seemed to Milt he shouldn't chance getting things wrong. He said as much to Ma Reed and she said he should do what he thought best. Early in the afternoon he put on his overcoat and wrapped a scarf around his head that belonged to Mr. Reed and set out for the Donner camp. He hiked across the scrub that grew in the lake valley and rounded the range of hills that formed the valley's north wall. He headed northeast and soon found the shallow wash that led to the feed of creeks near which the Donners had camped. He felt a little lightheaded at first but his body soon caught up with him and the exercise counteracted the cold wind and made him warm. He pushed aside dead brush in the wash and kicked at the patches of snow. With the ground half clear the hike didn't take long but as he came down the hill he noticed flurries of snow and knew what they meant and fought the urge to turn back. Instead he hurried on across the meadow to the Donner tent where Mrs. Donner welcomed him.

Her size always surprised him. She was smaller than either of her older girls and yet she seemed to fill the shelter. He felt good around her just as he did around Ma Reed. When either of them was nearby there was no place else to look.

—We haven't any coffee Milt said Tamsen but can I offer you some broth?

—Yes ma'am said Milt. Hi Mr. Donner.

George Donner raised up from his cot.

—Hello Milt he said. I guess you boys didn't make it.

Milt took the cup of broth.

—No sir we didn't. Charlie Stanton got fussy about them mules that Sutter loaned him. They wasn't keeping up and Will Eddy said to leave them but Stanton wouldn't.

—Did he think Colonel Sutter would object? asked Tamsen.

—Yes ma'am he did. He even told the Indians Sutter'd hang them if they came in empty-handed.

—That don't sound like what we was told said George Donner.

The little girls had been playing by the fire. Now they stopped to listen. Milt sipped the hot broth.

—I wasn't sure Mr. Donner so I come on over to find out what you wanted me to do. If Sutter's that tight about a string of mules he ain't likely to give me all them supplies you wanted if I just walk into his place out of the blue.

With that Tamsen saw why Jim Reed had appointed this otherwise unexceptional man his foreman.

—That's thoughtful of you Milt said Tamsen.

George Donner sat up on the edge of his cot. Milt saw that his hand was swathed in bandages. Eliza crawled over to her father's feet and he stroked her head. Milt felt a surge of warmth and thought of Patty Reed in the cabin by the lake.

—We was going to try the crossing again tomorrow said Milt but it don't look too good for it out there right now.

—Has the weather changed again? said George Donner. I ain't been out but a short spell this morning.

—It's clouded over said Milt. There's a west wind from over the mountains. I caught a few flakes of snow coming in. He handed Tamsen the empty cup. Right good broth ma'am.

—Thank you Milt said Tamsen. I expect we're all sick of broth by now.

—Food's food ma'am said Milt. We don't get that much to eat no more. Pretty soon we'll have to start in on the hides.

—How are the people at the lake holding up? asked Tamsen. They had quite a few cattle left didn't they?

—The Graves and the Breens did ma'am said Milt. We didn't have many at all but Ma Reed managed to buy a few from them folks. Most people is hungry but not hurtin. Baylis Williams is sick though.

—What's wrong with him?

—It's like he just don't want to go on. He gets as much to eat as the rest of us but he don't eat it. Sometimes he carries on like a baby. Crying and then just turning his face to the wall. Eliza has a time with him.

—Poor boy said Tamsen. He doesn't understand what's happening to him I expect. She looked at her husband and then back to Milt. It's late in the day. Will you have supper with us and stay the night? Tell us about your mountain climb?

—Might as well ma'am said Milt. It don't look like them boys is going to get away any time soon. He squatted down in front of Eliza and grinned. How're you little punkin?

Pat Breen wrote wind about WNW   Cloudy   looks like the eve of a snow storm   our mountainers intend trying to cross the Mountain tomorrow if fair   froze hard last night

November 26

Pat Breen wrote began to snow yesterday in the evening   now rains or sleet   the mountaniers dont start to day   the wind about W.   wet & muddy

After the snow commenced the night before Will Eddy

hiked angrily from cabin to cabin calling off the crossing. He told the teamsters they might as well go on back to the Donner camp where they had their own shelter and food to wait out the storm. They assembled at the Graves cabin because it was the farthest down the trail. They usually kidded and shoved each other around but the spirit of that had left them. There were 6 of them going back to the Donner camp. Sam Shoemaker, Joe Reinhardt, Jim Smith, Walt Herron, the half-breed Antoine and Gus Spitzer. John Denton hadn't even come over from the Donners. Jean Baptiste had stayed behind to help Mrs. Donner in exchange for more pay and a bigger ration. The 6 hiked out with their heads hanging and got to their shelter at the Donner camp a little before midnight. Denton and Baptiste were sleeping in the best cots and the fire had gone out. The men bedded down.

They looked each other over in the morning. They were a sorry sight. They'd all lost weight. They had lice. Walt Herron and Antoine got themselves dressed and went out to cut wood. Baptiste was already up and gone to the Donner tent. Denton wasn't well. He worked feebly to shore up the dripping roof by stuffing the leaks with strips of cloth. The wind gusted through the coat hung over the doorway and the room filled with smoke.

—Bacon and eggs said Shoemaker.

—What? said Smith. He knuckled his eyes to clear them.

—Bacon and eggs. That's what I could eat right now. A big platter of bacon and eggs.

—Ah hell said Smith. Shut up about it. We ain't got none and we ain't goin to git none.

—Don't you expect to be relieved? asked Denton.

—Shit said Smith we ain't never goin to see Californy. We're goin to die right here in this pukin hut.

—I don't give a shit no more said Shoemaker.

—I don't neither said Smith. It don't make me no mind.

—Does your legs feel swollen? asked Shoemaker. I cain't hardly bend my knees.

Smith felt down his legs.

—Yeah they do. Why's that I wonder.

—Hunger probly said Shoemaker. I could just about eat a horse.

—Eat them goddamn mules said Smith.

—Ain't that the shits? That little bastard Stanton not takin us down the trail cause he didn't want to give up them mules? Hell, we oughta a beat the shit out of him and made him show us the way.

—That stubborn little bastard said Smith. He wouldn't of done it even if we'd creamed him.

—I don't give a shit said Shoemaker. I'm sick of the whole business. Ain't nobody here a thousand miles cares if I live or die.

Denton stepped off the cot and sat down. His hands shook from the effort of working overhead.

—That's not true Sam he said. We all care about each other. We're in this business together and we'll get out of it together.

Shoemaker measured Denton with bloodshot eyes.

—Go fuck yourself Englishman he said. He spat into the fire.

November 27

Pat Breen wrote Continues to snow, the ground not covered, wind W dull prospect for crossing the mountains

The snow melted as it fell. Tamsen Donner walked through mud crossing from her tent to the Jacob Donners. The feeder creek was swollen with runoff and she got her feet wet. She picked her way from sage to sage. The dead gray plants spread out on the ground like giant spiders. Tamsen didn't try to visit the teamsters in their hut. Jean Baptiste kept her up on their doings and she had no sympathy to spare for them. They were grown men and ought to be able to look out for themselves. She understood that they were discouraged but saw no way that she could help them. It was otherwise with her brother and sister-in-law. Betsy was holding up as well as could be expected but Jacob had taken to his bed. He didn't even have George Donner's excuse of an infected hand.

—Betsy? she called. It's Tamsen. She opened the flap and ducked in. Her eyes took a moment to adjust to the gloom. The fire was reduced to a few coals and the snow blew freely down the smoke hole. Betsy Donner sat on a log next to the fire. Some of the children played on the cots. The 2 youngest, Lewis and Sammy, were at play on the floor. Jacob lay abed.

Betsy Donner got up. She was a short stout woman with a plain face. She wore her brown hair back in a bun. Her hands were knuckled from hard work. They plucked nervously at her skirt.

—Tamsen. She spoke quietly. I was just thinking about you. Come over and sit down.

Tamsen moved near the fire and sat on the edge of one of the cots.

—How is Jacob, Betsy? Tamsen looked over at Jacob Donner's blanket-covered form.

—He's asleep Tamsen. He's not good. I don't know what's wrong with him.

—Is he eating anything?

—He ain't eating enough to keep a bird alive. I have to coax him to get him to eat that.

—What's happened to your fire? Have you run out of wood?

Betsy looked down at her hands. Her shoulders began to shake.

—I just can't keep going she said. It's just all too much for me.

Tamsen moved to the crying woman and cradled her head in her arms.

—Hush Betsy she said. You've done magnificently. Tamsen knelt and took Betsy's face between her hands. We'll be all right darling. I'll ask one of the men to cut you some wood. They ought to be doing that anyway. But what can we do for Jacob?

Betsy stopped crying and looked at Tamsen.

—There's nothing to do for him Tamsen. He don't care no more.

Tamsen stood and looked down at the sleeping man. No. He didn't care any more. No more than her George cared. They had lived through their years of hardship. They had pulled up and come this way to find ease and they hadn't the strength to begin again with hardship. George wasn't yet lost. If they could achieve relief he would knit. But Jacob might not hold out that long.

—Let me see if I can find someone to cut you some wood said Tamsen. She turned to the door.

November 28

Pat Breen wrote Snowing fast now about 10 o clock snow 8 or 10 inches deep soft wet snow,   weather not cold   wind W

George Donner sat with Milt Elliott in the Donner tent.

—It don't look like nobody's going to make it over this weather he said.

—It's starting to pile up out there said Milt. I'd better see to getting back before I get completely snowed in here Mr. Donner.

—Do you think you can make it? said Tamsen.

—It ain't too bad yet said Milt.

—Look here said George Donner. I've been studying this problem about Sutter. Suppose I writ him a letter and promised to pay for any goods I ordered. Don't you think that would take care of it?

—He's probably heard about you from Mr. Reed said Milt. I'd think your signature would be enough.

—Mother said George. Fetch me the writing things will you?

—I'll get them said Leanna from beside the trunk. She opened the trunk and took out paper and pen and ink and brought them to her father.

—Here said George let's see. He read aloud as he wrote.

Donners Camp Nov 28 1846

This is to certify that I authorize Mil What's your full name, Milt?

—It's Milford Mr. Donner.

—*Milford Elliott and make him my agent to purchase and buy whatever property he may deem necessary for my distress in the mountains for which on my arrival in California I will pay the Cash*

—Colonel Sutter may prefer some of our goods said Tamsen. He may not have need of cash.

—That's true Mother said George. *the Cash or goods or both.* What do we need most?

—*Salt* said Leanna making a face.

Tamsen laughed.

—It's true dear. We're all just crazy for a little salt these days.

—*2 gallons Salt* said George Donner as he wrote it down. He smiled at his girls. *And $3 worth sugar*

—We have sufficient meat I suppose said Tamsen.

—But nothing else said George. All right. *150 lbs Flour 3 Bus Beans 50 lbs Cake Tallow*

—And the animals said Milt. I expect you'd best offer to buy them.

—*5 pack mules and two horses* wrote George Donner. *Purchase or hire.* No sense in buying them unless you have to Milt.

—Yes sir.

George Donner signed his name to the letter and handed it to Tamsen to fold.

—You'd better take that there and get moving Milt he said. This snow ain't getting any lighter.

November 29

Sunday. It had snowed through the night. The snow was deepening fast. At first it had fallen in wet fluffy flakes but now it fell in a fine powder so thick the people couldn't see from one cabin to the next. When Pat Breen woke in the morning he saw snow piled at his front door. It had blown through the door flap and spread in the shape of a fan on the dirt floor. Breen got up shivering in his longjohns and stared at the snow thoughtfully while he pulled on his trousers and shirt and boots. He went to the door to piss and found the snow up to his knees and pissed anyway drilling yellow holes in the snow. No sign of the snow abating. There was no part of the air outside the cabin that wasn't full of snow. It fell from some giant sifter. The Lord Almighty was baking a cake.

Breen stood by the fire watching Peggy frying meat. He held his hands out to warm them.

—We're sure to lose them cattle he said.

Peggy looked up from her cooking.

—Why's that?

—Likely they'll get lost in this snow.

—While you warm his majesty by the fire then.

—I've had the gravel woman. I ain't been well.

Peggy forked the fried meat onto the plates she had laid out on the hearth. The children gathered round.

—You'll not be better for starvin Pat Breen she said.

After breakfast Breen collected Pat Dolan and John and Edward and wrapped in coats and scarves they went searching for their cattle. Both Dolan and Breen had cattle left alive. Moving through the soft snow was a struggle. It wouldn't hold them up and they had to kick free at every step. It filled their boots and soaked and chilled their legs. Both men had brought their guns. They found the cattle huddled together under the pine trees at the edge of the cabin clearing. They were miserably thin. The boys tried to rouse them but they wouldn't move. They were down in the slush under the pine trees and wouldn't get up. Edward had never seen an animal big as an ox shiver before. Set in their emaciated faces their eyes seemed huge. They looked to the men as if the men might offer them help. Breen knew most of them by name but he felt little sympathy for them now. They didn't look like oxen any more. They looked like an idea for oxen without the finish on it.

They set their guns to the first oxens' head and fired. The reports started the other animals to their feet and they moved off a little ways in the trees. The men wanted the space anyway for butchering. Breen and Dolan began to gut the dead animals where they lay. Even the guts were thin and as the men cut into the bodies the smell of death came up more pungent for the cold snowfilled air. It might have come from the chimney of some underground charnel house. It thickened the air in the shelter of the pine trees and mingled strangely with the smell of pine and drove away the cold. Pine and cold and the smell of death went strangely well together as if the 2 were sauces or spices for the third.

Attracted by the gunfire Bill Foster came over from his cabin. The bear meat was about run out. Foster all but drooled when he saw the beef the Irishmen had killed. He asked if he could buy a yoke of the animals. Breen had 3 oxen left and Dolan 2.

—What's it worth to yi Bill? said Breen looking up steadily from his work.

Foster shuffled his feet in the snow.

—What do you want Pat? I ain't got all that much worth havin.

—Not much up here to have said Breen. I got mouths aplenty to feed meself.

—Ah Pat said Dolan so does old Bill.

—So he does said Breen. Anything you have of gold Bill?

Foster grinned and pushed in under the pines.

—I sure as hell do. I got my Pappy's gold watch. He pulled the watch out of his pocket on its chain. It's a beaut. Still keeps good time too. He spun it before Breen's eyes.

Breen snatched it with a bloody hand and turned it over feeling its thinness. He held it to his ear and listened to it tick.

—How do you wind it then?

—It's got a key said Foster. Just like a old granddaddy clock.

Breen spun it again on its chain.

—What's it worth then?

—It's sure worth twenty-five dollars said Foster. I could get more than that in California I bet. Only goods they got there is them as come round by boat.

Breen cradled the watch and studied its face.

—I'll give you a yoke of oxen for it entire.

Foster grinned then with Breen.

—Done.

Breen showed Foster his animals and Foster hiked back for ropes to lead them away. While he was gone the Breen boys looped ropes around the guts as the men cut them from the carcasses and dragged them out onto the snow. It melted around the piles and sunk them partly below the surface but it would not entirely give way. Where the guts touched the snow they stained it red. The red began at the edge of the snow and raced out on the snow like the fire of a fuse. The men killed and gutted 2 more oxen and the boys picked among the guts. They stripped the chitlings and dragged them to a pile in the snow beside the cabin. They didn't neglect their dogs.

Bill Foster returned with John Landrum Murphy. They tied ropes around the necks of the 2 oxen and kicked and shouted and dragged the animals away.

Breen and Dolan didn't try to skin the carcasses. They had a day's work with the killing and gutting. Snow fell throughout the day.

Pat Breen wrote still snowing now about 3 feet deep, wind W   killed my last oxen today   will skin them tomorrow   gave another yoke to Fosters   hard to get wood

November 30

Pat Breen wrote Snowing fast   wind W   about 4 or 5 feet deep, no drifts   looks as likely to continue as when it commenced   no liveing thing without wings can get about

11 people sat crowded into the Reed cabin. One of them lay abed. Baylis Williams was sick. A blotchy rash marked

his pale albino skin. He lay with his eyes half open breathing through his mouth. His sister Eliza tended him under Margaret Reed's direction. He did whatever the women asked him to do except that he wouldn't eat. Broth spooned into his mouth he pushed back out with his tongue. The broth stained yellow the pale scraggly hairs that grew unkempt on his chin. He moaned sometimes at night but otherwise made little sound.

Charlie Stanton usually sat on one of the beds with Milt Elliott. Margaret Reed kept busy at the hearth with Virginia and Patty beside her. Eliza sat at the foot of Baylis' bed. Luis and Salvador squatted against the wall beside the door.

The storm was slowly shutting out the light that had filtered into the cabin through the doorflap. Patty Reed had watched the darkness of the snow rising up from the ground. She studied the things people did to make way for the snow. At first people going out had kicked the snow aside but as it went on piling up they found other arrangements. Now that the snow was higher than she was tall they had packed down a ramp that slanted upward from near the bottom of the door to the top of the snow. They used it to go out to do their business and not much more. The soft powder buried them up to their waists when they tried to walk in it and there wasn't much chance of getting around. Patty thought that they couldn't make the snow go away so they were pretending it had always been there and making room for it. In a dream when something terrible was waiting up ahead you found a different path even though the different path took you a way you didn't want to go. So that the thing that was waiting had made you do something you didn't want to do even when you thought you were outsmarting it.

Smells filled the cabin. The smell of meat cooking. The cold smell of the snow that was somehow crisp and wet at the same time. The smell of their gas that they couldn't contain when they were living on meat. The smell of the pine logs burning in the fire and the fresh smell of pine from the broken stems of brush on the walls of the cabin. Wet wool. Musty buffalo robes and rank hides left from the cattle they had butchered. Sour bodies too. The smell of sweat. They were used to the smells but whenever one of them went out to do his business the smells hit him as he came back in.

Charlie Stanton smoked a pipe. Margaret Reed came to think of Stanton's tobacco as blessed. It masked the other smells in the close quarters and reminded her of her husband too.

Luis and Salvador talked about Water Babies. The Water Babies were small with gray and clammy skin. They had long black hair that floated behind them on the water. Luis had seen a Water Baby once beckoning to him from the Sacramento when it was in flood. The Water Baby had mewed at him like a woman hungry for a man. It had been hard to turn away and run back to the fort. Salvador nodded vigorously at Luis' story. He himself had had a similar experience. The Water Babies did not live up here in the mountains but he wondered if the *Hanglwuiwui* knew that he and Luis were in the cabins with the lost ones. The one-eyed and one-legged giant *Hanglwuiwui* lived in the mountains and ate the People. The fathers said there were no Water Babies and no *Hanglwuiwui* but those things had been here before the fathers came. It was not good to be hungry as they were hungry. If they could get the mules to stop their stubbornness they could go over the mountains and back down to the fort. The mules were perverse as old women though. If the mules were lost in the snow he and Luis could not be blamed for that. Little Charlie was in charge of the mules and should know that they could not live in so much snow. After the snow they could go on without the mules and perhaps get out of the mountains. Coyote would find the mules in the time of blossoms when the snow melted away. Coyote would eat the testicles of the jacks first to build up his strength and then he would eat the mares. Coyote knew how to make the most of an occasion.

—Mr. Stanton said Margaret Reed from the hearth. Have you ever seen so much snow?

Stanton was smoking his pipe. He removed it slowly from his mouth.

—Yes ma'am I have.

—Where was that Charlie? asked Milt Elliott.

—Upstate New York said Stanton. Where I'm from.

—That's right said Margaret Reed. You told us that.

—We had mountains said Stanton though nothing like these beauties. It would snow like this too. He puffed on his pipe. Once it stopped we'd get a good crust on it though and move right along.

—Do you foresee any difficulty with getting over the mountains once this snow lets up? asked Margaret Reed.

—It shouldn't be too bad ma'am.

—Think we can get them mules over this time? asked Milt.

Stanton looked sheepish.

—I guess I did overdo the business about the mules Milt. No. I won't insist we take the mules this time. We can leave them behind for the folks here. They may need them for food before it's over.

—Ugh said Patty Reed. Who wants to eat a old mule.

Her mother smiled.

—None of us do Patty but we may have to. Would you rather eat a hide?

—Ugh said Patty. I'd rather not eat at all. She lowered her voice. Is that what's wrong with Baylis Ma?

Her mother put her arm around her.

—I'm afraid so honey Margaret Reed said. He can't find it in him to eat. She turned back to Stanton still holding her daughter. Do you think a relief party could make it up to the camp after the storm is over Mr. Stanton?

Stanton considered the question. He blew a ring of smoke that caught the Indians' attention.

—If we can make it down they can make it up. The trouble will be getting pack animals up in this snow. Without the pack animals they couldn't bring much in the way of relief unless they sent an awful lot of men. I don't know. Maybe Sutter will turn out his Indians. He's got hundreds of them working for him on all that land of his around the fort. He could almost line them up two or three to the mile from here to Johnson's Ranch.

Patty smiled at the idea of a line of Indians from the lake camp to the pass and over the mountains to the green valley they said was below. She looked at Luis and Salvador. With their blankets thrown back they were playing finger hazard. Throwing fingers from their fists and matching or missing. They played it by the hour with grunts and chuckles as they lost or won. She had adopted them and they were hers. Luis and Salvador were hers and her doll Penelope and her dog Cash. Cash had caught a mouse under the bed in the corner of the cabin. It was a good thing too with so little left to eat.

Jim Reed rode south from Sutter's Fort. Colonel John Charles Fremont had offered him a captaincy in the Topographical Engineers. It would have required his presence all winter in command so Reed accepted a lieutenancy instead. He believed his people had enough beef to survive the winter. He wanted to relieve them as soon as possible but Sutter insisted no one could cross the mountains until spring. All the Americans in the area had ridden south to fight the Mexicans for California. He was riding among them. If they liked his brand of leadership it would be easier to convince them to form a party of relief. McCutchen was going on down to Sonoma to see what he could scare up.

Pat Breen did no skinning. He didn't even attempt to gather wood. Much to his wife's disgust he cut splits for the fire from the logs that supported the cabin walls. It was easier than going out in the storm.

December 1

Pat Breen wrote Tuesday   Still snowing   wind W snow about 5½ feet or 6 feet deep   difficult to get wood

no going from the house completely housed up looks
as likely for snow as when it commenced

Lewis Keseberg sulked in his bed. His foot throbbed
and his stomach growled. He was sick of eating beef. The
taste of unsalted beef gagged him. The smell of beef cooking
in the close cabin. The poles of the roof slanting down overhead were stained with water from the melting snow. He
was a *Gymnasium* graduate and a man of business and he
could do no more to help himself than lie on his bed and eat
poor beef and stare at the roofpoles. It was not possible that
he had been so stupid. Fate played her hand. He should have
chosen the voyage by ship but Phillipine had been with
child. He had wanted to see the American wilderness. Men
had written of it in Germany as if it were a paradise. As if
it welcomed one with dignity and benevolence. He should
have known better than to trust such men. He had met some
of them in St. Louis. They were dreamers. They thought
they could removed themselves from the hardness of life by
removing themselves to a new place. That was the American
taint. A laziness. A lack of discipline. If Stanton and the
others had had discipline they would all be over the mountains by now. If they had listened to him. He could have led
them. Welded them together with sternness and discipline.
They would not have waited for the weak, but what benefit
were the weak to them now?

Phillipine lay on the other bed. Her dress was open and
her breasts exposed. She was trying to nurse the baby. It
made smacking noises sucking at her breast. Keseberg
studied the other breast. The dark tissue around the nipple
was constricted by the cold. The baby smacked and sucked.
Ada slept beside her mother. Her knees were drawn up to
her chest.

The baby began to cry. Phillipine stroked its head and rearranged it on her body but it stopped sucking and cried
louder. She looked at her husband with tears in her eyes.

—What is it? he said irritably.

—I have no more milk.

Keseberg propped himself up on his elbow.

—You should eat more then. The baby went on crying and Ada stirred. Stop that! said Keseberg.

Phillipine sat up holding the baby and pulled her dress together and rocked the baby in her arms. It cried for a time and then subsided. Keseberg watched his wife. She was silently crying as she rocked her child.

—There must be no *weakness* he said menacingly. Phillipine nodded her head in time with her rocking. There must be no weakness Keseberg said again. We are not Americans who huddle with fear in our cabins. We do not expect Sutter to save us.

—What else do we do? asked Phillipine timidly.

—We eat and gain strength. We discipline ourselves. When we are ready we go over the mountains. We do it ourselves because we are strong.

The baby had fallen asleep. Phillipine studied its face hopelessly.

—But I have no more milk.

—Feed it broth then! said Keseberg. He pointed to the baby. Put it down and come here.

Phillipine started at the change in his voice. She looked at her husband and her eyes widened. He sat up on the bed and carefully lowered his wounded foot to the floor.

—Here said Keseberg. I have need of you. He patted the bed.

—But if Ada?

—Here!

Phillipine laid the baby on the bed. Its mouth sucked in its sleep. She stood and brushed the tears from her eyes. She had not yet buttoned her dress. She could feel her nipples erect in the cold. She stood before her husband. He reached under her skirts and she gasped.

—Remove them! he said hoarsely and dropped his hand.

—But it is light here.

—Damn the light!

Shaking with shame she lifted the back of her skirts and

pulled down her underclothes. They caught on her shoes and she almost fell but his hand gripped her arm and supported her. She pulled them over her shoes and stepped free. Keseberg jerked her to the bed. She tried to keep her knees together but he threw back her skirts and forced them apart.
—No! she said. You must not look there!

He pinched her thigh. She winced and the tears came again but she struggled no more. He studied her while she stared at the roof. She saw the stains there and the dead brown pine needles that clung to the stubs of branches left on the poles. Her belly was cold. She felt her sex constricted and blushed with shame. Ada was still sleeping. Keseberg turned on the bed. He sucked in his breath and cursed as he moved his injured foot. Then he fell on her. He was grinning but his eyes were cold. He released himself and reached to open her body but felt that she was dry. He dropped his grin and glared at her and then leaned to one side and spat on his hand and wet himself and guided himself in and thrust quickly and soundlessly shuddered and was through.

He withdrew. She dropped her knees and he carefully turned over onto his back.
—You have no passion he said. You are cold.

She turned her head to look at her children sleeping on the other bed beyond the fading fire. Beside her Keseberg's stomach growled. In the silence of her crying the sound filled the room.

Fighting the wind, Charlie Stanton stumbled through the soft snow to the edge of the clearing outside the Reed cabin. The mules were gone. He had found no trace of them except the shelter they had made under the pines south of the cabin. They had wandered away from the shelter but the snow covered their tracks. They must have wandered out into the storm to find food.

The snow blew hard across the clearing. Stanton could see only a few feet away. Someone shouted from behind him and he turned around. He saw a dim figure wrapped in scarves and then he recognized the voice.

—Uncle Billy! he called. Over here!

Graves kicked his way to Stanton through the snow.

—Cain't find my horses! he shouted.

—They've wandered off!

—Hell, I know that! You seen any sign of them?

—The mules ran off! shouted Stanton. The two men moved closer together. I can't find the mules Uncle Billy.

—Where you looked? said Graves. I been over to the other side of the cabin. No sign over there.

—They're not over here.

—We ain't goin to find them in this storm said Graves.

Stanton winced.

—We'd better tell the others. They'll lose their stock too.

—You tell the others said Graves. I'm goin back inside. He turned abruptly and moved away.

Stanton headed for the shelter of the trees. Mules were too smart to wander out in a snowstorm. They must have known where they were going. Had some other grove in mind where the browse was better. You couldn't hear a damned thing in the wind.

He found the place where the mules had sheltered. The snow had begun to fill it in. Wherever they were they were long gone. He should have sent the Indians out to check them every day. You had to stay on top of things. You had to be responsible. He had coveted the cabin and the fire and now the mules were gone. They couldn't have gone far. He'd find them after the storm.

He clapped his hands to warm them and hitched up his trousers. For the first time in his life his belly was flat. He felt weak. Puny. He liked the feel of a belly under his hands. He liked to fold his hands over his belly before a fire. Stanton shook his head. He was thin and cold. He thought of the warm cabin. Before he went back to the cabin he'd have to warn them about their animals. If he went to the Breens perhaps one of the boys could go on to the Murphys and tell Will Eddy. He couldn't make it all the way over there. He balled his hands and flailed the snow and pushed on.

Pat Breen wrote our cattle all killed But three or four of them, the horses & Stantons mules gone & cattle suppose lost in the Snow   no hopes of findng them alive

December 2

Pat Breen wrote Continues to snow   wind W   sun shineing hazily thro the clouds   dont snow quite as fast as it has done   snow must be over six feet deep   bad fire this morning

In the Murphy cabin Will Eddy watched his wife and the Murphy women cook the noon meal in separate pots. When Foster returned with Breen's oxen he insisted that the Eddys keep their food separate. He said he had too many mouths to feed. Foster sat now beside the hearth whittling at a pine chip. Eddy thought the sharing would have been to Foster's advantage. There was fat on the bear meat. The beef was poor. There wasn't much of either.

Foster lashed a sliver off the pine chip.

—Lem!

The boy started up.

—You and John Landrum get off your butts and get some wood.

John Landrum was playing cat's cradle. He bent his fingers and opened the cradle.

—Aw Bill he said. It's about dinnertime.

—You don't want to freeze your ass said Foster you better get out there and cut some wood.

Lavina Murphy poked her son-in-law with her spoon.

—You cut out that cussin Bill Foster she said.

Foster pulled the spoon out of her hand.

—Don't tell me what to do Ma he said. He licked the spoon. What you cookin there, skunk? Tastes like *skunk.*

Lavina wearily took back the spoon.

—You know it ain't skunk Bill.

—Tastes like skunk. Tastes just like skunk. Hey you brats he said. Get out and cut some wood like I told you.

—Don't call me no brat John Landrum said.

—Call you whatever the hell I like Foster said. Get out a here fore I whip your ass.

The boys reluctantly put on their coats and hats and took the ax and left. Foster returned to his whittling.

—Bill? said Eddy.

—Yeah hunter what you got to say?

—There's a way over them mountains. Eddy spoke softly. His wife turned from the fire and smiled at him.

—Hell yes there's a way over them mountains said Foster. All you need is some wings.

—No said Eddy. Snowshoes.

Foster flipped his knife. It stuck in the dirt floor.

—What the hell's snowshoes?

—Stanton told me about them said Eddy.

—That ain't much of a testimony.

—Stanton grew up in the Catskills up in New York.

—I thought he come from Chicago.

—Told me he was a Chicago man Lavina Murphy said cautiously.

—Before that he come from the Catskills Eddy said.

—Them mountains? asked Foster.

Eddy nodded.

—They wear snowshoes up there to get through the snow. Look like big paddles.

—We ain't got no paddles said Foster.

—They ain't really paddles. Frames with rawhide webbing like a canebottom chair.

—This meat's about ready Lavina Murphy said.

—Shush up Ma said Foster. Frames with rawhide. You reckon that'd hold a man up on the snow Will?

—Stanton says it does.

—You about ready Ellie? asked Lavina Murphy. We're about ready.

—Hell woman said Foster. All right. Little Bill, go out and get your brothers.

—Yes sir said Bill Murphy.

—Listen Will said Foster. You think we could make some of them snowshoes?

—We got the rawhide said Eddy. All we need to do is figure out the frames.

—Jesus Foster said and then you just walk right on top the snow as nice as you please. He stood up. Jesus. Why the hell didn't Stanton say something before?

—It just come to him the other day said Eddy.

—We all set around here starving when we could of gone over them mountains. What was that little bastard thinkin of?

—Snowshoes don't make no difference in this storm said Eddy.

—Don't guess they do. Foster scratched his beard and then grinned. Storm ain't goin to last forever though. He turned to his mother-in-law at the fire. Gimme some food Ma. We got some planning to do.

Eddy and Foster talked through the meal but part of Eddy held back. He watched his wife and the 3 Murphy women and the children eat their stew. They had eaten hurriedly and hungrily before but now they dawdled over their food. Played with it with their spoons as if it was too hot. Toyed with it but not because it was a toy. They toyed with it because it had become precious to them. He felt the urge to do the same. To study each chunk of meat as it floated in his bowl. Look at the way the fibers were arranged. The patterns of the melted fat on the snowwater. The veins that ran like tunnels back into the meat. The smell that made his stomach ache. People shouldn't have to feel that way about food. Food shouldn't be that important. They treated it the way he used to treat a piece of fine wood. They were tough. They were so tough they didn't know how tough they were. They could die here and they would still follow the rules. Still be polite to each other and do their business outside. Say please and thank you while they wasted away. He'd been sitting around too long. Licking his wounds. Living off the triumph of his bear like the bear would last them all winter. He'd have to do more. Have to go. Cross the mountains and get help. They couldn't count on Reed. Reed would get across if anyone could but they couldn't count on Reed. They had to count on themselves. These people were too fine to let down.

Eddy dug into his stew while Foster talked on.

December 3

Pat Breen wrote Snowed a little last night bright and cloudy at intervals all night, to day cloudy snows none wind S.W. warm but not enough so to thaw snow lying deep allround Expecting it to thaw a little to day

The teamsters at the Donner camp woke to silence and knew the weather had changed. They crawled from their beds and went to the door and pushed back the flap and saw that the snow had stopped. John Denton got their fire going while they climbed the ramp of snow before the door and fanned out to piss. They woke up from the stupor of the past week and talked excitedly of making another attempt across the mountains. They hadn't heard about the snowshoes yet but they thought if they could make it to the lake camp they could talk Stanton into guiding them down to Sutter's Fort. They hurried back inside the shelter and crowded around Denton's fire. Dutch Charley Burger went out again with the ax and hacked a hunk of meat off one of the quarters of beef they had stacked outside their door and brought it in and hung it on the hook over the fire. They hadn't eaten much in the past few days. Their excitement brought on hunger. They didn't wait for the meat to cook but cut pieces off the outside as soon as they were seared. Jim Smith farted as they talked and they all laughed.

John Denton understood their mood and got out of the way. He had kept the fire going during the storm while the others lay abed. Fed them too and shoveled their manure from the corner out the door. They ignored him now and he was grateful. It would suit him nicely if they all went away. Despite the beef he was weak. He had dizzy spells whenever he stood up. Once, squatting by the fire, he had almost blacked out and fallen in. He'd stuck his hand into the fire trying to catch himself and the pain of the burn brought him back to his senses.

Reinhardt, Smith and Gus Spitzer worked at making up packs. Shoemaker started on a pack and then forgot what he was doing and stared at the half-folded blanket in his hands. The 2 Germans talked to each other in their native tongue until Smith abruptly told them to speak English or shut up. They packed tobacco and hunks of beef. They took their money out of hiding places in their beds and slipped it into their packs. They packed aware of each other's eyes. Smith coughed and spat. He fingered his wool coat and studied Denton's sheepskin and saw Denton staring at him and looked quickly away.

Reinhardt finished packing first. As he stood up he noticed for the first time that the wind had begun to blow again. He dropped his pack and threw back the doorflap. Fresh snow billowed in. He cursed in German and flung the flap closed and sank to the floor. Smith and Spitzer stopped packing. Reinhardt began to cry. He sat slumped by the door gasping and crying. The other men did nothing. They stared at their hands. Denton poked the fire. Shoemaker had fallen asleep with his head lolling backward against his bed. The wind whistled around the shelter half-buried in the snow.

Pat Breen wrote the forgoing written in the morning it immediately turned in to snow & continued to snow all day & likely to do so all night

December 4

Pat Breen wrote Cloudy that is flying clouds   neither snow or rain this day   it is a relief to have one fine day.   wind E by N   no sign of thaw   freezing pretty hard   snow deep

[155]

Sunlight and shadow lightened and darkened the canvas flap on the door of Pat Breen's cabin. The cabin was crowded with Breen's children. They made little noise. They were sunk in lassitude. Chilled from the cold and weakened by a hunger poor beef could not feed. Pat Dolan had taken the 2 older boys out to cut wood. Breen had declined the invitation. Peggy didn't bother him about it. She had decided he could do as he liked as long as they had supplies. He was no more use to her than another child.

Breen took pride in their provisions. With Dolan's beef they had enough to last the winter. No point to risking his neck in the mountains. All this hurry to cross the mountains. If the others had been as careful as he they wouldn't be in such a bind. Stanton was to be blamed as much as anyone. He told them to halt up in Truckee Meadows for fodder when they should have pushed on. Stalled them in the pass worrying about his damned mules. He deserved a goodly share of the blame for his poor judgment.

The others could go on. Some as were running out of beef. Mrs. Reed's people were said to be going onto hides already. She could thank her hotheaded husband for that. The Lord helped those who helped themselves. The ones who went would make it easier for the ones who stayed. It wouldn't do to show off. The time might come when he would need to keep his gun ready.

Breen walked to the cabin door and pulled back the flap. The boys had packed a ramp up from the threshold to the top of the snow. He couldn't believe the extent of the snow. It reached higher than the door. The cabin had become a cave. Wouldn't hurt none. It helped keep the cabin warm. The wind wouldn't whistle through the way it had before.

—Are yi going out then? said Peggy. She was sitting on the hearth sewing.

—No woman I'm not said Breen.

—Aren't yi the regular homebody.

—Nothing t' go out for said Breen.

—True enough said Peggy. Nothing t' stay in for neither.

December 5

Pat Breen wrote fine clear day   beautiful sunshine
thawing a little   looks delightful after the long snow
storm

Now after the snow the cabins at the lake camp were like
storm cellars dug out below white ground. Their roofs wore
covers of snow. Smoke curled up through holes melted in
the snow. Paths packed down like trenches connected the
cabins. Other paths led into the woods where the men hiked
to cut wood. The trees seemed to have no trunks. They grew
out of the snow as if they had germinated far underground
and only in maturity pushed through to the sun.

The people shared Breen's enthusiasm for the sun. Many
had come out of the cabins. Men and boys cut wood. Women
spread blankets out on the snow to freshen them and dug
away at dwindling piles of beef stacked under the snow outside the cabin doors. Children planning snowball fights
found they lacked the energy for the contest and contented
themselves with standing in the sunken paths watching the
adults pass them back and forth between the cabins. The
people had felt buried and now they felt restored. If the
weather could change so abruptly then perhaps they could
make the trial of the mountains after all. And Reed and
McCutchen and Sutter's people could relieve them from
the other direction. The pass glared beyond them in the
morning sun. The sky was bluer than any sky they had ever
known. The sun's light at the corner of their eyes was almost purple. Even in the cold it seemed to sting their lips
and burn their skin. They drank it hungrily as they went
about their work. They weren't aware how often they stumbled. The men found their axes unaccountably heavy. The
women had trouble making the climb up from the cabin
doors.

At the Donner camp only the women and children responded to the sunlight. The teamsters lay abed. They
smoked incessantly and made little effort to eat. Jacob Donner was sick and desolate. He hardly spoke any more and

had to be chided to use the chamber pot. George Donner
tossed and turned with the fever that fought the infection
that was engulfing his arm. Red streaks ran up his arm
from the swollen wound on the back of his hand. Tamsen
now soaked the arm several times a day in hot water but the
infection refused to give way. She prayed for relief. Their
supply of beef was running low.

Jean Baptiste was cutting wood. Toward the end of the
storm they had almost run out of wood and except for meal-
times the shelter had been miserably wet and cold. Tamsen
thought Jean Baptiste a strange little man but there was no
doubt he had affection for them. He played with the children and worked hard to keep them in firewood when he
could. He spent a good deal of time flirting with Mrs. Wolfinger too but the German woman seemed to accept the
flirtation as her due. Tamsen wondered how much the little
half-breed admired Mrs. Wolfinger's beauty and how much
he admired her wealth but she dismissed the thought as unworthy. It didn't matter anyway so long as their play kept
their spirits up.

Tamsen set herself the task of getting her husband out of
the tent. He came unwillingly, blinking in the unaccustomed
glare, but the sunlight was good for his arm.

December 6

Graves had solved the problem of the snowshoes. He and
Stanton worked together in Graves' cabin with a will. The
challenge of making snowshoes had brought Graves out of
his melancholy. Despite his premonition of death he had
decided to try for the passage over the mountains with the
younger men and women who planned to go. He had built
a bench out of planking pulled up from a wagonbed. His boy
Billy and Stanton and Will Eddy had assembled a pile of oxbows beside the bench on the floor. The oxbows were made of
seasoned hickory bent in a U shape. They had held the oxen
in their yokes on the long pull west. They were about the

thickness of a baby's wrist and too heavy for snowshoes. Carefully and laboriously Graves and Stanton were sawing the bows into thin flat strips light enough to make the snowshoes frames but strong. Eddy said he'd find out how many people wanted to go. Graves insisted that each traveler contribute his own hide for lacings. Luis and Salvador agreed to cut the lacings from the patches of hide. They singed the leftover scraps in the fire and ate them.

With the loss of the mules the people in the Reed cabin were reduced to eating hides. The cabin stank now with the smell of singed hair. Margaret Reed and Eliza burned the hair off pieces of hide over the fire and then scraped them clean with a knife and boiled them in the cooking pot. Hours of boiling dissolved the hides into a ropy glue which they ate without salt or seasoning. No one but the Indians had been able to eat the glue the first few times they tried. Patty had vomited through 3 meals before her stomach accepted the insult but all knew they would learn to eat hides or starve and so they learned to eat hides. Baylis Williams refused.

For variety they roasted the bones left over from their beef days. Long charring in the fire reduced the bones to a soft crumbly substance that could be scraped away and swallowed. It gave them no nourishment but it helped fill their stomachs. The Indians were adept at catching the mice that sometimes found they way into the cabin. They broiled them whole and ate hide, guts and all. Then they removed the bones from their mouths and organized them into skeletons beside them on the floor.

Patty had vowed she would never eat a mouse but now she wasn't so sure. She grieved for her little dog Cash. There was nothing to feed him except scraps of hide. He took them gratefully and chewed them for hours but he was too weak to play.

Pat Breen wrote Sund. The morning fine & Clear now some Cloudy wind S-E not melting much in the

[159]

sunshine, Stanton & Graves manufactureing snow shoes for another mountain scrabble no account of mules

December 7

Pat Breen wrote beautiful clear day wind E by S looks as if we might have some fair weather no thaw Baylis Williams lay dreaming. He had taken no food for days. Sometimes he sipped the water his sister Eliza poured down his lips but as often he clamped his teeth and it ran off his chin and wet his pale throat and the gray homespun shirt he wore. He could no longer leave his bed. When he fouled it with his thin stool Margaret Reed led the children to the far end of the cabin and played with them while Eliza cleaned her brother as best she could. He was losing the swelling that had made him look fat. Becoming skeletal. The bones of his face stuck out now. His eyes drew back in their sockets and the sockets darkened as if they were bruised. His albino paleness made him look bloodless. He looked like a skeleton lying in his bed except that spots of flush marked his cheeks still from the low fever he had been running.

He did not know he was starving. He dreamed he was a child playing on the farm. Drove the cows in to milk and drank the warm milk his mother squirted at him from their teats. He smelled Thanksgiving. Turkey and pumpkin pie. The table would break up before him in a swirl of colors and he would whimper and Eliza would attend him and then the table would return again and he would smile. Eliza thought he was smiling at her and smiled back. He dreamed his father's death lying on the big family bed twisted with lockjaw. He was a little boy standing at the door holding his aunt's hand. His aunt opened the door slowly and a hole seemed to open before him into a terrible blackness. He saw his father's hand clutching the cover like a claw and hid his face in his aunt's skirt.

An owl chased him through the night. He could see the owl

in the darkness. The owl swooped and caught a mouse. It squeaked in the owl's claws and when he found the owl's tree the skulls of mice lay in little heaps on the ground below the nest.

He was warm and wet and someone changed him.

His stomach hurt and his mother gave him castor oil. He kicked and flailed and spit it out.

Mr. Reed had cut off his head. Thrown his body away. It turned into an owl's body and flapped on the ground like the chickens when they butchered them on the farm. His head was white and lay among the other heads at the foot of a tree.

The warm milk washed over his face and into his mouth. The brown cow eats green grass and gives white milk and golden butter. The smell of the cows in the barn at milking time. The warm barn in the cold winter with the cows sleeping in their stalls. Warm bread and golden butter. The taste of the bread. Grass green. The bread filling his mouth.

December 8

Pat Breen wrote fine weather Clear & pleasant froze hard last night wind S.E. deep snow the people not stiring round much hard work to get wood sufficient to keep us warm & cook our beef

The teamsters had run out of beef. They only had hides left. John Denton prepared them as best he could. Dutch Charley Burger had been cutting wood for the fire but he decided to cut no more. If the other men weren't going to help he was getting out. There wasn't any meat left anyway. Denton could do as he liked.

Burger announced that he was leaving for the lake camp. Gus Spitzer begged to go with him. He said he couldn't make it by himself.

—I go to Kesebergs' said Burger. He won't help you.

Spitzer was pulling on his overcoat.

—Breen will he said. He owes me. I help him on the trail.

—Ain't nobody going to help nobody no more said Shoemaker forlornly from his bed.

—Goddamn said Burger. All right. Come along then.

Spitzer put on his hat and stumbled behind Burger to the door.

—You got to help me along Charley said Spitzer.

—*Ja* said Burger I help you along. He took Spitzer's arm and pulled him up onto the snow. By God he said Keseberg *feeds* me he will.

The 2 men struggled together through the snow. Sometimes the crust held but for long stretches they waded in snow to their waists. The creek was frozen over and bridged with snow. They heard it bubbling as if far underground. No trace of a trail was left between the 2 camps but they struck out southwest by the sun. Through the forest of tall pines. Burger saw a lump of gum on the stub of a pine branch and stopped to break it off and pop it into his mouth. He cracked it until it softened and then chewed it to ease his hunger. Spitzer sucked on pieces of the snowcrust. Whenever he stopped to rest Burger cursed him and threatened to leave him and go on. He didn't like Spitzer's sniveling. He wanted to stop as much as the other man but knew better. Better to go on while one still had strength.

Late in the afternoon the men struggled up the last hill before the stream valley below the lake and saw the smoke of the cabins. They stumbled down the hill falling in the snow and dragged themselves past the Graves cabin. No one was out. They found the path to the Breen cabin and pulled themselves on. They had not quite reached the cabin when Spitzer collapsed.

—Breen! Burger called. Pat Breen!

John Breen looked out the door.

—Who is it?

—Dutch Charley Burger! Call your poppa! Spitzer needs help!

Spitzer lay gasping for breath. Pat Breen came out of the cabin bareheaded and climbed up to the men.

—Be he sick? Breen asked.

—Starving Pat he's starving said Burger.

Breen stuffed his hands into his pockets and looked down at his feet.

—And aren't we all starving he said. I've not got enough for me own.

Burger's voice went cold.

—*Also* he said. He helped you back on the trail.

Breen shuffled his feet.

—Ah he did that now.

—Take him in or leave him here to die said Burger. I give not a damn.

Breen shrugged.

—John! Edward! Give us a hand!

The boys came out and Burger wiped his glove across his mouth and hiked around to Keseberg's door. He lowered himself down the ramp but did not push back the flap.

—Herr Keseberg! he called.

—*Ja?* Keseberg's voice came from inside. Who is that?

—Charley Burger!

—Why Charley said Keseberg where have you been? *Herein!*

Burger pushed aside the doorflap and stooped and entered the cabin. After the glaring snow he could see only a green glow before his eyes.

—And Charley said Keseberg have you gone blind?

Burger turned to face the voice at the side of the cabin.

—*Nein* Herr Keseberg. It is only the snowglare. Soon I shall see. His eyes adjusted and he made out Keseberg lying on the bed. Phillipine and the children lay on the other bed. The fire was dead.

—Why have you come to visit me Charley? said Keseberg.

Burger saw that he was grinning.

—We have no more beef. I want to work for you.

—You want to work for me said Keseberg. But before you went away.

Burger swayed on his feet.

—I am weak Herr Keseberg. May I sit down?

—Sit down, sit down said Keseberg. He gestured to the cold hearth. Sit down at our noble fire. My wife does well don't you think?

—I think you could use my help Herr Keseberg said Burger.

—*Ja* I could use your help Charley but how am I to feed you?

—I would eat only a little. I could cut your wood and keep your fire going.

Keseberg laughed.

—And you would cut my wood and work my fire and eat only a little then.

—A man must live Herr Keseberg said Burger.

—Sometimes I would disagree with you dear Charley but for now I would like a fire. Go and cut wood and build me a fire Charley and then we will eat. Keseberg grinned again. Do you prefer the loin or the brisket? Or perhaps you would like sausages and beer? He lay back on his bed. Go and cut wood then!

December 9

In the early morning Milt Elliott readied himself to hike over to the Donner camp. Stanton wanted George Donner's compass for the mountain crossing. Milt thought some of the teamsters would want to make the attempt. He didn't suppose Mr. Donner and Uncle Jacob were up to it however.

Noah James decided to come along. With the food getting low Graves had told him he ought to look to the Donners for support. He had been their teamster after all. Stanton was willing to loan them snowshoes in return for his errand. He insisted they get back to the lake camp by Sunday the 13th. He expected that the snowshoes would be finished by then and the party could leave.

Late in the morning it began to snow. Milt and Noah found the snowshoes heavy going but better than fighting the snow. The storm was something else. The wind blew hard and obscured their way. Burger's trail quickly filled in. Fortunately Milt knew his way from previous trips. The trees couldn't guide them because they were buried more deeply now in the snow but Milt remembered the shape of the hills between the 2 camps. They covered the 7 miles in 3 hours with frequent stops to rest. Saw the smoke from the tents and hurried in.

George Donner felt better than he had in weeks. The past few days of sun had helped his arm. He was grateful to his wife for getting him out of the close tent. He had taken more food and the fresh air had stirred him. He accepted Stanton's letter from Milt Elliott with interest and read it aloud to the men and his wife.

—9th Dec 1846
  Mrs. Donner
    Donnersville
     Cal

They laughed at that. George noticed the salutation. He deserved it. He had allowed his wife to take charge. To do the duties he ought to have done.

—You will please send me 1# your best tobacco. The storm prevented us from getting over the mountains. We are now getting snowshoes ready to go on foot. I should like to get your pocket compass as the snow is very deep & in the event of a storm it would be invaluable.

Milt & Mrs Graves are coming right back, and either can bring it back to you.

The mules are all strayed off. If any should come around your camp—let some of our company know it at the first opportunity.

         Yours
          Very Respectfully
          C. T. Stanton

—Why he's in fine spirits said Tamsen. She took the letter
from her husband and silently read it through. Do you
think you can get back right away Milt?

—Yes ma'am. Milt had taken off his overcoat and stood
before the blowing fire trying to warm his hands. If we can
get over to Sutter's we sure can get back.

—Wonder what's happened to Jim Reed said George Donner. He sat easily on the edge of his bed.

—I just don't know Mr. Donner said Milt. It ain't like him.

—Could the incident with poor John Snyder have disturbed
him? asked Tamsen.

—Wouldn't let that keep him from relieving his family
said her husband. Jim's brave as they come. George went
to the family chest and unlatched it and took out a tin of
tobacco. Look here Milt he said. We've got enough tobacco
to send some back to Stanton and any of the others as need
it. Why don't you take this whole tin?

—Don't you want to keep some for yourself?

—I've got plenty more here. You ain't going to try to go
back in this storm are you?

Noah James had stood silently near the door. He spoke
up.

—No way Mr. Donner. We're stuck here till she blows over.
They ain't about to leave over to the lake camp till it blows
over.

Pat Breen wrote Commenced snowing about 11
Oclock wind N:W snows fast took in Spitzer yesterday so weak that he cannot rise without help
caused by starvation all in good health some having
scant supply of beef Stanton trying to make a raise
of some for his Indians & self not likely to get much

December 10

Pat Breen wrote Snowed fast all night with heavy
squalls of wind Continues still to snow the sun peep-
ing through the clouds once in about three hours

Milt and Noah spent the night on the dirt floor of the

Donner tent before the fire. They kept the fire low between 2 green logs because of the wind. In the morning the tent was dark. Snow filled the space outside the door flap. The Donner girls were frightened by the darkness in the tent but Milt dug the door out and a little light came down the ramp. Snow blew through the flap however. Tamsen cooked small portions of beef for them with Mrs. Wolfinger's help and all drank some broth. George Donner never slept well any more because of his arm. He was usually irritable in the morning.

After breakfast Tamsen asked her visitors to take a look at the teamsters.

—I haven't heard from them in several days she said. We ought to see if they're in need.

Milt and Noah put on their coats and hats and went out in the storm. The sky was dark gray and filled with blowing snow. The snow whitened their eyelashes and their whiskers. Their snowshoes didn't work very well in the powder but they kept them on. They had trouble finding the teamsters' shelter and guessed their fire must be out. The shelter was completely buried in the snow. It revealed itself only by the pattern of the snow mounded on the bent-over trees that formed its roof. They searched for the door and found it below a sink in the snow. They called and heard John Denton feebly return their call from inside. They dug away the snow with their hands and cracked back the frozen doorflap. A wave of close air hit them from inside. They bent low and went in.

The fire had gone out and snow from the smokehole lay piled over the dead ashes. The teamsters lay abed wrapped in blankets and old coats and rags. They hardly looked alive. Even in the cold the smells of vomit and loose bowels filled the shelter. Piss froze in yellow pools beside the cots.

—My God I'm glad you came said Denton weakly. I thought we'd die here.

—Mrs. Donner sent us over said Milt. She was worried about you.

Denton began to cry.

—I thought we'd die. Oh damn. Could you build a fire?

Milt turned to Noah.

—I'll get a fire going. This here's just pitiful. Whyn't you go on back to Donners and scratch up some food.

—Yeah said Noah. He looked disgusted. I'll do that little thing.

After Noah left Milt found the teamsters' ax and waded through the storm to the nearest grove of trees. He cut branches with quick swings until he had an armload and then struggled back to the shelter. Inside he broke the branches and scraped the hearth bare and kindled a fire. It crackled and caught and filled the shelter with smoke that set the men in the beds coughing. He saw that the smoke-hole was blocked and poked through the snow with the ax handle. The wind caught the fire then and pulled it up into a bright blaze and the shelter cleared.

Milt found a pot and filled it with snow and melted the snow over the fire. When the water was warm he took a cup and carried it around to each of the men. The fire stirred them. Denton drank the warm water eagerly and then in turn Shoemaker, Smith and Reinhardt. Milt brought them more. He soon had them sitting up shakily on the edges of their cots. He took blankets from their beds and folded them and arranged them in a semicircle around the fire. Then he helped the men to the blankets and sat them up.

Noah pushed through the door flap and shook off the snow. He face glowed red in the firelight from the cold. He pulled a piece of meat the size of his fist from his coat pocket.

—Miz Donner said this was all she could spare. He handed it to Milt.

—It ain't much said Milt.

—It'll have t'do. They ain't got much and they got kids to feed. He looked the teamsters over. You boys is sure a sorry sight. He unbuttoned his overcoat. Thought you could take care of yourselves.

—We ran out of food said Denton.

Sam Shoemaker looked back dully at Noah.

—Ain't none of your business anyway.

—It's my business when I got to go traipsing back and forth in a goddamned snowstorm said Noah.

Milt found the cooking pot in the corner where someone had thrown it but it was full of frozen glue. Half-cooked pieces of hide stuck out of the brown mass. He decided to use the pot he had heated the water in. He took the pot from beside the fire and carried it to the door and scooped more snow into it. The snow made the warm water steam. He went back to the fire and hung the pot and cut up the lump of meat into it. The boys were going to need some nursing. Well enough. With the storm he didn't have anything better to do.

Pat Breen wrote very difficult to get wood to day now about 2 Oclock looks likely to continue snowing don't know the debth of the snow may be 7 feet

December 11

Pat Breen wrote snowing a little wind W sun vissible at times not freezeing

Eddy had come over to the Graves cabin in the morning to see how the snowshoes were going and found Stanton about half crazy. The storm had spooked him and his failure to turn up the mules or borrow any beef. He wanted George Donner's compass and he wanted tobacco and he wanted Milt and Noah back with the snowshoes they had borrowed. It would take an extra day to make 2 more pair. He was sick to death of sawing oxbows.

—Look here said Eddy we can't leave till everyone's had a chance to make up their minds if they want to go. I got to see everyone around here and talk to them. The more we can get to go the better for the folks as stays behind.

Stanton sat at the workbench. He had stopped sawing. He picked at the sawdust. Graves was working by the fire drilling holes in the frames with a hot nail. Billy Graves and the Indians were busy lacing.

—I know Will said Stanton but we've got to get away as

fast as we can. We're getting weaker every day. It'll be hell crossing the mountains, just hell.

Eddy took out his pipe and began packing it with tobacco.

—How far you figure it is?

—A man can ride it in two days when the snow's down. Say sixty or seventy miles. He perked up. That's to Johnson's Ranch. It's another day's ride to Sutter's.

Eddy lit his pipe.

—Fellas've been getting over to Donners in less than a day. Ought to be able to make ten miles a day with the snowshoes don't you think?

—I don't know about the women said Stanton.

—Hell Charlie. Ain't no women sick around here. You noticed that?

—My gosh said Stanton. That's true. That doesn't mean they can take the mountains though. He fiddled with the saw. He hated the saw and hated the necessity of making more snowshoes. Every strip took hours of work. It exhausted him. He'd never felt so tired in all his life.

—They'll do just fine said Eddy. He pushed back his stool and stood up. I'm going to get a list started here. He walked over to Graves. How many of your folks planning to make the crossing Uncle Billy?

Graves set the hot nail carefully back into the coals and looked up.

—Me first of all. I ain't done all this work just to be left behind.

Eddy grinned.

—You think a old man like you can make it over them mountains?

—Why hell yes boy I can make it. I was hoofing around on mountaintops afore you was even born.

—They was little pissant mountains though wasn't they?

—Only little pissant I know about is smokin a pipe said Graves grinning.

—Okay Uncle Billy said Eddy. I'll put you down. Who else?

—Sarah and Jay say they're going. Mary wants to go but I don't see it.

—I'm just as strong as the rest of you Mary Graves called across the cabin.

—Ayeah said Graves. Strong-willed that is.

—Anyway I'm going said Mary.

—How about Bill? said Eddy.

Graves shook his head.

—He's got to stay back here and look after the others. Miz Graves needs him to cut her wood. Miz McCutchen ought to go though. She don't want to. Graves lowered his voice. Don't want to leave her baby. We told her Miz Graves'd take care of it. Whyn't you speak to her Will?

Amanda McCutchen sat at the end of her cot dully watching her baby sleep. She was a small woman with gray eyes and light auburn hair. Like the others her face and hands were swollen.

Eddy squatted in front of her. She glanced at him and then turned back to her baby.

—I can't just leave Harriet she said.

—Mrs. Graves is a good mother said Eddy. She'd take good care of her.

—I'd never forgive myself is something happened. Will wouldn't forgive me neither.

—He knows the case is hard Mrs. McCutchen. If it wasn't he'd be here to take you down the mountains.

Amanda began crying.

—I miss him so Mr. Eddy. Just miss him so.

Eddy spoke softly.

—Then you ought to leave Harriet in these good hands here and go on to him.

—I ain't even got no more milk said Amanda. She sniffed and sat up. Reckon I ought then. Ain't doing nobody no good here. Grudge me the little food I eat.

—Then you'll go said Eddy. I'll put you down.

—I'll go Amanda said. One thing's good as another I reckon.

Eddy wrote her name on his list and returned to Stanton's bench and sat down.

—That's five he said and you and me is six and seven.

Stanton stopped sawing. The planning cheered him.

—And Luis and Salvador eight and nine. I think we'll make it too. These snowshoes are just the thing.

—What about Mrs. Reed? asked Eddy.

—She's got the children. Antoine's going.

—Who'll cut the wood over there?

—She thinks she can get Milt to stay or maybe move in with one of the other families.

—Ten then said Eddy. He tapped out his pipe. I'll get on back. Check out the other cabins here tomorrow. Got to get a pile of wood up for Ellie. He stood. Keep at it Charlie.

—I said I'd do it said Stanton testily.

—I knewed you would Eddy said.

December 12

Pat   Breen   wrote   Continues   to   snow   wind   W
weather mild   freezeind little

In the Breen cabin Pat Dolan oiled his new snowshoes with tallow. He scooped 2 fingers into the tallow pot and rubbed the softened fat into the rawhide. Into the knots that held the laces to the frames and over the frames themselves. He whistled as he work. Simon, Peter and James Breen sat at his feet watching. They had never seen snowshoes before. The idea of a man walking on giant shoes filled them with awe. Everything got bigger in the mountains. The snow was deeper and you had to wear bigger shoes.

Pat Breen watched Dolan with disgust. There was no point in Dolan's going. A fool's errand to cross the mountains in the middle of winter when there was beef left.

—Ah they're brave shoes said Breen. Watertight and shipshape are they Pat?

—Yir a sharp fellow Pat said Dolan grinning. I'd say a mite of envy there though.

Breen snorted.

—Envy is it. It's a foolish thing yir doin when there's no need.

—There's need said Dolan. Think of the sufferin Pat Dolan is sparin the mithers and the little ones. A hero ever after. Recorded ever after in the annals of the great country of California. Pat Dolan, a simple Irish fellow, bravely crossed the terrible California mountains in the dead of winter to bring succor to the poor souls trapped there by the awful snow. Will yi write that in yir diary then Pat.

—Not a word of it said Breen. Isn't enough pages to fill with word of fools.

—Pat said Dolan the supplies are low. Every one of us that leaves make it easier for them as has to stay. Mrs. Reed's already livin on the hides.

—It's a hard case said Breen but we all look out for our own.

Dolan lined the snowshoes in front of the boys. He sat up and looked at Breen as he wiped off his hands.

—Will yi make me a promise Pat he said.

—Sure I will said Breen.

—Yir t' share what's left of my beef with the Reeds.

—I'd rather you'd stay and share it yirself said Breen.

—I'll be over at Sutter's takin my ease said Dolan. Truthfully, I want Mrs. Reed to have my supplies.

—If that's yir wish said Breen.

—That's providin we don't need them Pat Dolan said Peggy from the hearth. She was drying beef for Dolan's pack.

—Share what yi can said Dolan solemnly. If yi don't the time may come when some as need it badly will try to take it by force.

—Ah but I've got this great brave husband to guard me said Peggy.

—I wouldn't give tuppence for my life if I stayed around here and ate beef while others were starving said Dolan. I've no family to feed. He turned to the boys and pointed to the snowshoes. D'yi want to try them out? They nodded in unison and he picked up the shoes and headed for the door with the boys following behind.

December 13

Pat Breen wrote Snows faster than any previous day wind N:W Stanton & Graves with several others makeing preperations to cross the Mountains on snow shoes, snow 8 feet deep on the level dull

Lavina Murphy insisted that all the grownups at the cabin should go. Food was too short to stay. She said she'd been taking care of children all her life and didn't see why she should stop now. Bill Foster was all for the arrangement but Sarah didn't want to leave her little boy. Harriet had lost her husband and now her mother was telling her to leave Naomi and the baby. Eddy grimly backed the widow. There were 10 children in the cabin to feed and not much bear or beef. Ellie was too weak for the crossing. She would have to stay and help Mrs. Murphy and care for Jimmy and Margaret. It was terrible to leave them but it was worse to stay and eat the food that might keep them alive until relief.

John Landrum balked worse of all. He was 15 and strong enough to make the crossing but someone had to stay and cut wood. He argued with Bill Foster and suddenly took a swing at him and knocked him down. Foster got up with blood in his eye. The fight had been a long time coming and he was ready for it but Eddy held him back. John Landrum flung himself on his bed and pounded the blanket in rage. Finally he gave in.

Lem and Bill wanted to try. They didn't have snowshoes but they said they could follow in the tracks of the people in front. If they could go it would help and Eddy didn't turn them down.

The storm had blocked Milt Elliott's return from the Donner camp. He lived at the teamsters' and nursed the men. Tamsen Donner was unwilling to give them any more beef. Even her husband had argued with her but she was adamant. They were grown men and ought to look after themselves. Milt boiled hides for them but they hardly ate. They were weak and sick. So was Jacob Donner. Noah James had moved into Uncle Jacob's tent to help as he could. He kept the fire going even in the storm.

December 14

   Pat Breen wrote fine morning   sunshine   cleared off last night about 12 o clock   wind E:S:E   dont thaw much but fair for a continueance of fair weather

The storm was over. People were getting ready to go. Mary Graves had named the group the Forlorn Hope and the quaint phrase was passed among the cabins. It stuck. People heard it and laughed. The Forlorn Hope. The women were sewing their heaviest dresses into pantaloons. They blushed to do it but knew they had to if they were to travel through the snow. The risk was severe but no more severe now than the risk of staying behind.

Snow covered the cabins. The creek was buried and the lake was a meadow of snow. Snow hung heavy on the pines. It whitened the bluffs to the south and the hills to the north. The mountains beyond the pass were white with snow and the clearings filled with snow and the cabins snowcaves marked only by the packed ramps at their doors and the wisps of smoke that rose from their buried chimneys where the heat of the fires melted back a circle of snow and water dripped down the chimney walls.

No one would carry even a change of clothes. A blanket and a little food were as much as they could carry. They set their ration at 3 strips of jerky per day. 3 pieces each the size of 2 fingers. 6 days' ration because Stanton and Eddy had calculated they could make 10 miles a day. A man could walk 5 miles an hour over solid ground. They would carry Foster's rifle in the hope of finding game and a hatchet to cut wood. Several pistols. A little coffee, all that was left in camp. Loaf sugar.

They were taking charge of their destiny again. They would no longer sit numbly waiting for relief. The preparations nerved them and they felt more vigor than they had in weeks.

December 15

Pat Breen wrote Still continues fine   wind W:S:W

The last day of preparations was a grim day despite the bright sunlight. Amanda McCutchen winced whenever her baby cried. Will Eddy stayed close to Ellie and the children. He knew he might never see them again. Ellie knew it too. The mountains could consume them all.

Dutch Charley Burger decided at the last minute to go. Anything was better than living any longer with Keseberg. The man was bitter and vicious and niggardly about food. Burger had no snowshoes. He expected to follow the trail the others made just as the Murphy boys planned to do.

At the Donner camp Milt Elliott continued to nurse the teamsters. He'd changed his mind about the crossing. Tamsen Donner urged him to go on to the lake camp and attempt the mountains but he refused. The teamsters needed his help and Ma Reed had no one to look after her interests. Mr. Reed would relieve them soon enough. California was only a word for a place that seemed to him far away. He'd stick with people he knew. People who needed his help.

Margaret Reed felt the reprieve of Dolan's gift. It would be work to collect it from Peggy Breen but she thought she could prevail. She gave Dolan a gold watch and a Masonic medal to seal the bargain. He was to hold the objects as collateral against her husband's repayment. She had not known Dolan was an ally although he had enjoyed playing with Patty and the boys during the evenings on the trail. They must have kept up his spirits. Patty especially affected people that way. Jim's Irish birth also bound the bachelor to their need, and the deep ways that men are bound to mothers.

The men and women of the Forlorn Hope went early to

bed that night but there was restlessness in all the cabins. The choice of going or staying had not been free. The strong would go and the weak would stay. Those who stayed felt they had the lesser choice. That was why the Forlorn Hope took only a minimum of food. To balance the choices. But the decision also increased the risks. No one slept well.

Toward midnight Baylis Williams stopped breathing. One minute he was alive and the next minute he was dead. He had fasted for days but his death still took Eliza by surprise. She had turned away from her brother and turned back and found him dead. She shrieked and threw herself onto his body and began to wail. Margaret Reed woke and went to the girl and held her in her arms. Baylis was the first to die at the lake camp and the first death since Bill Pike's almost 2 months before. Margaret knew then that it wouldn't be the last and thought of her husband and prayed he would find a way to come to them. The snow had buried them alive. She no longer envied the Forlorn Hope. They might as well be going naked into Hell. The snow would conspire against them as it conspired against those who had to stay behind and they would be lucky to escape with their lives. Baylis was the first victim of the snow. She could not think the snow anything but innocent but she understood suddenly how implacable innocence could be and she was grateful that she had known a man and born children. Innocence as intense as the snow's innocence was really a kind of terrible rage. Baylis's death had served a purpose. They would all take strength from it. It would fuel their desperation.

December 16

Will Eddy and Pat Dolan carried Baylis Williams' body out of the Reed cabin and buried it in the snow at the edge of the clearing while Eliza and Margaret Reed stood by. The burial was quick work and while it proceeded the others of the Forlorn Hope gathered outside the Breen cabin and prepared to depart. They were awkward in their snowshoes.

They practiced walking on the loose snow and often fell down. They giggled and laughed and handed each other up again.

They struck out in a line with Eddy breaking trail. The fine powder the storm had left gave little support even to the snowshoes. Eddy found he had to lift his knees nearly to his waist to clear the shoes from the snow. It would be hard going at best.

Stanton was behind Eddy and behind him were Bill and Sarah Foster. Uncle Billy Graves, Mary Graves, Amanda McCutchen, Pat Dolan, Harriet Pike and Sarah and Jay Fosdick followed in the middle of the line. Next came Luis and Salvador and Antoine. Dutch Charley Burger and Lem and Bill Murphy brought up the rear. They soon discovered that the snow was too deep for the snowshoers to pack an adequate trail. The 2 little boys and the big German floundered alike in the snow. The boys sank up to their waists with every step and had to claw their way out of the holes they made. Their sisters Sarah Foster and Harriet Pike saw their troubles and dropped back to help them along but the going was still rough.

Pat Breen wrote fair & pleasant   froeze hard last
   night & the Company started on snow shoes to cross
   the mountains   wind S.E.   looks pleasant

At the Donner camp, in the early morning, at about the same time that Eddy and Dolan were burying Baylis Williams, Jacob Donner died. His wife and George and Tamsen Donner had sat with him through the night. He hadn't been well for months. That fact gave them consolation but they knew he hadn't died of hunger. He died because his courage failed. Tamsen and George comforted Betsy as best they could. Noah James was still there to look after her. She would need him. She was beside herself with fear for her family's prospects in the days to come.

The lake was a snow barren unmarked by any sign of life. 8 feet of white and dazzling snow covered its thick winter ice. The Forlorn Hope struggled along its banks high above the ground on the snow. The cold air burned their noses but the wind blew lightly and they found themselves sweating inside their heavy clothes. At the beginning they had shivered and gone dizzy with hunger but as they pushed on along the lake shore their bodies adjusted to the load. They stumbled less as they found the knack of the snowshoes but their thighs ached from lifting their legs and their backs ached from leaning forward to keep their balance. The glare already stung their eyes and continual squinting gave them headaches.

The men took turns breaking trail while the women followed along behind. They paced themselves badly because the cabins still smoked only a little way behind them. They could feel no progress so long as the cabins were in sight but with the sun overhead at noon they had advanced only halfway up the lake. Eddy regretfully called a halt. They flopped in the snow and chewed dried beef and scooped handsful of snow to wet their mouths. The beef swelled as they chewed it into a gray ball. The snow hardly moistened it. It tasted nauseatingly of pine smoke. Yet they had made a beginning. They were out in the open under a sky so blue it reminded them of the skies in Illinois and Missouri after a spring storm had washed the dust from the air. It was the finest air in the world and the sun shone warm on the snow. They had started toward California after 2 months of holing up in the dingy cabins now behind them. If they got along well they might be at Sutter's by Christmas.

—Chain up! Chain up! Eddy called and set the women laughing. The beef had strengthened them and they set out in good spirits. Eddy knew they wouldn't cross the pass that day and determined to camp at the head of the lake where the wagons they had abandoned long ago still stood mounded over with snow. There might be provisions left in the wagons and they could use the wood to make a fire.

At the Donner camp Noah James finished digging a grave in the snow. With George Donner helping and Aunt Betsy and Mrs. Donner and the children looking on he lifted

Jacob Donner's body and lowered it into the grave. Mrs. Donner said a prayer and Noah shoveled snow to cover the body.

Sam Shoemaker was dying in the teamsters' shelter with Milt Elliott and John Denton looking on. Joe Reinhardt and James Smith lay silently abed behind them. Shoemaker's mind was gone. He had talked to his parents in the voice of a small boy but the voice was gone husky now. It was almost a whisper. He asked his mother to build a fire for him and he stretched his shaking hands out above the bed to warm them. He talked wildly of food and brought his hands to his mouth and said *please* and *thank you* and then his throat rattled and he died. Eventually Milt stood and pulled the blanket over his face. John Denton began sobbing.

—He is dead? asked Reinhardt.

—Yeah said Milt. He's dead.

—We are all dead said Reinhardt. It is a curse.

—Ain't no curse said Milt. You fellas quit eating.

Reinhardt turned away.

The Forlorn Hope stopped at the head of the lake at about 4 in the afternoon. The women were dispatched to the wagons to search for provisions. The men took turns at the one hatchet cutting green logs to make a platform for the fire. Bill Murphy was crying. Even with the help of his sisters he had hardly kept up. They had dragged him into camp and they knew he couldn't go on. Lem begged Stanton to make him snowshoes and when the women came back to the camp from the wagons with a leather saddlebag Stanton agreed. Dutch Charley Burger also had struggled in the snow without snowshoes. He was too heavy for makeshift shoes and without waiting for the fire to be built he took Bill Murphy by the hand and the 2 started back, the big man dragging the crying boy. They could see the smoke from the cabins at the other end of the lake. In its first day the Forlorn Hope had traveled 3 miles. The pass rose before them and beyond it the unknown.

December 17

Pat Breen wrote Pleasant sunshine today wind about S.E Bill Murp returned from the mountain party last evening Bealis died night before last

In the early morning Milt Elliott woke to find the fire in the teamsters' shelter gone out and the wood supply low. He was the only one left with strength for woodcutting. He hated to leave his warm bed but he got up quietly and took his snowshoes and went out. He was awed as always by the total silence of the valley. In Illinois birds would be chirping to one another in the trees. At dawn and sundown the animals and the birds always came alive. But in the mountains nothing moved by day or night except the people trapped there in the snow. The sun breaking across the snow suddenly flooded the valley with light but it didn't cheer him. He was cutting wood to warm dying men. Feeding dying men food they wouldn't eat that didn't sustain them. Yet he couldn't let them die.

John Denton struggled up from sleep. For weeks he had dreamed almost every night of summer fields in England where he played as a boy. Fields where sheep grazed on green grass. He was dreaming the same dream again when he woke in the dim cabin. He started up. The fire was out. He looked around for Milt. Milt was gone. Smith and Reinhardt lay piled with coats and quilts just as they lay during the day. Shoemaker was dead and Jacob Donner was dead. Milt had left them now to die. The fire was out. Milt must have given up on them and gone back to the lake. His snowshoes were missing. They had nothing to eat but hides. No prospect of anything to eat but hides. Denton thought of his dream. It terrified him. He was dreaming his way back into the past. He had let Milt care for him along with the others. Acted the invalid. Acted the weakling. Milt had left to remind him that if he would live he must do for himself. Uncle Jacob had died with beef at hand. Sam had refused the horrible glue of the hides. If he crossed to the lake camp he might find occasion to go over the mountains. The shelter reeked of death. His own dying. He didn't want to die. Let these two die. They were dying anyway. Milt thought him no better than they. Milt had already gone and his going proved him alive. Denton decided he would go too.

The Forlorn Hope climbed toward the pass, following Stanton's memory of the trail that twisted up among outcroppings of mottled granite. Mary Graves brought up the rear of the line. She felt stronger today than she had felt yesterday. Felt a sense of purpose in the work of the climb. They had breakfasted on coffee and a little beef and set out early. Now it was afternoon yet they weren't exhausted. The pass was a goal and they fought to reach it before the end of the day. Without a word the feeling had come back along the line that the goal was in sight. Mary looked at backs covered with heavy wool. Heads cloaked in caps and mantles and scarves. Each back bore a makeshift pack. The packs were pitifully thin. They hardly supported the blanket rolls tied on top. Mary remembered a book she had read as a child. In the front was an engraving of a party of men climbing a snow-covered mountain. The line in front of her looked like that, like a Norwegian fur company among the icebergs. It was a funny thought. There were men who lived in the ice and snow through entire winters and never suffered and never complained. They must have laid up stocks of food or knew where to find game. But they climbed through snow just as her Forlorn Hope was climbing and if they could do it perhaps the Hope could too. She knew at least that she wasn't going back. She could be of no use to those who stayed behind.

At the head of the line Eddy and Stanton pulled themselves up onto a massive flat rock blown clear of snow. They moved out of the way of those who followed and sat down grinning to unlace their snowshoes. When Eddy got his snowshoes off he walked back to the rim of the rock and handed the others up.

—It's the top of the pass! he shouted. The others were grinning too. We made it! It's the top of the pass!

They caught their breath standing on the rock and looking back into the lake valley. The hills sloped down to the glare of the snow-covered lake. Smoke rose from the cabins beyond.

—We're about as near heaven as we can get said Stanton.

Eddy pounded him on the back.

—Jesus Christ Charlie he said. You're a wonder of a guide.

Stanton blushed.

—Anyone could guide us this far.

—Aye said Pat Dolan but yir goin to guide us the rest of the way Charlie.

—Look at the cabins said Mary Graves. They're so beautiful down there in the snow.

—It looks like a little village said Sarah Foster.

—It ain't no village said Bill Foster it's misery and botheration.

—I got a good feeling about this here Forlorn Hope said Eddy.

—I do too said Mary Graves.

Eddy smiled at her.

—That's good he said. If you ladies hold up we'll get along fine.

—We'll hold up Mr. Eddy said Harriet Pike. You men see you do the same.

Uncle Billy Graves snorted. He had taken off his boots and was sitting on the rock rubbing his stockinged feet.

—This here ain't no contest between the sexes he said. If it was I'd take the prize. I'm twiced as old as any of you.

—I'm twiced as little said Lem Murphy.

—Hey Lem said Eddy how you doing? He went over to the boy and pounded him on the back. You been moving right along today. Everything okay?

—Yeah I'm okay said Lem. Kinda cold right now.

Eddy stood up.

—Let's get on here he said. We done a day's work. Get off this rock and make camp over yonder. Build a fire on that bare rock over yonder and spare us cutting green wood.

Coffee and beef and sleep in the snow. The men and women slept together to keep warm in the bitter cold at the top of the pass. Will Eddy huddled with Lem Murphy. His back pressed against Mary Graves' back. She slept against Will Eddy protected in the circle of her father's arms.

Pat Breen wrote Milt. & Noah went to Donnos 8 days since not returned yet, thinks they got lost in the snow.

J Denton here to day

December 18

Pat Breen wrote Beautiful day sky clear it would be delightful were it not for the snow lying so deep thaws but little on the south side of shanty

The excitement of the afternoon before had left the people of the Forlorn Hope. They woke fatigued from the cold and the height and with little talk glumly ate their meager ration of beef. They hiked down into the valley beyond the summit. It opened to the northwest.

Stanton had trouble keeping up. He was weak with hunger and his eyes burned. The glare on the snow was terrible. His head ached with the effort of squinting to shut out the light. He saw spots and a green glow that obscured the figures ahead of him and narrowed his view. Despite the sun the wind blew furiously around him and he was cold. He shivered and couldn't stop shivering and the strain weakened him further. The valley had changed. When he crossed it before there had been only a foot or 2 of snow on the ground but now he guessed there must be 25 feet or more. If that much snow had fallen in the months since he returned eastward from Sutter's then the snow would extend much farther down the mountains than he had estimated. The snow would fill Bear Valley and perhaps beyond. He had calculated their rations believing they would reach grass and perhaps game at Bear Valley or just beyond. If the snow went farther down the mountains then they would run out of food. They had only made 5 miles in their first 2 days of travel and looked like they might make another 5 today. And he was going blind.

A spasm shook him and he began to cry. They were letting him fall behind. They weren't even helping him. He had gone twice over the mountains for them and come back and twice saved their lives. Sutter's had been a wonderful place. The old colonel treated him with respect. He'd had a bed in the main house and meals at Sutter's big table. Talk of California. Of the American emigration. The Mexicans were restive. Sutter's great hot chili and the Indians eating like pigs out of troughs set up in the yard. Cornmeal mush that smelled like heaven.

The wind stung his face. His lips were cracked and sore. He felt as if he were skinned and his clothes were hanging on his bones. His legs ached with lifting the snowshoes in and out of the snow. He wasn't used to the work the way the others were. He had ridden mules when they had walked. Walked down Mary's River and up to the mountain lake. He was paying for his riding now. Everything he had ever done had gone against him. His store had failed and he had borrowed money from his brother he couldn't pay back. He'd lost the mules to the snow. He wasn't even sure now of the trail. The snow changed everything. It was white as salt. White as the sun. It took no pity on a man. His father had a name for him. His father called him a priss.

He sniffed and swallowed and looked up. He couldn't see through the green glare. He stretched his arms in front of his eyes and they ended in glare at the wrists.

—Help me! he screamed. Help me!

Half a mile ahead Jay Fosdick heard Stanton's scream but he was too tired to turn back. Let him crawl into camp. The rest of them had to. It'd come to sink or swim. Let the bastard sink or swim.

George Donner sat on Joe Reinhardt's bed listening to the strange babble of German and English pouring from the man's mouth. Milt Elliott was cooking up a broth of beef Tamsen had provided to nurse the German back to life but George saw there was nothing for it. The man was dying. Milt brought the broth and spooned it onto Reinhardt's lips but he let it drool from his mouth. Abruptly he shoved Milt's hand aside and sat up on his elbow.

—Herr Donner he said fiercely. My soul is sick. I have done a terrible crime. I shall burn in Hell for it. You must know Herr Donner you must pray for me.

George Donner patted the man's shoulder.

—Lie back Joe he said. It's all right.

—Herr Donner said Reinhardt. Spitzer, I killed that old man.

—Wolfinger? said George Donner.

—*Ja* Wolfinger. We kill him back there. Take his money. It is a mortal sin.

—He was lost anyway Joe said George Donner gently.

—*Ja* but we kill him. Reinhardt's eyes were wild. I am going to Hell Herr Donner you must save me from Hell! He was gasping for breath.

—Joe said George Donner. Joe. It's all right. He moved to push the dying man down onto the bed and heard him rattle and felt at the same moment the pain shoot through his injured hand. Reinhardt's mouth dropped open and he fell back. He seemed still to be screaming. George Donner moved hurriedly to close the mouth and brush shut the eyes.

Pat Breen wrote saw no strangers today from any of the shantys

December 19

Pat Breen wrote Snowed last night commenced about 11 Oclock. squalls of wind with snow at intervals this morning thawing wind. N by W a little Singular for a thaw may continue

In the morning at the Donner camp Jim Smith died. Tamsen Donner was there to close his eyes. She told Milt Elliott that he died like a tired child falling asleep. All the teamsters who had stayed at the shelter were dead now. Milt couldn't understand it. They hadn't died of starvation. They had just given up. One death followed another as if Death gave lessons. Denton had disappeared probably to the lake camp if his tracks meant anything. Milt had to bury another body in the snow. He would stay with the Donners for that but then he was going back to Ma Reed. That was where he belonged. Jean Baptiste and Noah could look after the Donners now. They had enough beef to last them until relief came if it came soon.

With Eddy in the lead and Luis and Salvador following the Forlorn Hope groped west through the snow in the high river valley. Mary Graves followed close behind the men but the others were strung out in a line that reached back almost 2 miles. Stanton was in the rear far from the last of the line. His feet were numb. They felt like blocks of wood. A little of his vision had returned during the night but it was rapidly clouding again in the spells of sunlight. He was terrified of being left behind. His terror drove him onward even though he stumbled often and fell in the snow. Ice caked his beard. He forced himself forward following the trail of snow disturbed by the snowshoes of those in front of him. They counted on his terror propelling him forward and he hated them for that.

Mary Graves knew her feet were freezing. She was wearing a pair of her father's boots. They were big and heavy but superior to any of her own shoes especially with the snowshoes straining them. Her father had fallen behind. She couldn't help him. She had felt confident of her strength before but now it seemed to be failing. Her mind drifted into strange moods when she imagined they had almost reached their goal and when she looked up from her imagining she discovered that she had slowed down or wandered off the trail. She shook her head then to clear it and angled back onto the trail and pushed ahead and then found herself wandering again. Sometimes panic choked her and she wanted to scream but she held the scream in until it faded away. There was a place at the back of her mind that wouldn't lie still. It squirmed as she had watched a prairie wolf squirm once when it was attacked by the family dogs. It sent shivers down her back. If she let it go it would drive her mad and devour her but if she held it back too long she feared she couldn't stand the pain. It lurked and waited and she knew she couldn't control it. She forced it through her body and into her legs to drive them up and down lifting the chains of the snowshoes. As long as she thought of the snowshoes she could keep the thing down in her legs but whenever she thought of where they were and where they were going the thing broke loose and went wild.

Looking up she saw smoke rising from a gorge to the north of the trail. Smoke meant a camp and a camp meant food and warmth.

—This way! she shouted to Eddy. Over this way! Look at the smoke! She broke and tried to run but could manage only a fast clumsy walk in her snowshoes.

Eddy took in the gorge and saw what Mary saw.

—It's only mist! he shouted. It ain't smoke! You're wasting your breath! He turned off the trail and angled back to block her before she reached the edge of the gorge. He feared she would fall in. Mary! he shouted. Stop! It ain't nothing! He reached her 10 yards from the edge and grabbed her and fell with her into the snow.

—It's smoke Will! she yelled hysterically. It's smoke! They made it! They come to save us! She struggled to break free but he was too strong for her. Why are you holding me? she hissed. I want to get to camp. They got food for us. They got a fire.

—It's not smoke Mary said Eddy it's just mist.

The Indians had stumped over to see what the white woman was screaming about. They heard the word *smoke* and studied the mist from the gorge and shook their heads.

—Not smoke said Luis.

Mary Graves shook herself free from Eddy.

—We've got to go down there and see she said.

—Trail not that way said Luis.

Mary pushed herself to her feet.

—Oh *damn* you all she said. I know that's smoke. I seen it with my own eyes. She faced the gorge. Hello! Hello! We're here! Up here!

—It ain't no use said Eddy. There ain't nobody there.

She turned on him.

—There *could* be someone there and if there is wouldn't you be ashamed to pass them by without even trying to stop them?

Eddy dropped the gun from his shoulder and held it out and fired it into the air. The report echoed from the gorge and then there was silence.

—It's just mist said Eddy. Mary Graves sat down in the snow and cried. Eddy shouldered the gun again and gave her his hand and pulled her up. Don't take on Mary he said. We all wish it was over.

They hiked back to the trail. The others had never left it. They had only stopped wherever they stood and watched. When Eddy took up the march they began again to follow. Stanton was nowhere in sight.

Pat Breen wrote it continues to Snow

Uncle Billy Graves was thinking of Vermont. He remembered snow in the mountains. He had driven the cows to the barn in a snowstorm when he was just a boy and thought he would never make it. He'd gritted his teeth against the storm and driven on. His pappy had pushed them to learn the hardness of farming in a rocky land. It never seemed to matter how much you hurt so long as you got the job done. He'd given up worrying about his aches and pains long ago. You just pushed on until you were ready to drop and then you pushed on the more. He was old now and didn't feel the strength he used to feel. There was a breath on his back like the breath he had felt the day he went with Eddy to haul in the bear. The breath of the grave. Graves. That was a kind of a curse right there. It'd waited for him all his life while he tore the gristle off his bones to make his way. Waited for him right there in the mountains whistling through a gap in some rock. He felt like a dried-up egg. When you shook it next to your ear you could hear something rattling inside. Something that had died and dried up in there without ever once seeing the light of day.

Pat Breen wrote Sun Shining

Lem Murphy was cold. He wished he was back in the cabin again. Bill was lucky he'd give out and gone on back with Dutch Charley. His hands was all sore and he didn't have no gloves. Harriet didn't care nothing she just went on. The snow'd quit but the sun hurt his eyes. He'd cut off little pieces of the fire rug and crisped them and et them. They didn't taste like nothing but they made your belly full. He wished he had his horse. If he had his horse he'd of rid over the snow and got clear to Sutter's and back by now.

Pat Breen wrote cleared off towards evening

With the sun setting Eddy stopped to make camp. Bill Foster came up with the hatchet and he and Eddy took turns hacking at a pine to cut the baselogs for the fire. Eddy figured they'd make 5 miles that day. Before them the river valley widened out into bottoms that looked like the lake above the cabins. It was one place they might have found a relief party but no sign of life marked the snow. South of them a domed mountain towered up. There were 25 or 30 feet of snow in the bottoms. Eddy couldn't believe the snow. There must be more snow in the California mountains than anyplace else in the world.

Stanton stumbled into camp an hour late. He was nearly snowblind and shivering with exhaustion. Mary Graves led him to the fire. It was another hour before his shivering stopped.

December 20

Pat Breen wrote night clear froze a little now clear & pleasant wind N W thawing a little

The people of the Forlorn Hope shook themselves awake at dawn. They brewed the last of their meager store of coffee and drank it with the last of their sugar. They warmed their strips of beef over the fire. Some of the men lit pipes. The tobacco dulled the pain in their bellies. No one wanted to leave the fire. They sat around it wrapped in their blankets trying to store up enough heat to keep them through the day. Will Eddy was the first to lace on his snowshoes and push himself to his feet. The Indians followed and then several of the women and only then the men. The women were holding up better than the men. They even laughed together around the fire sometimes at the ridiculous way they looked. Eddy laughed too but none of the other men. Even Pat Dolan was morose at their prospects. Finally the men came on and the line strung out across the bottoms.

Stanton fell behind again. The Hope hadn't even reached Bear Valley and he knew California was days farther away. He had 5 strips of beef left in his pack. As much as any of them if they had resisted cheating themselves. It would carry them to Bear Valley but Bear Valley would be filled with snow. After that they would starve. California was a lifetime away. New York was no farther. His brother and his sister-in-law sat now before the hearth in the old stone farm house where he was born. He had left his diamond pin with Sutter with instructions to send it on. *Capt. Sutter will send the within, in the event of my death, to Sydney Stanton, Syracuse, N.Y.* He had given Alice the diamond pin when Sydney loaned him the money. She thought the pin was a pledge and returned it to him but it was a gift and she would have it back. Now she would have it back. She had sent it to him with a poem clipped from a newpaper. It was a poem in a mood of tender pathos and even now it moved him almost to tears. "The Withered Flower." He had it by heart. He had read poetry with Sydney and Alice and seen Sydney grow restless but Alice had been moved. She knew the gentleness of his spirit.

> O! dying flower, that droop'st alone,
>   Erewhile the valley's pride,
> Thy withered leaves, disordered strown,
>   Rude winds sweep far and wide.

The scythe of Time, whose stroke we mourn,
    Our common doom shall bring.
From thee a faded leaf is torn,
    From us a joy takes wing.

As life flies by, oh! who but feels
    Some sense, some charm decay?
E'en every fleeting moment steals
    Some treasured dream away.

Some secret blight each hope destroys,
    Till at length we ask in grief,
If, than life's ephemeral joys,
    The floweret's be more brief.

Somehow she had known that he would find himself in this wind-swept valley alone. The scythe of Time and the fleeting moment were the days yet to travel and the disappearing rations. But the secret blight was the blight on his soul since his mother's death. No man had ever felt more alone.

The people of the Forlorn Hope had stopped to rest and to chew a little beef at the side of the bottoms below a divide. Somewhere beyond the divide was the gap in the western ridge that would lead them into Bear Valley. Stanton came up while the others were resting and sank down before them onto the snow. They were dull with fatigue and hardly noticed him. Walking in the snowshoes was an ordeal even on the bottoms and now they faced the climb up to the divide. Then his sobbing took their attention.

—You've got to help me he said hoarsely. I can't make it by myself any more.

Mary Graves pushed herself up and went to Stanton's side.

—It's all right Mr. Stanton she said. You *will* make it.

—No I won't said Stanton I'm going to die.

Bill Foster snorted.

—Ah shit Stanton stop your sniveling.

—There's women here Bill said Eddy. Watch your language.

—I don't give a goddamn who's here said Foster make that sniveling son-of-a-bitch shut up.

Eddy turned to Stanton.

—Bawling won't do you no good Charlie he said. You got to just push on.

—I'm going blind! screamed Stanton. I'm going blind!

—Shut that up! yelled Foster. He climbed to his feet and started toward Stanton but Eddy grabbed his leg and jerked it back and Foster fell down.

—Leave him alone said Eddy evenly. He's just scared.

—He's a sniveling little puke said Foster.

—If someone could just *help* me said Stanton brokenly.

—Ain't no one can help you said Foster. We cain't hardly help ourselves.

—We just got to go on said Eddy measuring the faces of the others around him. There's nothing else for it. The faces were hard. Eddy waited for Stanton's fit to subside and then laced on his snowshoes. Let's get going. We got to climb this here hill.

One by one the others stood and turned in behind him and the Forlorn Hope climbed toward the divide leaving Stanton still sitting in the disordered snow.

Pat Breen wrote Mrs Reid here. no account of Milt. yet Dutch Charley started for Donnghs turned back not able to proceed tough times, but not discouraged our hopes are in God. Amen

Christmas tugged at Breen's conscience. All else failing of relief, he had decided to try prayer.

December 21

Pat Breen wrote Milt. got back last night from Donnos camp sad news Jake Donno Sam Shoemaker Rinehart, & Smith are dead the rest of them in a low situation snowed all night with a strong S-W wind to day

Cloudy   wind continues but not snowing,   thawing
sun shineing dimly   in hopes it will clear off

At the campfire beyond the divide Will Eddy decided to
lighten his pack. Ellie had prepared it for him and he
hadn't bothered to inventory it before he left. Anything he
could throw away would spare him that much wasted effort.
He pulled out the scraps of paper Ellie had used to wrap
the beef in. He found a pair of spare moccasins and decided to keep them. If he couldn't wear them he could eat
them. Feeling in the bottom of the pack his hand closed
around a lump only a little smaller than his fist. He pulled
it out and peeled back the paper. It was a lump of frozen
meat.

Jesus Christ.

He stuffed the meat back into the pack and looked around.
No one seemed to notice. Ellie had packed him a hunk of
bear meat. It must weigh half a pound. He'd had it all
along and didn't even know. Had as much meat almost as
the full ration they'd packed for the whole trip.

His fingers worked the paper free and he pulled it from
the pack. Ellie had written him a note. *My dearest husband.*
I believe that you will find this gift when you need it. You
must save it until the last possible momet. I believe it will
save your life & help you to hurry back to us for we need
you so. Your own dear Eleanor

She'd robbed her own store for him. It was an act of
mercy. She'd always been a woman he could count on. It
wouldn't do to let the others know. He'd better save the
meat and eat it on the trail when they were behind. Save
it anyway until all the beef gave out and even save it some
after that. The last possible moment. That wouldn't be so
long. He stuffed the note back into the pack and bent and
put it on.

—Let's get moving he said. We ain't going nowhere settin
around the fire.

They laced their snowshoes over painfully swollen feet
and one by one stood up. Stanton sat leaning against a tree

beside the fire as the others moved out. Mary Graves turned
back to him.

—Are you coming on Mr. Stanton?

Stanton stared into the fire puffing his pipe.

—Yes he said I'm coming soon. You and the others go on.

—You ought to come on now said Mary Graves gently.

—It's all right Mary. I'll be along soon.

She stood watching him. He hadn't eaten that morning.
If the others wouldn't help then there was nothing she
could do. He was a decent man. He had made the shoes they
were walking on. And sustained them in that way and in
the desert before.

—Mary! Uncle Billy called back to her. Come on!

She turned and left the campfire.

Through the day the Forlorn Hope slogged along the
eastern slope of a ridge. A stiff wind blew the snow. The
men had the advantage of their beards but the women contrived to wrap their shawls over their faces like masks
until only their eyes peered out. Clinging to the slope was
an unendurable effort and gradually without much awareness of what they were doing they turned down the hill.
For a time they followed a snow-filled stream canyon that
ran west but near the end of the day the canyon bent to the
south. The Indians moved up to Will Eddy and indicated
that they ought to continue west but west now was only the
canyon wall. Eddy realized that they needed Stanton's
knowledge of the trail and decided to call a halt. Stanton
had come up before. He was likely to come up again if
they made camp and waited for him.

Stanton sat still leaning against the tree. The fire had
gone out long before and he had made no effort to rekindle
it. He was dull with cold but he had managed through the
day to load and reload his pipe. He was smoking the last of
his tobacco. All day the lines of a poem he had written ran
through his head. They were like a song heard in the morning that he couldn't stop humming. He wanted to think of
something else but they blotted everything else out. They

[195]

went round and round with the smoke from his pipe and the whistle of the wind.

> When death shall close my sad career,
> And I before my God appear—
> There to receive His last decree—
> My only prayer there will be
> Forever to remain with thee,
> My mother.

To My Mother in Heaven. When death shall close my sad career and I before my God appear there to receive His last decree my only prayer there will be forever to remain with thee my mother. The time had come. It wasn't so bad as he had supposed. It was what he had waited for. He knocked his pipe against the tree and fumbled it into the pocket of his coat and then unbuttoned the coat and opened it to the wind and folded his hands across his hollow belly and fatigue welled up in him and the swell of the litany my mother and he closed his eyes against the blackened snow and sleep took him easily at the camp beyond the divide.

December 22

Pat Breen wrote Snowed all last night

With no food in camp except the bear meat hidden in Eddy's pack the Forlorn Hope set out at dawn following the only trail they knew down the stream canyon south. Over the ridge behind them lay Bear Valley and the food Reed and McCutchen had cached in Jotham Curtis's wagon but only Stanton could have found the trail. He had not come up during the night and they feared the worst for him. They debated going back to find him but with their food gone they knew they would only put themselves in worse danger. They drank hot water to stay their bellies and stumbled on. They hadn't traveled a mile when a storm broke from menacing low clouds swirling across the mountains beyond the canyon. The clouds came on and closed overhead and in minutes they could see no more than the canyon itself. They shouted up and down the line to halt and came together at an outcropping of rock that partly blocked the wind. They couldn't go on in the storm. They were too weak to fight the wind while they fought the snow. Eddy and the Indians moved out from the protection of the rock and began cutting wood. Breaking off branches to feed a fire. The women came out and dragged the wood back. They said Stanton might still come up but Mary Graves knew otherwise. Stanton had left them for a better place. Hell itself would be a better place. They were already half out of their minds with hunger.

Pat Breen wrote Continued to snow all day with some few intermissions had a severe fit of the gravel yesterday I am well to day, Praise *be to the God of Heaven*

December 23

Through the night the storm raged over the Forlorn Hope. It dumped a foot of snow on their camp. They struggled to keep the fire alive. In their hunger they slept poorly and couldn't stay warm no matter how close they huddled to the fire. Before dawn Eddy contrived to cut off a few bites of the bear meat. He kept his head inside his blanket so the others couldn't see him chewing. A less practical man might have worried at eating when the others had nothing but Eddy reasoned that the Hope needed a leader if it was to get out of the mountains alive and a leader needed more strength than those who followed him. He promised himself that he would save them or die trying and he ate.

The clouds looked worse in the morning than they had the day before but the snow let up and laboriously they tied on their snowshoes and climbed the canyon to a high knob above its wall. From the knob they could see miles in every direction and what they saw appalled them. Snow covered everything in sight. To the east lay the buttes that ran down from the river valley. To the north rose mountains on which hung the solid gray ceiling of the storm. To the west ran a high ridge with no break anywhere in its line. Southward cut the canyon in which they had camped and other canyons beyond. The streams must lead to a river and the river must lead out of the mountains. The Indians were confused. They were valley Indians and had seen the trail only once, when they came over from Sutter's with Stanton. The snow had changed the landmarks and they no longer knew where they were. Stanton was nowhere in sight. They still believed he might come up with them and they went into camp on the height to watch for him.

Pat Breen wrote Snowed a little last night clear to day & thawing a little. Milt took some of his meat to day all well at their camp began this day to read the Thirty days prayer, may Almighty God grant the request of an unworthy sinner that I am. *Amen*

December 24

Pat Breen wrote rained all night & still continues to rain poor prospect for any kind of Comfort Spiritual or temporal, wind S: may God help us to spend the Christmass as we ought considering circumstances

Out in the snow Pat Dolan's mind also turned to the church but whenever he thought of the rituals of his religion he found himself concentrating on the round white purity of the Host. The priest said it was bread but the priest said it was also the body of Our Lord and Savior Jesus Christ. It was bread transsubstantiated into the flesh of the Savior. Dolan had never thought about the mystery of the Mass before. The Savior had ordered all true Christians to eat of His Body and drink of His Blood. If the Savior hadn't ordered it it would be a horrible thing. The most horrible thing in the world. If the snow could be transformed they could eat that but the snow was everywhere and everywhere it was only snow. The Host was before his eyes in the careful fingers of the priest and then he extended his tongue and the priest laid the Host on it and he was filled with sweetness and a sense of great peace yet he was eating the body of the Son of God. It was a mystery beyond all mysteries and he had never thought of it before.

It made his flesh crawl because it seemed to him suddenly that the Savior had asked them to do a terrible thing but maybe that was the point. To bind them to Him body and soul in a ritual beyond all human understanding. The thought and the meaning of the thought for them filled his mind and only his numbness held him still in the snow.

The bear meat relieved Eddy's hunger and in the morning he roused and routed the others and without much said they laced on their snowshoes and moved into line behind him. The Indians were stoic as always but even the men didn't grumble. There was nothing to do but go on and Eddy intended to make them go as long as he was alive to drive them.

They stumbled down into the stream canyon and followed it south. Eddy found himself pulling out ahead and slowed down to let the others catch up. The sky was set over the canyon like a cast iron lid but ahead was even darker. They stumbled through deep snow so shadowed that it seemed dirty yet no footprints broke its powdery surface ahead and even the trees in the canyon were solidly mounded with snow with no green showing.

The storm burst over them. It swept up the canyon like a flood and battered them to a standstill. The snow that had fallen before had been nothing compared to the snow that swirled around them now. Here was a storm like the storm that had confined them to their cabins at the lake and they knew as immediately as it came that it wouldn't let up for days. Eddy veered to the side of the canyon and waved the line over and halted behind a snowhill that covered a tall pine. The people were confused. Some were cursing and others were crying. They crowded together behind the tree. Bill Foster shouted that they had to turn back.

—We can't turn back! Eddy yelled against the wind. We got to go on! There's nothing back at camp! It's just as far back as it is down to the valley!

—We've got to go on! Mary Graves shouted and the other women nodded vigorously.

Uncle Billy started screaming.

—We're going to starve! Don't you people know we're going to starve!

—We go on said Luis to Eddy and then all were silent. The wind wailed through the canyon.

Abruptly Pat Dolan pulled away. He was waving his arms.

—We're not to starve! he said. Our Lord Jesus Christ has led the way!

Was he crazy and raving.

—Our Savior told us to eat of His Body in remembrance of Him! said Dolan. If we can eat of the Son of God then we can eat of the dead! We aren't to starve! Pure as the snow He was yet He showed us the Way!

Others had thought of it too and thrust the thought aside. Now it was out and it hung in the air before them.

—For I am the Way and the Life! said Dolan rushing now. And he who believeth in Me shall not perish but shall have Everlasting Life!

Eddy bolted to Dolan's side.

—Draw straws then! he shouted. Draw straws then! The men draw straws!

Foster was out and furious and then they were all out and moving back from one another.

—Shut up! shouted Foster. You're talking shit! Nobody's goin to eat nobody!

—Shoot it out then! shouted Eddy. Two men shoot it out! That's okay! That's decent!

Foster tried to push Eddy down but Eddy didn't budge and Foster fell back raving into the snow.

Already the Indians had started out. Mary Graves followed them and Amanda McCutchen and Harriet Pike. The 2 Sarahs stayed with their husbands but began to pull them away. The men realized what was happening. Eddy turned first and pushed past the women and the Indians to the head of the line while the other men stumbled up and fell in behind.

The storm beat against them. They pushed on down the

canyon fighting the wind. Eddy was dizzy with hunger but
the others had moved beyond dizziness to a flat dullness
that rarely admitted the thoughts that now obsessed them.
They denied and denied but denial did not spare them the
storm or the horror. The thoughts of food that had preoccupied them for days now mingled with thoughts of
bodies they had seen. Their own bodies. The bodies of
babies lying on quilts being changed. The arms and the
mouths of the men or women they loved. To think of food
now was to think of the terrible thing before them and to
deny that was to deny the thought of food. But they could
drive on and wear themselves out and perhaps someone
would die. Stumbling and falling in the snow they drove on.
They found another canyon opening west and turned into
it and farther down it bent south and another canyon
opened west and they turned into that one.

Darkness neared and the snow blew around them until
they could hardly see. The snow was pitiless. Eddy began
to fear that they would be cut off and shouted back to make
camp. With the Indians he chopped the green logs for the
fire platform but their hands were so numb they could
hardly hold the hatchet and they deliberately chose the
smallest trees they could find. For more than an hour in
the blizzard of snow they hacked at the trees to cut wood
and after they were through and the fire was started they
sent 2 women out to cut more. Eddy had counted the days
they had been gone and knew it was Christmas Eve and he
cursed the season bitterly. He had never had much truck
with religion and it seemed to have failed them completely
now.

Exhausted and numb the people of the Forlorn Hope
huddled around the fire. While going out again for wood
Eddy had managed to gnaw off a few more bites of bear
meat. It was almost gone. He returned to the fire and
wrapped his blanket around him and hunched down in the
snow. The others had fallen asleep or lay in sleep-like
trances. Eddy found himself next to Antoine. The team-

ster was small and swarthy. His face had withered with hunger into a dark skull and he lay now at the very edge of the fire with his eyes shut breathing raggedly. Then Antoine's hand flopped over into the fire. Eddy thought Antoine would jerk it away but it began to smoke and he did nothing about it and it doubled up and began to draw together like a claw. Eddy reached out then and pulled it from the fire. He wondered if he should have left it where it was and rejected the thought with disgust but a little later Antoine shuddered again and his hand again flopped into the fire and as Eddy watched sickly it curled and smoked and slowly burned black.

Later in the night the storm blew wild and Jay Fosdick piled on more logs. The fire flared high in the banshee wind but abruptly it burned through the platform and settled and began to melt the snow. Eddy saw the danger and saw that the wood they had cut would not last the night. With his blanket wrapped around him he took the hatchet and pushed through the snow to the nearest tree and shook the branches to free them of snow and began hacking them away. He swung the hatchet over his shoulder and felt the head fly. He cried out and spun around but he saw no sign of the head. It had buried itself in the snow. He swore and searched. It was gone without a trace. Their only hatchet was gone. He could cut branches with his knife but they could cut no more logs. He was crazy with rage and he swung back to the tree and tried to break branches off with his mittened hands but they were green and difficult to break and when the fit of rage passed he gave up and groped his way back to the fire.

By midnight the fire had melted down 8 feet below the surface of the snow. A pool of icy water at the bottom threatened to put the fire out. Eddy had watched it sinking and furiously calculated to save it. He took 2 branches from the woodpile and used them as tongs to stand the biggest logs on end. It was a precarious arrangement at best but the flames burned up the logs and Eddy piled branches on the upright ends and the needles caught and flared and the fire was bright again.

Luis sat in a stupor against the side of the firehole. He was cold and the cold woke him and he stood and moved closer to the fire but stumbled over his own feet and fell. His head hit an upright log. The fire seared his forehead and he yelled. The log tipped and knocked down the other logs and the fire fell into the pool of water and hissed and bubbled and went out.

People started moaning. Eddy climbed from the hole.

—Get out! he shouted. Get out of that goddamned hole! He grabbed a stick and poked at the people still huddling beneath him. Get out! You'll freeze to death down there!

Their only chance now was to bury themselves in the snow. As the people crawled out of the hole Eddy shouted at them to lay their blankets on the ground and sit on them and make a circle. Luis and Salvador came up and he showed them where to sit and then Bill and Sarah Foster and Harriet Pike. Pat Dolan crawled up dragging Lem Murphy and Eddy put their blankets over their heads. Amanda McCutchen came up and joined them. Mary Graves tugged on her father. He didn't want to move. Eddy yelled down to him that he was dying and Graves yelled back that he didn't give a damn. Eddy slid into the hole and helped Mary drag her father out but the old man lay down on the snow and refused to get up. Mary saw that he was going and called to her sister and Sarah Fosdick pushed out of the blankets and came over. Graves told them to use his body to save themselves. They shook their heads and he glared at them.

—That ain't nothin wrong he said. You do like I tell you now.

He clawed at his chest and died. Eddy shouted to the women to come on. They touched their father's face and then crawled to the shelter and Eddy guided them inside and laid his own blanket over them and crawled in beside Mary Graves.

The snow fell on through the night. It covered them over. Crowded against each other in the darkness they found to their surprise that they were warm.

December 25

Christmas Day. *Pat Breen wrote* began to snow yesterday about 12 o clock snowed all night & snows yet rapidly wind about E by N Great difficulty in getting wood John & Edwd. has to get I am not able offered our prayers to God this Cherimass morning the prospect is appalling but hope in God *Amen*

Christmas reminded Tamsen Donner of another Christmas years ago when she had honored the Savior's Birth alone. 3 babies and a husband gone. Tully had been like Mr. Donner. A man whose strength lay in patience, not in invention. She seemed to favor such men. It was strange that Mr. Donner had wanted this journey. She'd expected him to stay put in Illinois. She'd thought his ripe years would secure her own. When Tully and the babies died she'd vowed to take life as it came ever after. One thing at a time with time to savor it. Teaching school and studying flowers and making a good man a home. The vow had seemed self-evident. She meant to cling to simple things. But it opened out like a tree. Branch forked into branches that forked again into twigs and each one had its burden of flower and fruit. When the Savior was born on Christmas Day He could not have know the ways His life would take Him. Could not have known the betrayal and the scourge and the terrible Cross. She had her own Cross now and it was no more than she could bear. Tully and the babies had set her for it. If they hadn't died of the cholera she might have pleaded with Mr. Donner to stay in Illinois and he might have done it. But the cholera was in Illinois too and 3 more babies and she would have gone to Hades and beyond to spare them the death the first 3 died.

Breakfast at the Reed cabin on Christmas morning was a pot of glue but Margaret Reed had other plans for Christmas dinner. When the last ox had been slaughtered she had seen the meat stacked in a corner of the cabin where it would preserve itself by freezing but she cleaned the tripe herself and hung it outside the cabin on the end of a log on the north wall where no one walked. At the bottom of a trunk she had hidden a handful of beans and another of rice and a few dried apples and a small square of bacon. Through the weeks since then she had fought the urge to retrieve her provisions. Her children needed more than hides to sustain them. They needed to remember that they were Reeds and had once been prosperous and even in extremity could be resourceful. They needed hope against the hardship yet to come. They needed a little magic even and if their mother could play Santa Claus at Christmas then perhaps they could continue to believe that their father would return for them. As she believed.

In the morning she went out and dug into the snow for the tripe. It hung where she had put it. She pulled it free from the log and carried it inside and called her children. They clapped with delight when she laid the frozen tripe on a board by the fire to thaw but when they saw the beans and rice and bacon and apples they were ecstatic. She sent them to haul in snow and when they had done so she melted enough in the big cooking pot to fill it half full. The beans went in first and cooked for more than an hour before she diced the tripe and dropped it into the pot with the rice. All through the morning the children sat at the pot and watched it boil and smelled its heavenly smells. She added the diced bacon and a film of oil formed on the broth. Now the children cheered whenever a piece of meat or a bean boiled to the surface. Finally the apples went in and the smell changed to something sweet, some distant memory of autumn and orchards.

The children had their bowls in hand long before the stew was ready. Milt was there and would have his share and well-earned too because he cut the wood for the fire. The ladle dipped to the bottom of the pot and brought up tripe and bacon and rice and beans and apples all cooked together and into the bowls it went and the children dug at it with their spoons. They were ravenous not only for the food but for the taste of food after weeks of tasteless beef and sticky hides and charred bones. Margaret Reed was afraid they wouldn't enjoy the meal. As she served the last bowl to Virginia she smiled on them all, Virginia and Patty and Jimmy and Tommy.

—Children she said eat slowly. There's plenty for all.

12 people still lived crowded together in the snow shelter Eddy had made. They slept through the night leaning against one another while the heat of their bodies melted the snow that piled above the blankets over their heads and water slowly soaked their clothes. Even through Christmas Day it was dark as night in the shelter but no one cared any more. Hunger dulled them until nothing mattered except breath and heat. The bodies around them kept them warm and as the day wore on they pressed closer together until they seemed one crowded damp body growing in a circle in a snow-covered cave.

Pat Dolan was raving. He wanted to escape. He wanted to go ahead. With the storm howling around the shelter he kicked and shoved his way free of the bodies and tore back his blanket spilling snow and light into the circle. He turned onto his hands and knees and scuttled outside. Harriet Pike flipped the blanket back into place and again the shelter was dark. They could hear Dolan screaming outside. He was calling Eddy to follow. Eddy was the only man he could trust. The others would stay there and die. The others would kill him and eat him.

Eddy pushed his way out of the shelter. He had to drag Dolan back inside or the man would freeze to death. Dolan was up to his knees in the snow. He had stripped down to his trousers. His coat and his shirts lay blowing on the snow. Eddy grappled with him but he fought maniacally.

—Get inside! Eddy yelled. You'll freeze to death out here!

—Yiv got to come with me! shouted Dolan. It's death in there yi bastard it's death in there!

They wrestled in the snow. Eddy gave up and pulled away. Dolan was crazy and crazy strong. Maybe the cold would bring him around. Eddy crawled back into the shelter.

Dolan ran away into the storm and for a time there was silence and then Bill and Sarah Foster felt him flop down against them and complained and Eddy went out and dragged him back inside and held him down. He thrashed for a time and then grew quiet. Fell asleep. Later he stiffened and they knew that he was dead.

The storm blew on through the evening and the night. They slept together like children. Eddy held Mary Graves as he might have held Ellie and his hands moved over her thin body and when he was aware of what he did he felt ashamed. He had no desire except the desire to feel the life of another human being. Mary made no effort to move away. Once in the night Eddy woke to a sharp pain in his hand and realized that someone beyond Mary was trying to bite him and jerked his hand away. Another time he woke to screaming from the other side of the circle. Lem Murphy had gone wild like Dolan. The people beside Lem held him still.

They were wet with snowwater and buried under the snow. Alive at their own burial in the cold and the dark. No one thought any greater calamity could befall him now. The ritual they would perform on the dead bodies when the storm finally passed would only crown their suffering. They no longer had the strength to care. They were already dead and buried under the mountain snow. Whatever they did after the storm would be forgiven them. But they feared to begin.

December 26

The Forlorn Hope slept under the snow. The storm blew on through the night and the morning. Their strength was ebbing and in their wet clothes they were freezing. When Eddy could no longer bear his shivering he crawled out into the snow to the fire hole and beside it found some branches and dragged them back to the shelter. Inside he uncapped his power horn and with flint and steel tried to strike a fire. The spark caught the powder and the horn blew up burning his face and hands. He yelled and slapped at his face. His eyebrows were singed off and his face and hands blackened. He scooped under the blankets for snow and pressed it to his face and it eased the pain. Opposite him Amanda McCutchen and Sarah Foster had also been burned and the shelter stank of black powder. The smoke set everyone choking and Mary Graves threw back her blanket to let in some air. To her amazement the sun had broken through.

—It's over! she shouted. She laughed and pushed herself unsteadily to her feet and snow cascaded into the circle.

The others were yelling and laughing with her. They crawled out from under the wet blankets. The sun blinded them. The clouds were breaking up and the sun shone on the snow. The snow was so dry and fine it hardly seemed cold to them.

Eddy stumbled from the shelter. His face was streaked with soot and red and puffy from the explosion. He gestured to Mary and she came over to him. He handed her the flint and steel.

—Get a fire going he said through cracked lips. See if you can light a tree.

Mary took the flint and steel to Bill Foster.

—We've got to light a fire she said. Can you do it?

—I can do it said Foster. Need some dry tinder. Everything's wet around here. Foster felt the inside of his coat and stuck his hands into his pockets but nowhere did he feel anything dry. He went from person to person asking them for cloth for tinder. Sarah Pike felt her mantle and discovered that the layers of cloth slipped across one another. Foster pulled out his hunting knife and slit the mantle and found a loosely woven cotton lining that seemed dry. He cut off a piece. Eddy had found a dead tree and with the help of the Indians was shaking it free of snow.

It towered up 20 feet above the deep snow. Foster knelt beside it and held the flint in the pad of cotton and struck it with the steel. On the fifth try the spark caught and Foster blew it to a smoulder and then to a tiny flame. Eddy was there with a twig he had shredded with his knife. The twig caught and he held it under a larger stick and soon the stick caught too. Sheltering it with his body he blew it to a flame and held it under a bunch of dead needles at the bottom of the tree. The needles flared and the fire roared up one side of the tree. The others had dragged their blankets around the tree and now they lay down in the snow while the fire grew. Their excitement at the sun had already exhausted them. They were too tired even to move away from the tree. Branches burned loose from the trunk and fell around them hissing in the snow and still they didn't move. The sun was warm and the tree was warm and they no longer cared for anything else but warmth and food. They watched the branches fall. They seemed to fall for hours before they hit the snow.

When he was warm Bill Foster stood and hitched up his pants and pushed his way through the snow to the packed circle where the Hope had waited out the storm. Pat Dolan's body lay half-naked on the snow. Foster kneeled beside it and unsheathed his hunting knife. He looked over his shoulder to the burning tree and saw that Eddy and Mary Graves were watching him and jerked his head back around. He touched Dolan's cold bare belly and his flesh crawled and he took his hand away. His back throbbed as if someone might put a ball into it at any moment. He touched Dolan's belly again and discovered that his mouth was watering. He waited no longer then but touched the point of his knife to the point of the curve directly below the center of Dolan's rib cage and pressed it into the skin. The blade drew no blood and he pressed it harder feeling the plate of gristle under the skin move down. He pushed and the blade cut through the skin and then he bent his wrist and sawed down the center of the belly to Dolan's belt. He pulled out the knife and with both hands opened Dolan's belly exposing the viscera. He grasped the heart in its sac and with the other hand sawed it free and laid it on the snow and then he wedged his fingers around the liver and brought the lip out of the cavity and cut the tubes below it and pulled the liver out and laid it beside the heart. He could stand no more and he wiped his knife on his trouserleg and sheathed it and picked up the heart and the liver and carried them to the tree and dropped them on the snow. Everyone was watching him now as he again unsheathed his knife and cut a branch from the tree and shaped it into a spit and spitted the heart and then their eyes enraged him.

—Goddamn it to hell you want it too! You want it too! Go get it! Go get it and eat! You got to eat!

Jay Fosdick lurched up and moved to the corpse. Sarah Foster knelt beside her husband and took the knife and began slicing the liver. The other women broke off branches from the unburned side of the tree and sharpened them into spits. Tears ran down their faces but they made no sound and didn't look at each other. Eddy watched but didn't take part. He had no need yet of such food. Luis and Salvador studied the scene with impassive faces. Soon they moved away to another tree and shook it free of snow. Luis returned for a light and went back and lit the second tree and the 2 Indians sat beside it alone. As soon as Sarah Foster had cooked a strip of liver she took it to her brother Lem who lay in a stupor on the snow. He was too far gone to know where the meat had come from but he couldn't be roused and so could not eat. After trying for a time to shake him awake Sarah turned aside and ate the liver herself.

Pat Breen wrote Cleared off in the night   to day clear & pleasant   Snowed about 20 inches or two feet deep yesterday. the old snow was nearly run soft before it began to snow   now it is all soft the top dry & the under wet   wind S.E

A quarter-moon rose in the starlit sky over the camp of

the Forlorn Hope where Lem Murphy now lay dying and
the others lay sated with flesh around a good fire. The moon
lit the snow to silver but did not illuminate the clear air of
the black sky. In the middle land where he was born Eddy
had loved the bright moonlit sky above the dark earth at
night. It seemed fitting to him here in the mountains where
the people around him had suffered more terrible things
than any he had ever imagined that the light should glow
from the earth and the sky be dark. Everything else was
turned around and it seemed right that the earth should
glow like the moon and the sky give back no light. At least
the storm was over. They had a chance to make it through.
But he wondered if any of them would ever be the same
again. It was practical that they should eat the dead but at
the back of his mind it made him cringe. It was like looking
down into a wound in your own body or seeing your own
hand lying severed on the ground. The Indians cringed too.
They must have known the ghosts it awoke. The earth
glowed as if lit from below. Below where all the people of
all the years of the world were buried. Eddy supposed men
always in a sense ate the dead. Life grew up from the
earth and the earth was a moulder of worms and corpses.
He noticed that no one ate their kin. He'd heard of ship-
wrecked men who drank their own piss or blood when they
were thirsty enough but the juices that came out of your
own body weren't the same. He wouldn't eat the dead until
he was almost dead himself but he wondered why the idea
bothered him so. It was no more complicated than eating an
ox you'd raised up from a calf and given a name to and
laughed and swore at along a thousand miles of trail. Oxen
had soft eyes too. Up in the mountains where the earth
glowed like a glowworm under a quarter-moon you had to
make up the rules as you went along. Tomorrow they'd better just swallow their gorge and get to work drying meat.
They had a reprieve from storm for a few days and they still
had a long way to go. Down into a place called California
that had never been more than a name but now would never

be pronounced by any of them without a shudder along the spine.

December 27

Pat Breen wrote Continues clear froze hard last night Snow very deep say 9 feet thawing a little in the sun

The Forlorn Hope remained in camp cutting up the dead and drying the meat. Eddy had not yet eaten of the dead but Luis and Salvador could hold out no longer and they joined the others.

Cutting up the corpses was grisly business. The women left that work to the men. But slicing the thin bluish muscles into strips for drying began to seem no different from slicing the meat of the oxen. For the time being Eddy confined himself to making drying racks from pine branches trimmed from live trees. People avoided their own. Mary Graves and the Fosdicks took nothing from Uncle Billy's body and the Fosters and Harriet Pike took nothing from Lem Murphy. Dolan and Antoine supplied them. Once to her horror Sarah Foster saw Lem's heart roasting on a spit over the fire. It seemed to her then that nothing worse could happen to them and like the others she felt a growing division from herself. She was watching what she and the others were doing from some high mountain far away. She could see herself accepting a strip of meat from Bill and squatting down beside the fire to slice it out into pieces thin enough to dry. She could see the others moving back and forth from the silent bodies lying in the snow. They were tiny figures and they moved like ants back and forth stopping sometimes to wave arms like whiskers before passing each other and moving on. The Camp of Death. That was the name they had given it. The Camp of Death. There was no other world anywhere. The world was surrounded by mountains congealed with snow. The mountains ran out from them in larger and larger circles and beyond the mountains were places they only knew in dreams. The other places had no substance any more. They might be there or they might not. Probably they were not. Only the Camp of Death was real or else why was she there doing things that she could never in those other worlds bring herself to do?

Pat Breen wrote today chopt a tree down   it sinks in the snow & is hard to be got

December 28

Pat Breen wrote Snowed last night   Cleared off this morning   snowed a little   now Clear & pleasant
The Forlorn Hope remained in camp resting and drying meat.

December 29

Pat Breen wrote fine clear day   froze hard last night. Charley sick. Keysburg has Wolfings Rifle gun
The Forlorn Hope still at the Camp of Death.

December 30

Pat Breen wrote fine clear morning   froze hard last night   Charley died last night about 10 Oclock   had with him in money $1.50 two good loking silver watches one razor 3 boxes caps   Keysburg tok them into his possession   Spitzer took his coat & waistcoat Keysburg all his other little effects gold pin one shirt and tools for shaveing

At dawn after 5 days at the Camp of Death the Forlorn Hope started again for California reduced now to 3 men, 5 women and the 2 Indians. Eddy had eaten the last of the bear meat on the 28th and had not eaten since. He took up the rear of the line with the Indians at the head. They had no idea where they were. They steered vaguely west. The sun behind them seemed far away, reduced to a small fierce point. Men and women alike walked painfully on feet so often frostbitten that they now oozed blood with every step. Their snowshoes had been soaked and dried until the laces were rotten and often broke.

The snow was not as deep as it had been. The trees began to emerge as they hiked from stream canyon to stream canyon. They had a sense that the world was rising up before them. They were hiking downhill but the lessening snow made it seem that they were hiking up. The snow had packed in the days of sun since the storm and made easy traveling. By dusk the Forlorn Hope had advanced 5 miles.

They cleared the snow away from beneath a dead tree and for the first time since they left the cabins they found themselves standing on hard ground. They fired the tree and got warm. Eddy sat down before the tree but made no effort to help arrange the camp. He stared glassily into the fire. He felt comfortable. He wasn't even hungry. He remembered the shop in Illinois where he had worked at his trade. The smells of the different woods he had cut and roughed out and stored in racks at the side of the shop. Sweet cherry and strong oak and the nutty smell of hickory. Walnut he used for the rails inside of carriages. He loved it more than any of the other woods for its dark depth. Sanding walnut was slow work. You always sanded a day or two longer than you thought the wood needed. Then came the hour when you heated linseed oil and brushed it on and the secrets of the wood lept out at you. Looking into the oiled walnut then was like looking into the ice of a lake. You could see down into it and see how it had formed. He always expected to see a leaf or an insect frozen into its depths. Oak he loved for the fight it gave you and cherry for the smell.

Mary Graves knelt beside him but he didn't look up. —Will? she said softly. She put her hand on his shoulder and shook him. Will? What's the matter? Eddy smiled at her then without speaking. Will she said you've got to eat. He shook his head. You've got to *eat*. You're dying. Do you know that? You're *dying*.

Eddy heard the words dimly. Mary thought he was dying. He'd never felt better. He was back in his shop. The tree was burning in front of him and Mary was beside him.

—I'm fine he said just fine.

—You're not fine said Mary. You're in the same state the others were before they died. You've got to wake up and eat.

There was justice in what Mary said. If he was sitting by a burning tree with the snow behind him then he couldn't be in Illinois. Graves had gotten that way before he died. Didn't want to do anything. Wandered off somewhere. Forgot where he was. Eddy guessed he'd better eat. If he didn't eat he'd die. Will Eddy over there by the fire would die and never get back to his shop.

—All right Mary said Eddy. I guess I'd better eat.

She went to the cooking fire on the other side of the tree and with a stick lifted a strip of meat from the rack. She carried it to Eddy who took it in his fingers and quickly dropped it and picked it up again carefully and blew on it and began to tear off bites. As the taste filled his mouth he was suddenly ravenous and he chewed quickly and swallowed and bit off more. Mary ran to the fire and got more meat and hurried it back and he ate until she thought he had eaten as much as he dared. When she stopped bringing him food he looked at her expectantly and she shook her head and almost immediately he fell asleep.

Later that night Eddy revived. He was hardly awake before the memory of what he had done shocked him like a nightmare and he understood for the first time what the others must have gone through. He felt no guilt but something inside him shrank away from the act.

They talked until midnight. Eddy rejoined them again as leader. They talked about all that had happened to them and how it might have been different and at the height of the conversation Eddy vowed to them then that when they got to California he would kill Lansford Hastings.

December 31

Pat Breen wrote last of the year, may we with Gods help spend the comeing year better than the past which we propose to do if Almighty God will deliver us from our present dredful situation which is our prayer if the will of God sees it fiting for us Amen—morning fair now Cloudy wind E by S for three days past freezeing hard every night looks like another snow storm Snow Storms are dredful to us snow very deep crust on the snow

The Forlorn Hope hiked on over the snow breaking always west. Now the streams in the canyons ran clear of snow except where bridges of snow had formed on fallen trees or on bushes that in summer overhung the water. The snowbridges had piled up sometimes 25 feet high over the obstructions. Beside them the stream had undercut the snow and the snow had fallen away so that the bridges were seldom more than 2 or 3 feet wide. Over the bridges the Forlorn Hope crossed the streams precarious on clumsy snowshoes. Late in the day they were following down a ridge slick with snow. Eddy thought the slope too dangerous and worked his way up to the top. On both sides of the ridge deep canyons dropped to streams far below. He led the Hope along the ridge and coming out from behind a mountain to the west they suddenly saw a stretch of ridges descending beyond it and beyond the ridges a broad green plain. It had to be the valley of the Sacramento. They stopped struck by the first green they had seen in months and laughed and hugged each other. Eddy moved them on. Another mile and the ridge they were following came to an end in a deep canyon that cut across in front of them to join the canyon below them to the west. They realized they would have to descend the canyon and climb its western wall to get to the valley and their excitement changed to gloom. They camped on the ridge for the night.

1847

January 1

Pat Breen wrote we pray the God of mercy to deliver us from our present Calamity if it be his Holy will Amen. Commenced snowing last night does not snow fast wind S.E sun peeps out at times provisions getting scant dug up a hide from under the snow yesterday for Milt. did not take it yet

The Forlorn Hope sledded more than they hiked down the steep eastern wall of the canyon. They squatted on their snowshoes and slipped over the snow but often they found themselves piling into snowdrifts that blocked their way. They were so weak they had trouble digging free. The canyon was half a mile deep but they quickly reached the bottom. They crossed the stream on a snowbridge and began the laborious climb up the western wall. At first it was nearly vertical and they had to climb from rock to bush pulling themselves up with their arms. Above the vertical wall they found themselves on a more gradual slope marked with trees and covered with hard snow. They had to dig steps in the snow with their hands. The effort of digging was terrible. Eddy traded off with the Indians and even the women took their turn. Their bloody feet stained the snow. Jay Fosdick fell behind. Eddy called back to him to try harder

or he would die. No one could help Fosdick. It was enough
to climb the towering wall.

Margaret Reed had dreaded the time but the time had
come. The children's dog Cash would have to be killed. They
had fed it on scraps of hide. It was hardly alive but the
children had turned to it and cared for it and now they
cried. Patty was heartbroken but didn't complain. Jimmy
vowed he would never eat again. Even Milt hated what he
had to do but he took the dog outside and bashed its head
with a club of firewood. It flopped on the snow and tried to
crawl away and he bashed it again and it lay still. He
brought it back into the cabin and while Ma Reed kept the
children away he slit its throat and caught the blood in a
pan. It was all they had except for mouldy hides. The
children were horrified but they were also hungry and
eventually they ate.

The Forlorn Hope camped for the night on the level
ground above the canyon. Fosdick had not come up and
even his wife Sarah hadn't the strength to help him. She
called down to him from the rim of the canyon but no call
came back. That night they ate the last of the dried flesh
they had prepared at the Camp of Death and were once
again without food.

January 2

Pat Breen wrote fair & thawey   snow got soft   wind
S-E   looks thawey   froze pretty hard last night

The Forlorn Hope waited in camp through the morning
for Fosdick and finally at noon he struggled in. There was
nothing left for him to eat. They set out west through the
woods and made a few miles progress away from the canyon to a place where the snow was only 6 feet deep. They
camped there for the night. Salvador called for Eddy and
showed him his feet. The toes were black and shriveled and
several had fallen off.

January 3

Sunday. *Pat Breen wrote* continues fair in day time

freezeing at night   wind about E   Mrs. Reid talks of
crossing the mountains with her children   provisions
scarce

Cash was gone and the Reed family was back on hides.
They had eaten the dog hide, bones and all. They were out
of meat and had little prospect of buying or borrowing any.

The Forlorn Hope stumbled on through the woods. Oaks
began to show up among the pines and cedars. Eddy estimated they made 7 miles by the end of the day despite their
weakness. There was only 3 feet of packed snow on the
ground where they camped and they saw that they would
no longer need their snowshoes. They ripped out the lacings and crisped them in the fire and ate them. They weren't
much for food but they filled the belly. Eddy dug out his
spare moccasins and gave one to Mary Graves and together they cut them up and roasted them.

January 4

Pat Breen wrote fine morning   looks like spring
thawing now about 12 o clock   wind S:E   Mrs. Reid
Milt.   Virginia & Eliza started about ½ hour ago with
prospect of crossing the mountain   may God of Mercy
help them   left ther children here   Tom with us Pat
with Keysburg & Jas with Graveses folks, it was difficult for Mrs. Reid to get away from the children.

Jay Fosdick could hardly travel. His wife supported him
on one side and his sister-in-law Mary Graves on the other
but the Hope made only 2 miles. They came to bare ground.
It was excuse enough to camp. They pulled branches off the
trees and built a fire. They had nothing to eat but their
moccasins and boots but their feet were so swollen they
could no longer wear their footgear and they set about cutting it up and roasting it.

Halfway through his meal Foster spat out a mouthful of
boot and cursed.

—Goddamn it he said I ain't going to eat no more of this
shit. You Eddy he said pointing at Eddy. Them Indians

ain't no good to us any more. We ought to knock em off and eat em.

Luis and Salvador lay apart from the others as they had at each camp. Eddy looked in their direction and frowned back at Foster.

—Shut up that stuff Foster. They're just as in this as the rest of us.

—They're Indians said Foster. They ain't white men. They don't got no right to live when white men is starving.

—They came up to *relieve* us Mr. Foster said Mary Graves. How can you talk about killing them?

—Niggers and Indians is all the same said Foster. They're just like animals.

—Goddamn you Foster said Eddy you ain't going to kill them Indians.

—I'll kill them if I like said Foster.

—If you want to go that way said Eddy then let's draw straws. Take our chances all of us.

—I don't want to draw no straws said Foster. Ah shit. I'll eat this goddamned boot.

Eddy left the fire and walked to the Indians.

—Luis he said. There's talk over there of killing you boys. You better light on out of here.

Without a word the Indians got up and limped away into the woods.

When it came to killing people for food Eddy decided he'd had as much as he could stand. Back at the campfire he shouldered his gun.

—I'm moving on he said. We're out of the snow now. There's got to be game hereabouts. You people can find your way. If you hear me fire you'll know I shot some game. You can follow the sound of the shot.

He turned to go but the women were up and hanging onto him. Harriet clung to his leg and Amanda McCutchen threw her arms around him. They pressed their bodies against him until he could feel their bones through their clothes. Amanda was trying to turn his head and he hadn't strength to resist and suddenly she was kissing him and working her hands through his hair. He pushed her away and she fell down.

—Don't leave us she moaned. He shook himself and dragged free of Harriet's hold on his leg.

—Will! shouted Mary Graves. I want to go with you! She hurried to his side. I want to go with you. I can keep up. I've got the strength.

—Come on then he said.

—But let's stay here till morning. It's too late to go today. It's almost night. It's too late for hunting.

Eddy considered and then nodded.

—It is. All right. I'll wait till morning.

January 5

Pat Breen wrote Beautiful day thawing some in the sun Wind S-E snow not settleing much we are in hopes of the rainy time ending

Eddy and Mary Graves set out in the morning following the bloody trail of the Indians. They quickly distanced the others. Bill and Sarah Foster and Harriet Pike and Amanda McCutchen struggled forward out of sight behind them. Last of all came Jay and Sarah Fosdick. Fosdick was about done in.

Eddy looked for deer sign. 2 miles beyond the morning camp he spotted a place beside a tree where the grass was matted down. He grabbed Mary's hand and veered from the trail over to the nest.

—Mary. Do you see? There was a deer here last night. Big one by the looks of it. Do you see? His eyes filled with tears. He thought a branch had lashed his face but then he realized he was crying and he sank to his knees. Mary knelt with him. It was crazy. He hadn't cried since he was a boy. Hadn't cried at the Camp of Death. Hadn't cried when Mary brought him the meat from the dead. It was crazy and he was crazy but the crying felt good and he was glad he wasn't crying alone. He turned and pulled Mary to

him and bent her head up and held her and kissed her. Her
arms were around him and his face was buried in her hair
and he could taste her tears mixed with his own. He felt
peaceful but then he remembered the deer and he pulled
back.

—Mary don't you feel like praying?

She smiled at him while the tears welled from her eyes.

—Oh yes. I feel like praying but I've never prayed in my
life. She stroked his head. Do you pray Will?

—I don't know how to pray. I want to pray. Looking at her.
God we need that deer. God give us that deer.

—God give us that deer said Mary. I'll always believe in
You if You give us that deer.

—Amen said Eddy. Come on.

He pulled Mary to her feet and they moved ahead
following the trail of the deer. They reached the edge of the
flat woods that had begun above the canyon and started
downhill. Near the bottom of the hill Eddy froze. He
pointed to the southwest. A large buck stood still in a
clearing not 100 yards away.

—Oh my god whispered Mary Graves oh my god.

Eddy raised the gun to sight it. His arms quivered and
failed and the barrel dropped back down. Eddy swore and
again tried to raise the gun and again his arms failed. Mary
began to cry.

—*Be quiet* Eddy hissed *it'll hear you.*

—Oh she said I'm afraid you won't kill it.

—Be *quiet* Eddy hissed again. He had to get the barrel
level to sight it. He took a deep breath and jammed the butt
into his shoulder and forced his cheek against the stock
and jerked the gun straight up into the air. The buck
stood still sniffing the wind. Thank god for the wind. Eddy
clamped his arms and slowly let the barrel fall. When it was
level with his eyes he sighted the buck's antlers and as it
continued to drop he saw the shoulder and compensated
sideways with a little jerk and then squeezed the trigger

and fired. The gun kicked and nearly knocked him over but he saw the buck's tail go down before the animal leaped into the air and bounded away.

—Oh merciful god screamed Mary Graves you missed it!

—I didn't miss it said Eddy and he lept down the bank into the snowdrift at the bottom and dropped the gun and ran on. The buck crashed through the brush with Eddy behind it. 200 yards away it suddenly collapsed. Eddy was running and Mary was running and as he came up to the buck he unsheathed his knife. The animal was still kicking on the ground trying to get up. He fell on it and slit its throat and the steaming red blood gushed and he pushed his face into the gush and the blood was wet on his face and he gulped it as it splashed into his mouth and then Mary fell on top of him drinking the blood their mouths working together and their bodies writhing and then the blood stopped pulsing and the man and the woman rolled together beside the body on the ground.

After awhile they got up and dragged the carcass of the deer out of the brush into a clearing. Blood caked their faces and their clothes. They broke branches from the trees and with flint and steel Eddy started a fire and then they gutted the deer. Eddy cut strips of liver and spitted them and started them roasting on the fire while Mary prepared the fat guts and when the meat was cooked they ate their fill and fell asleep in each other's arms.

When they awoke it was night. Eddy went back with a torch and found the gun in the snowdrift. At the campfire he cleaned and loaded it and fired it to signal the others.

Jay Fosdick heard the gunfire. He had collapsed long before and lay with his wife in the snow in the woods.

—There he said Eddy's killed a deer. If I can only get to him I can live.

He tried to get up to crawl toward the sound but his arms wouldn't hold him and he lay back down and began to cry. Sometime during the night he died. Sarah Fosdick wanted to die too. She pulled herself free of her blanket and threw it over her husband's body. She hoped she'd freeze to death. She lay through the night shivering in the snow.

January 6

Pat Breen wrote fine day clear not a cloud froze very hard last night wind S:E Eliza came back from the mountain yesterday evening not able to proceed, to day went to Graves, the others kept ahead

Sarah Fosdick woke to the dawn light. She hadn't died and now she was glad. She didn't want to die. She left her husband's body and stumbled forward. Somewhere ahead she would find a camp and Eddy's signal had meant she would find food. She had traveled only a little way forward when she heard a noise ahead of her. Bill and Sarah Foster came through the trees. They couldn't be coming back to help her because they hadn't helped her before so they could only be coming back for one reason and the reason chilled her more than the morning cold.

—We wanted to see if you was all right Foster said when they came together.

—Jay's dead said Sarah Fosdick.

Foster was confused. All night he had dreamed of having Sarah Fosdick's heart but she was still alive. When she pushed on past him he turned and followed her and his wife followed behind.

By the time they reached Eddy's camp he had finished butchering out the deer and was drying the meat at the fire. Amanda and Harriet had already eaten their fill. Eddy fed Foster and his wife and Sarah Fosdick. Compared to what they had eaten before the meat was juicy and fat. It satisfied them more than they had been satisfied in months but it wouldn't be enough to feed 7 people for long. Eddy said someone would have to go back for Fosdick's body and Bill Foster got up to go. Sarah Fosdick wanted to go too. Eddy said she should spare herself but she insisted. He looked at her as if she was mad. Probably she was. Probably they were all mad. He shrugged and she followed Foster and his wife back through the woods. When they found the body she watched as Foster cut away the clothes but she turned away when he opened the belly and extracted the liver and the heart. Then as if he were butchering an animal Foster dismembered Fosdick's arms and legs and called to his wife to help and the woman came forward and accepted the 2 legs with the boots still on the feet and dragging them from her hips like a runaway horse dragging the broken shafts of a carriage she stumbled off toward the camp. Foster stuffed the organs into his pack and put it on and picked up the arms and followed After awhile Sarah Fosdick gathered a few mementos into her pack and came on behind.

January 7

Pat Breen wrote continues fine   freezeing hard at night   very cold this morning   wind S.S.E.   dont think we will have much more snow   snow not thawing much not much dimeinished in debph

With the meat dried and packed away the Forlorn Hope set out west. They followed down a mountainside to the bottom of another deep canyon that ran north and south blocking their way. No snowbridge crossed the cold mountain stream in the canyon bottom and late in the day they waded the water and camped on the western bank of the stream and built a roaring fire to dry themselves out.

January 8

Pat Breen wrote fine morning   wind E   froze hard last night   very cold this morning   Mrs. Reid & company came back this morning   could not find their way on the other side of the Mountain   they have nothing but hides to live on   Paddy is to stay here   Milt. & Eliza going to Donnos   Mrs. Reid & the 2 boys going to

their own shanty & Virginia   prospects Dull may God
relieve us all from this difficulty if it is his Holy will
Amen

The Forlorn Hope climbed the steep western wall of the
canyon. Their feet were swollen and split. They had cut
strips from their blankets to wrap them. The blood stuck
the wool to their wounds and congealed the mass into a cari-
cature of shoes.

They reached the crest of the wall at the end of the day
and found themselves in the green foothills of the mountains. An oak forest mixed with pines. They ate the last of
their meat.

It wasn't enough. Foster's rage had built for days.
Eddy's bossing pissed him and the delays the women
caused. After supper he took Eddy aside.

—We got to have more food he said.

—Be nice said Eddy. You going hunting?

—Shit said Foster. But look here Will. That woman
Amanda ain't no use to us. She cain't keep up. She's a
damned nuisance. Foster winked and grinned. We could
save her her pains.

—You son-of-a-bitch! Eddy spat. Amanda's got a husband
and a baby. He turned to go back to the fire but Foster re-
strained him.

—Sarah Fosdick then. Mary Graves. They ain't got no men.

Eddy shoved him away.

—Did you hear that? he shouted to the women. Foster
wants to murder one of you! He ran to the women with
Foster behind. Did you hear that?

Foster stood fast.

—I don't give a shit. You cain't stop me.

Eddy grabbed a club of firewood and slammed it against
the ground to test it and threw it to Foster.

—Let's see! he said and he pulled his knife.

Foster caught the club and backed up and then stopped
and raised the club with both hands holding it ready.

Suddenly the women grabbed Eddy from behind and caught his knife arm and threw him to the ground.

—Stop this! screamed Mary Graves. *Stop this!* She glared at Foster. Bill Foster you put down that club! There ain't going to be no killing around here now!

Foster stood stupidly holding the club. When his wife took it from his hands he made no protest but allowed her to lead him to the other side of the fire where he lay down.

—If that son-of-a-bitch comes near any of you I'll kill him said Eddy.

January 9

Pat Breen wrote Continues fine   freezeing hard at night   this a beautiful morning   wind about S.S.E. Mrs. Reid here   virginias toes frozen a little   snow settleing none to be perceived.

The Forlorn Hope had advanced only 2 miles out of camp when they came across bloody footprints on a patch of snow. Foster was jubilant.

—It's those goddamned Indians he said. They're still crawling around here somewhere. I'm going to get me some Indian meat.

Eddy knew he couldn't stop Foster. He gestured to the others to go on but Sarah Foster and Harriet Pike stayed behind. Foster trailed the Indians by their footprints and found them lying exhausted near a creek. They couldn't have eaten for a week. Luis looked up to see Foster standing over him grinning, gun in hand. He had dreamed it over and over again. A white man standing above him with a gun, grinning. It made no difference now. He had eaten of human beings.

—You going to die now Indian boy said Foster. He put the muzzle of the gun to Luis's head and Luis groaned and Foster fired shattering the skull. The body kicked in death and in a sudden frenzy Foster kicked back. He caught himself and grinned again and reloaded the gun and walked to

Salvador and shot him without a word. Then he unsheathed his knife and set to work on the bodies while Sarah and Harriet built a fire.

January 10

Pat Breen wrote began to snow last night   still continues   wind W N W.

The snow that fell on the lake camp fell as cold rain on the remnants of the Forlorn Hope. Eddy, Mary Graves, Sarah Fosdick and Amanda McCutchen wandered separately from the Fosters grimly conscious that Foster had become a dangerous man. They had thought that when they came down from the snow their ordeal would end but even in the valley they could find no food. Deer were plentiful but no one had the strength to track them and Foster had the gun. They ate grass to fill their bellies. The rain soaked them through. Eddy had heard a story once about a man in Iowa who had fallen into an abandoned well 200 feet deep and lived. He lay there for 2 days shouting for help and got none and finally he had to crawl out by himself and chase down his runaway team and go on. The man must have felt the world had emptied out of people. That was how Eddy felt but it didn't weaken his determination to find help. Ellie and the baby were suffering whatever he was suffering or they soon would. But most of all he wanted to save himself. It amazed him that he wanted so fiercely to stay alive with so much death and horror on his back. He couldn't even condemn Foster. Foster had gone crazy and it wouldn't take much for Eddy to go crazy too. So they stumbled on. The women treated him like a husband. He felt like he'd been married to all 3 of them for years. They were just skin and bones and so was he. Skin and bones and hearts that wouldn't stop beating even when they wanted them to.

January 11

Pat Breen wrote still continues to snow fast, looks

gloomy Mrs Reid at Keysburgs virg. with us wood
scarce difficult to get any more wind W

Eddy found an Indian trail and near' the end of the day
came upon fresh footprints. They hurried down the trail
around a bend and burst upon an Indian village. A cry
went up when the people in the village saw the ragged
bloody skeletons emerge from the brush and the women ran
inside their huts. Eddy called to them and soon the men
came over. The women and children followed and surrounded the Forlorn Hope. They had nothing to offer but
acorns and acorn bread. Eddy tried to eat the bread but it
made him sick. He vomited painfully and an Indian led him
into a hut and he lay down to sleep.

An hour later the Fosters came up. When they heard the
noise of the village they tore off their packs and threw
them aside. They thought the Indians might recognize their
own.

January 12

Pat Breen wrote snows fast yet new snow about 3
feet deep wind S:W no sign of clearing off

The Forlorn Hope staggered through the rain down the
trail to the next Indian village guided by the chief's son.
The word had gone ahead and they were well received but
the Indians had nothing to offer them except acorns.

January 13

Pat Breen wrote snowing fast wind N.W snow
higher than the shanty must be 13 feet deep dont
know how to get wood this morning it is dredful to
look at

The Forlorn Hope rested through the day. Acorn bread
wasn't enough to revive them and Eddy still couldn't keep
it down.

January 14

Pat Breen wrote new moon Cleared off yesterday

evening   snowed a little during first part of night
Calm but a little air from the North   very pleasant to
day   sun shineing brilliantly renovates our spirits
prais be to God, *Amen*

The Forlorn Hope still in camp. The Indians pitied them
and nursed them as they could.

January 15

Pat Breen wrote fine clear day   wind N W   Mrs.
Murphy blind   Lanth not able to get wood   has but one
axe betwixt him & Keysburg, he moved to Murphys yesterday   looks like another storm   expecting some account from Suiters soon

The Indians moved the Forlorn Hope to another village.
Dreams claimed them but their legs still did their bidding
and by that they knew they were still alive.

January 16

Pat Breen wrote wind blew hard all night from the
W.   abated a little   did not freeze much   this is clear
& pleasant   wind a little S of W   no telling what the
weather will do

The Forlorn Hope once again moved on. Heading for
Johnson's ranch on the Bear River. They would have come
out on the Bear if they had stuck to the mountain trail.
They had wandered off to the south in the watershed of the
American River. Come out somewhere south and east of
Johnson's. The Indians at the latest village knew where the
settlement was.

January 17

Sunday   *Pat Breen wrote* fine morning   sun shineing
clear   wind S.S.E.   Eliza came here this morning, sent
her back again to Graves   Lanthrom crazy last night so
bill says, Keyburg sent bill to get hides off his shanty
& carry thim home this morning,   provisions scarce
hides are the only article we depend on, we have a little
meat yet, may God send us help

The chief of the village where the Hope spent the night contrived to assemble a handful of pine nuts. He gave them to Eddy as a gift from one chief to another. Eddy ate them all and felt a surge of strength. He set out in the morning ahead of the others with a guide. The others had traveled only a mile when they gave out and lay down beside the trail to die. Eddy had gathered himself for a last effort. He clawed on. At midday he and his guide met another Indian on the trail. He promised the new recruit a measure of tobacco and with one man on each side of him he staggered on through the afternoon.

Near sunset he reached the first cabin outlying the settlement around Johnson's ranch. The Indians dragged him to the door and pounded and a girl open it.

—*Bread* Eddy croaked. *Bread.*

Harriet Ritchie almost slammed the door. She hated Indians and the thing they supported between them was bloody and filthy and it stank. But it spoke English and it looked like a white man and holding her breath she took it by its arm and helped it in. It collapsed on the bed. It didn't even turn over. She bent to lift its feet to the quilt and saw that they were lumps of blood-caked wool.

Her mother appeared from the other room.

—*Oh my god* said Mrs. Ritchie. She flinched and recovered. Harriet she said run and get your Pappy.

Late that night 4 men from the settlement reached the other 6 survivors back on the trail and built a fire and brewed coffee and baked bread. One of the men talked to Mary Graves and hurried back to the fire.

—It's the Donner party he said. There's more up in the mountains.

—I ain't never see nothing like it said another man. They's starved most to death.

January 18

Pat Breen wrote fine day clear & pleasant   wind W, thawing in the sun   Mrs. Murphy here to day   very hard to get wood

Harriet Ritchie's father and 3 men rode on horseback with more food for the stragglers and brought them in to Johnson's ranch about 10 o'clock at night. For the first 6 miles out from Ritchie's cabin the men followed the trail marked the day before by Eddy's bloody feet. Ritchie calculated that Eddy had made 18 miles that day. And brought word of the Donner party to California. He was some kind of man.

THREE

RELIEF

January 19

Pat Breen wrote Clear & pleasant   thawing a little in
the sun   wind SW   Peggy & Edward sick last night by
eating some meat that Dolan threw his tobacco on,
pretty well to day (praise God for his blessings,)
Lanthrom very low   in danger if relief dont soon come
hides are all the go, not much of any other in camp

Breen had more than hides. Breen had meat but was sensible enough to save it against later need and eat the dis-
gusting hides with the others. Margaret Reed and her children had moved to the Breen cabin leaving Milt and Eliza
with the Graves. The Reeds ate hides with the Breens and
cracked and cooked the bones the Breens threw out. But
Virginia was weakening on the poor diet and from time to
time Peggy Breen gave the girl a little meat. Peggy's
daughter was an infant and the Irishwoman cherished Virginia as only the mother of 6 sons could. Margaret Reed
knew the exchange and approved it. She no longer cared
what kind of food her children ate. Dog or mouse or hide or
bone were all the same to her so long as any could be found.
The cabin was crowded but it had a stone fireplace and a
good roof. And the amusement of its patriarch droning his
prayers on through the day and the evening by the light of

pine splits got up in place of candles. If prayers could save them they would have been saved long before.

Mrs. Ritchie's food had restored Will Eddy's mind if not yet his body. He lay on his bed in the Ritchie cabin grateful for the smells breezing in through the open door, trees and flowers and the sweat of horses in the corral. From the hearth came the unbelieveable sweetness of baking bread. He could see the greenness of the valley beyond the door and it soaked through his exhaustion like the sun itself. He was safe and in good hands but his safety wouldn't ease him while his family suffered in the mountains. Mountains. The word made him ache. He knew the mountains in the marrow of his bones. Mountains were places where you went to die not once but over and over. You died and woke up from death alive and gritted your teeth and put all you had into the effort of dying again and waking up again and gritting your teeth again and going on.

—Ma'am? Eddy questioned the woman at the hearth.

—Yes Mr. Eddy?

—We ought to get a letter started to send down to Sutter's. Get some men organized to try a relief.

—I know my husband intends that said the woman.

—I ought to write it out so it'll be ready when he gets back.

—Harriet's out feeding the stock said the woman but she can do it for you soon as she gets back.

Harriet Ritchie returned and took paper and pen and set up a stool beside Eddy's bed. She was a big heavy girl with brown eyes and blond hair. Eddy doted on her heaviness. The thing they could all do when they got out of the goddamned mountains was eat and eat until they were fat as pigs. It wouldn't matter what else they did so long as they got enough food to get fat on.

Eddy started the letter *To Whom It May Concern.* He described the conditions at the mountain camps when he left there more than a month before and estimated the supplies that probably remained. He guessed that by now most of the survivors in the mountains would be living on hides and that more would have died since Baylis Williams. He thought the next 3 or 4 weeks would tell the tale. He listed the names of the families still trapped and their numbers. He listed the dead of the Forlorn Hope and the survivors. He mentioned that Reed and McCutchen were believed to be in California and ought to be located and apprised of the situation. He offered to lead a relief party into the mountains as soon as he had gotten his strength back and he offered to pledge the men's wages. But he urged haste in the plainest possible words. He said that the Donner party couldn't survive the winter without relief. If they didn't get relief soon the people trapped in the mountains would likely die and the children first of all.

By the time Colonel Ritchie returned from looking in on Foster and the women at Johnson's the letter was done. Ritchie had brought back one of Johnson's Indians and he dispatched the Indian with the letter to John Sinclair at his ranch near Sutter's. Before the Californians had fought the Mexicans to a standstill Sinclair had been *alcalde* for the whole of northern California and Ritchie guessed he was still the proper official to appeal to now.

The Indian arrived at the ranch late at night but Sinclair was gone. Mrs. Sinclair received the letter and read it with horror. The condition of the women of the Forlorn Hope especially disturbed her and her first act was to gather up some underclothing for them from her own supplies. She bundled the underclothing and sent it back by one of the ranch Indians and sent another to carry the letter on to Sutter's Fort. There in the early morning Captain Edward Kern of Colonel Fremont's brigade received it. Kern was Fremont's mapmaker and had been put in charge of the Fort during the recent hostilities. Much to Sutter's chagrin.

January 20

Pat Breen wrote fine morning wind N froze hard last night. Expecting some person across the Mountain this week

Kern called a meeting immediately after chores. There weren't a dozen white men at the fort not counting Kern's guard and he couldn't commit his guard without orders from Fremont. Sutter was there looking agitated but anyone who had been at the fort more than a few days knew that Sutter almost always looked agitated. He commanded with a nervous hand in the best of times and playing second fiddle to a U.S. Army Captain of doubtful authority was not the best of times. Kern read Eddy's letter to the meeting. He said he wanted volunteers to make up a relief expedition into the Sierra Nevada and he was willing to commit the Army of the United States to pay every man a generous wage of $3 a day.

So the Donners were trapped in the mountains. Aquilla Glover felt as if he'd been kicked by an ox. He'd known the Donners in Owl Russell's train way back on the prairie. He'd heard of their taking the new Cut-off and wondered what became of them. He figured they'd turned off for Oregon like so many of the others. There was a turnoff from Mary's River that folks sometimes took. But up there in the snow and living off rancid hides.

—I'd be proud to lead a expedition said Glover. The other men turned to him. I knew the Donners back on the trail. Seems to me we all owe it to ourselves to do what we can. Any of us could've fallen into the same trouble ourselves.
—Not me said one of the men coldly. I come round by boat.
—There's women and children up there said Kern.
—They cut out their portion the man said. Anyone who'd go up in them mountains is crazy.
—Then I'm crazy said another man. Put me down.
—Your name? asked Kern.
—Sept Mootry. I come across from Indiana last summer.
—Thank you Mr. Mootry said Kern. Who else will go? He looked around the room.
—I will go. A stocky man in a sailor's blouse. Joe Sels will go if the Army will pay. How does Joe Sels know the Army will pay?

—You have my personal word of honor as an officer and a gentleman said Kern.

—We have armies in my country also Captain said Sels but never mind. I will go because there is need.

—Need never lined nobody's pocket Dutch said the man who came around by boat.

—Money never helped no one sleep at night neither said Glover.

3 men weren't enough. Kern conferred with Sutter and announced that they would wait until the *alcalde* returned from Yerba Buena. Sinclair had gone to the little town at the bay of San Francisco to deal with the new military authorities there. He was expected back the next day. They could wait that long.

January 21

Pat Breen wrote fine morning   wind W   did not freze quite so hard last night as it has done

The Donners still had beef and Tamsen wisely alternated it with hides. George's hand was no better but only a little worse. For a time the swelling had gone down and Tamsen thought it was healing but now it had begun to ulcerate. She soaked it every day and her husband seldom complained. Noah James took care of the Jacob Donners. Betsy had become a little silly. She was good to the children but sometimes she couldn't seem to cope. Noah made the difference and Tamsen tried to look in at least once every other day.

She wondered what was happening at the lake camp. They'd had no word since Milt left long ago. Surely by now the snowshoers had passed over the mountains. They ought to be seeing a relief party any day. It wouldn't have come to the lake camp without coming on to them. John Denton was gone too and she wondered if he were well. He'd been weak when he left. Nevertheless she was grateful for his leaving. It meant that much more food for the children.

They were taking the strain so well. They accepted whatever there was to eat without complaint.

She decided to send Jean Baptiste to the lake camp. The weather was good and it would be a good time to find out the news. He went willingly. He was as curious as she. After he left she called the children together and bundled them up and took them out onto the snow. Wrapped in a buffalo robe they leaned against a log and watched her sketch.

She sketched the hills to the west of the tent. They were smoothed by the deep snow but the trees made interesting patterns. They didn't grow randomly. They seemed to prefer the slopes and the gullies. They thinned out toward the tops of the hills. In the summer they likely found less water there and more sun. The wind would affect them too. Trees grew up around you and you never thought about them but when you did you understood that they also had a sense of life. It must be very dull and slow and yet there must be pleasure in the warming sun. The life of the world went on wherever you were. You could no more stop it than you could stop the earth from turning. God had started it that way long ago. Tamsen would welcome a more personal intervention however in their present circumstances. The Lord who aided Daniel in King Darius's den of lions might consider also aiding them.

Alcalde Sinclair returned from Yerba Buena and conferred with Kern and Sutter. With Sinclair on hand Sutter willingly agreed to guarantee the Army captain's offer of wages and they reconvened the meeting. Now that Sutter was backing the effort 4 more men volunteered. A sailor named Ned Coffeemeyer. A German named Adolph Brueheim who had been a passenger's servant. He went down on the list by his nickname, Greasy Jim. A half-breed Frenchman, Joe Varro. Sinclair threw in one of his ranch hands, a halfwit named Billy Coon. Billy Coon did whatever Sinclair told him to do. He could herd the horses. Aquilla Glover agreed to take charge of the expedition and rode out for Johnson's ranch to sign up the men there. The guarantee of wages would help his appeal for heroes.

Sinclair wrote his own letter to the Governor at Yerba Buena, quoting heavily from Eddy's. Sutter put the letter on his launch the *Sacramento* and sent the launch down its namesake river to the town on the bay. He instructed the pilot to look up Reed and McCutchen and let them know the ugly turn of events. He recalled all too painfully sitting with Reed calculating the beef the Donner party could live on. Eddy's figures made clear how wrong their calculations were. Sutter wondered what had become of the other oxen and his mules. He'd always thought highly of the Americans but now he questioned their foresight. If they didn't do better than their Donner people had done they could give California back to the Mexicans. He would almost not mind if it meant that Kern would leave his fort.

Pat Breen wrote John Battice & Denton came this morning with Eliza   she wont eat hides   Mrs Reid sent her back to live or die on them. Milt. got his toes froze the donoghs are all well

Milt froze his toes cutting wood. Chopping down trees was bad enough in the deep snow but half the time when they fell they buried themselves and had to be dug out. If they could be reached at all.

January 22

Pat Breen wrote began to snow a little after sunrise likely to snow a good dale   wind W came up very suddenly, now 10 Oclock

The sixth storm of winter struck the lake camp. It found life low at the Murphy cabin. The Kesebergs had moved over some time before. There was no one in the cabin strong enough to keep the wood up. Keseberg had helped but his foot still crippled him. John Landrum was sick. Sometimes he went out of his head. Lavina Murphy was nearly blind. She had all the children to care for. Phillipine Keseberg helped but Eleanor Eddy could hardly care for her own.

Her baby and the Keseberg baby lay together. Neither mother had any milk. They fed the babies gruel made with snowwater and the little flour left. The others lived on hides that had been used for roofing and turned putrid from the warmth of the cabins. It was food that sickened them even as it kept them alive.

The babies had enormous eyes. Their bellies bulged with hunger. They were thin as sticks and their heads looked outsized. They hardly even cried any more but slept fitfully or stared at the dark roof above their heads.

Beside the fire Keseberg studied his foot. A wound had opened on top the arch and continued to issue pus. He pressed carefully around the edges and cleaned away the pus with a scrap of rag. Something dark seemed to show from the heart of the wound. It looked like a piece of charred wood and he remembered that the stob that had pierced his foot had been a burned-off willow sapling. He called Phillipine and she came and looked and then located her sewing scissors for him. Keseberg dug the scissors into the wound. Slowly he extracted a thick splinter of char. It had worked all the way up through his foot.

January 23

Pat Breen wrote Blew hard & snowed all night the most severe storm we experienced this winter wind W sun now 12 oclock peeps out

Darkness in the Murphy cabin buried in the snow. The wood gave out the first day of the storm and no one dared fight the wind and snow to cut more. Even when the snow ended early in the afternoon no one moved to go out. They lay about the darkened cabin wrapped in quilts against the bitter cold. Sometimes the Murphy boys talked and sometimes the women talked but more often there was silence broken only by the occasional thin cries of the babies. People stared into darkness daydreaming or slept through nightmares so real they woke up shaken and afraid. They dreamed of endless storm or they dreamed of the wolves they sometimes heard at night scratching at the snow above the cabins. They remembered tables groaning with food in some other place in some other time.

January 24

Pat Breen wrote Some cloudy this morning ceased snowing yesterday about 2 Oclock Wind about S.E all in good health thanks be to God for his mercies endureth for ever. heard nothing from Murphys camp since the storm expect to hear they suffered some

Lewis Sutter Keseberg died at the Murphy cabin. Phillipine wept for her dead baby. The death charged Keseberg and furiously he hacked firewood off the cabin walls and built a fire. By the light of the fire he dug a grave beside the cabin door and buried the tiny body and packed the sandy dirt over it. Exhaustion hit him then. He limped back to his bed and flopped down and wrapped himself in his quilt. When he got his breath back he opened his eyes and watched the others gather greedily around the fire.

—John Landrum! Keseberg barked. Lazy scum go and cut some wood!

—He cain't hear you said Lavina Murphy. He's outa his head.

—Better for him he were dead said Keseberg but no voice took up his challenge.

Armed with a petition from the citizens of San Jose, James Reed rode out for Yerba Buena. He had not yet heard the news of the Forlorn Hope. Sutter's launch still picked its way carefully down the flood-swollen Sacramento.

January 25

Pat Breen wrote began to snow yesterday evening & still continues wind W

Thanks to Milt Elliott and young Billy Graves there was a good fire at the Graves cabin. When Jean Baptiste and John Denton had returned with Eliza from Breen's, Elizabeth Graves had refused to let the girl in. Milt changed her mind. He told her she'd shared the meat he got from Dolan and she had to share with Eliza too or he'd take his hides and move out. Milt had thought Uncle Billy Graves was a pinchpenny. It began to look like his wife was behind it all. Maybe they were a match for each other. She had her cares but Eliza had to have a place to live. Now that she was back the girl was eating hides with the rest of them. Ma Reed gave her hell. He'd told Eliza not to go bothering them but she was too addled to listen. Ma didn't have enough for her own.

The McCutchen baby was crying. Milt went over to her. She'd scratched herself raw.

—Miz Graves he said. Come here.

—Come here yourself said Elizabeth Graves. What'd you want?

—This little baby's all bunged up.

—Been scratchin itself said Elizabeth Graves. Got lice.

—It's tore its skin all over the bones said Milt.

—Ain't nothin I kin do about it. I got enough to do just to feed it.

—It's been crying for a hour said Eliza.

—Tie it down said Elizabeth Graves.

—What good'd that do? asked Milt.

—Keep it from scratchin. Ain't going to heal long as it keeps on scratchin.

—Seems like a hard thing to do.

—Things is hard all over Milt. Like you told me tother day. Here. She knelt beside the baby and slipped a loop of ribbon around one wrist and pulled the arm away from the body and tied it to the bed frame. With another piece of ribbon she tied the other wrist. That'll ease the poor little thing she said.

January 26

Pat Breen wrote Cleared up yesterday   to day fine & pleasant, wind S.   in hopes we are done with snow storms.   those that went to Suitors not yet returned

provisions getting very scant   people getting weak liveing on short allowance of hides.

Aquilla Glover rode into Sutter's with a man named
R. P. Tucker. He wore his beard around the edge of his
face like a sailor. Everyone called him Dan Tucker after the
song. They'd collected a few more men for the relief expedition from among the settlers around Johnson's ranch.
Dan Tucker and his boy George were willing. 2 Mormon
boys, John and Daniel Rhoads. Jot Curtis liked the wages
more than he disliked remembering the treatment he'd had
from Reed and McCutchen coming out of Bear Valley.
Glover told Kerns they were waiting for Will Eddy to get
patched up. He wanted to go with them and it looked to
Glover like a good idea. Eddy knew where folks were and
none of the men in the expedition had been over the mountains more than once and that in the late summer before all
the snow. They figured Eddy could guide them in a few
more days. He'd have to go on horseback. His feet were
still a mess.

January 27

Pat Breen wrote began to snow yesterday & still continues to sleet   thawing a little   wind W   Mrs. Keyburg here this morning   Lewis Suitor she says died
three days ago   Keysburg sick & Lanthrom lying in bed
the whole of his time   dont have fire enough to Cook
their hides.   Bill & Sim. Murphy sick

Bedridden at the Breens' Virginia Reed remembered the
time her Pa rode into camp on Glaucus with a whole haunch
of elk slung across his saddle. You should of seen the one
that got away he said. The men laughed and slapped her
Pa on the back and Governor Boggs stuck a cigar in his
mouth. Elk was the best meat she'd ever tasted. Sweet and
tender and juicy. Her Ma roasted it on a grill over a fire
she made with those nasty buffalo chips. Virginia had
gathered those nasty buffalo chips all along the Platte but
they didn't hurt the meat none. She got a big hunk of the

haunch. It was charred on the outside black and crunchy and bitter the way burned meat is and she held the hunk in both hands and bit right into the crunchy part. It was red and bloody inside. The juice ran out into her mouth. She could feel it running out because it salted her tongue where it ran and then she brought her teeth together and bit and the shreds came apart and she had a bite. She chewed it up so fast Patty teased her. She told Patty to shush because she was hungry and cold. It was cold on the Platte at night even in summer. She knew now she didn't know what hunger and cold were. They were terrible things that happened to you and no matter how much you hated them you couldn't do nothing about them. She'd heard Mr. Breen pray so much now that she began to think the praying would do some good. God wouldn't turn away from that much praying and the most beautiful words in the world. She'd never heard words like that in the church in Springfield except when someone read the Bible itself but this wasn't the Bible this was prayers someone writ just for special things. The prayers Mr. Breen had read aloud over and over were for deliverance from some evil or for some special mercy. She knew what she was going to do. If they were relieved then she was going to convert and become a Catholic. If they were relieved it would be Mr. Breen's prayers. *O Holy Father* she prayed *if You will send us relief I will join the Catholic church and be faithful to it all my born days.*

January 28

Pat Breen wrote full moon cleared off last night & froze some to day fine & warm wind S.E looks some like spring weather birds chirping quite lively full moon to day

At Sonoma Will McCutchen had stumbled across Caleb Greenwood, the old mountain man. Greenwood was tall as McCutchen but lean as a hickory switch. He claimed to be 83. Said he'd been out in the mountains forever. Had a hundred Crow brats to his credit. His son Brit Greenwood was with him in Sonoma and another mountain man named John Turner. They'd guided wagons over by Fort Hall last summer and come down the valley to hunt. Greenwood told Mac he'd gone east over the mountains the winter before with old Clyman and Lansford Hastings. Said Hastings was a son-of-a-bitch who didn't know his ass from a hole in the ground. Greenwood said he'd put together a relief party if they could scratch up some wages for his boys. He knew half a dozen old bullshitters around the valley who'd rather piss on snow than tule any day of the week. Weren't likely to bust their asses in the mountains without someone greased their palms a little though. Mac talked to the older settlers around Sonoma and got them to pledge a little backing but they thought his best bet would be to go on down to Yerba Buena and apply to the Navy. The Donners were U.S. citizens and the Government ought to be willing to put up some money to relieve them. Mac told Greenwood and Greenwood said he'd go.

January 29
   Pat Breen wrote fine morning   began to thaw in the sun early. wind S.W   froze hard last night   there will be a crust soon   God send *Amen*
   Margaret Reed was amazed at Peggy Breen. At first when they'd moved into the Breen cabin Peggy had seemed hard as a rock. She gave them the beds farthest away from the hearth and said in no uncertain terms that they were to leave the Breens' food strictly alone. She said they weren't welcome but Pat Dolan had been fool enough to give them rights to his little bit of meat and hides so they were there but she didn't have to like it. Margaret had accepted the words without complaint because there wasn't anything else to do. Mr. Breen hadn't even intervened as Jim would have done with gallantry. But as Virginia weakened Margaret saw Peggy feeding the girl on the sly and began to change her mind about the Irishwoman. It seemed now that be-

neath her hardness Peggy Breen had the same singlemindedness that Margaret felt. That whatever else befell them she was going to do her best to save her family and if that meant being harsh to others or even dying herself then so be it. It wasn't necessary to be harsh with others unless the occasion demanded it as it had when Eliza came over with her complaints about the hides. Margaret warmed to Peggy now and though there was still no sharing of food except with Virginia at least there was less anger in the cabin. Margaret helped Peggy clean. Patty played with the baby Isabella and with her agemate Peter Breen. Jimmy and Tommy got their share of Peggy's attention along with her own sons. It was Mr. Breen who seemed the strange one now with his earnest piety seemingly just discovered and his flexible health yet even he was growing stronger and more humane in adversity. He complained less and led more. As the others in the camp grew weaker Margaret supposed it was only sense that the Breens with meat to eat would grow stronger not only physically but also in presence. Who else was there to lead? John Denton was sick and Keseberg remote. Gus Spitzer lay abed hardly alive. Milt was Milt. None of them were faring all that well. Supplies dwindled. They hadn't many days of hides left. If relief was coming it had best come quickly.

January 30

 Pat Breen wrote fine pleasant morning wind W beginning to thaw in the sun

 Milt Elliott burst through the door.

—Ma! the Graves is strippin your cabin. They got your things and they're takin the hides off the roof.

 Margaret Reed started up.

—They've got no right Milt she said. She looked to Pat Breen. Can you help us Mr. Breen?

 Breen put down his pen and closed his diary.

—Send me boys over Mrs. Reed.

—John said Peggy. Edward. Get your coats on and trot

over to Mrs. Reed's old cabin and drag them hides back
here. Strip the roof.

The boys rushed into their coats and out the door.

—Sit down Milt said Margaret Reed. She was startled by
his appearance. He had lost weight and his eyes were dark.
Tell me what happened.

—Aw Ma after you sent Eliza back Miz Graves was mad as
heck. I don't know what got into her. He rubbed his hands
over his face. This morning she was sittin over there talkin
to Bill and Ellie and then they went out. They come back a
little later with your stuff. Looked like they was raidin your
cabin. I ast them what they thought they was doin and they
said they was taking your stuff cause you'd never paid
them for them oxen Uncle Billy sold you. Then I saw they
had one of the hides off the roof and I knew there wasn't
much left on the cabin and I lit out over here.

Margaret Reed turned to Peggy.

—So that's why Eliza came over here with her story she
said.

—Tis our meat they're after said Peggy. They thought to
play on your sympathy for the sarvant girl.

—It's a terrible business said Breen.

—Aye Pat said Peggy. Best load your gun.

Milt looked ready to faint.

—Milt said Margaret Reed lie down here and rest. I can't
thank you enough for warning us.

—It weren't nothin Ma. They still got their own hides over
there. Ain't got no cause to go stealin yours.

—They're afraid Milt. I don't blame them.

—Sure we don't need that kind of talk around here Margaret said Peggy Breen.

—You're right Peggy said Margaret Reed. Excuse me.

—The Lord willin we'll get on said Peggy. She turned and
poked up the fire.

In the evening Pat Breen wrote John & Edwd. went
to Graves this morning   the Graves seized on Mrs
Reids goods untill they would be paid   also took the

[249]

hides that she & family had to live on. she got two
peices of hides from there & the ballance they have
taken you may know from these proceedings what our
fare is in camp there is nothing to be got by hunting
yet perhaps there soon will. God send it *Amen*

For the first time Breen had addressed the world beyond
the camp.

January 31

Pat Breen wrote The sun dont shine out brilliant this
morning froze pretty hard last night wind N.W. Lan-
tron Murphy died last night about 1 Oclock, Mrs. Reid
& John went to Graves this morning to look after her
goods

Led by Aquilla Glover the Sutter's Fort contingent of
the first relief rode out for Johnson's ranch. The American
was in flood and the men spent the day building a raft and
ferrying themselves and their horses across.

Late in the afternoon Lewis Keseberg dragged John
Landrum's body out of the Murphy cabin and dumped it
unceremoniously beyond the entrance in the snow. It seemed
heavy to the weakened Keseberg but it weighed less than
100 lbs. Only the hands had not shrunken with starvation.
They were large and work-toughened and they stuck out of
the sleeves of the boy's shirt like the hands on clown sticks.

February 1

Pat Breen wrote froze very hard last night cold to
day & Cloudy wind NW. sun shines dimly the snow
has not settled much John is unwell to day with the
help of God he will be well by night amen

James Reed rode into Yerba Buena midmorning and
sought out the *alcalde* in a commandeered adobe building
by the wharf. The Navy controlled California whenever
Fremont's irregulars could be gotten out of the way. Navy
Lieutenant Washington A. Bartlett was acting *alcalde* for
Yerba Buena and the district of San Francisco. Reed told

him about the Donner party still believing it had beef to spare. Bartlett was bored with the farce of California wars where armies retired after the first exchange of fire and whole districts could be acquired simply by lowering sail in their harbors. He took the issue of emigrant relief earnestly and set out with Reed to interview the leading citizens of the town. Reed found quarters at a boarding house with the Reverend Mr. Dunleavy. Dunleavy had been in Owl Russell's train. He warmed to the work of arousing the citizenry. Bartlett sent a sailor to request an interview with the Governor, Navy Captain Hull. Hull returned word that he would see the *alcalde* and Colonel Reed on the 3rd.

After a long day's ride through flood-softened mudlands the first relief camped for the night a few miles south of Johnson's ranch. Glover sent word to Johnson that they would come in first thing in the morning.

February 2

Glover and his men rode into Johnson's at dawn and found the rancher already up and herding cattle into the corral beside the slaughter shed. Johnson told Glover he'd have to do his own slaughtering and drying but the ranch Indians would help out grinding wheat. He didn't have a mill but they could make coarse flour in the Indians' mortars. They ought to send someone to borrow the settlers' coffee mills. They'd work for grinding wheat too. Mrs. Johnson appeared then from the house with a platter of steaks for the men and before they began the butchering they set to.

The Johnson's ranch contingent rode in while the men from the Fort were finishing breakfast. Dan Tucker's son George came. Colonel Ritchie. Jotham Curtis looking dour at the prospect of hard labor despite the excellent wage. Billy Coon was sent to cut out the first steer and head it into the shed. Ritchie told Eddy to keep home but the leader of the Forlorn Hope couldn't stay away. He sat straddling a log beside the drying fire Glover had built and once the first steer was slaughtered he spent the day slicing meat in thin strips and passing them to George Tucker to hang on the racks. As soon as the strips were dried they came off the racks and were laid on squares of canvas and packed into bundles. Johnson himself spent the day rounding up horses and mules for the pack train. No one's mood was improved by the rain that began in the morning and continued through the day but neither did the rain slow them down. The men who had crossed from the States knew that rain in the valley meant snow in the mountains. Eddy knew the tag intimately. He was reminded of it whenever he shifted himself on the log to ease his bandaged feet.

At the Graves cabin Elizabeth Graves had been reduced to feeding the McCutchen baby snowwater but she hardly bothered any more. The baby was barely alive. It breathed fitfully and seldom opened its enormous eyes. It was head and belly lying under a blanket tied to a cot. Lice crawled freely on its body now and it no longer even cried. Milt was too weak to do any more than stagger out to cut wood. He went out in the afternoon and hacked at a tree for more than an hour before he dropped it into the snow and then almost lost it. He contrived to rope it out of its snow burial and dragged it home and saw that the blanket had been pulled up over the baby's head. Ellie Graves was digging a hole in a corner of the cabin with a cooking spoon.

Pat Breen wrote began to snow this morning & Continued to snow untill night now clear wind during the storm S-W

February 3

Pat Breen wrote Cloudy looks like more snow now cold, froze a little last night wind S.S.W. it was clear all last night sun shines out at times

At 9 o'clock an aide ushered Reed and Bartlett into the Governor's office. Captain Hull came out from behind his desk to welcome the American. The letter from the Gov-

ernor of Illinois which Reed had forwarded to Hull the day
before had done its usual good work. Reed briefly told the
Captain the situation and Hull said he had received a petition from San Jose that very morning.

—If all the people are going to do is forward me petitions
said Hull we're not going to see much relief.

—I think the people in Yerba Buena are willing to subscribe
heavily sir said Bartlett. Colonel Reed and I have talked
to many of them in the past two days

—I hope so said Hull. I haven't men nor means to fit out a
Navy expedition.

—That won't be necessary Governor said Reed. There's
plenty of men around here willing to make a try at it. We
crossed from the States with a large party. They knew my
people and they're raring to go.

—A public meeting would start things off sir said Bartlett.

Hull was passing out cigars.

—By all means he said. When do you propose to hold it?

—Tonight sir said Bartlett. If you'd give your approval.
He lit Hull's cigar.

—It's your town Lieutenant said Hull. By all means proceed. He turned to Reed. Colonel Reed, I'll do everything in
my power as Governor and as a private citizen to help you.
There's no question but that relief must be sent.

—Thank you Governor said Reed. I'll be eternally grateful
to you.

—Your people are Americans said Hull. Frankly, if they
were more of these damned Mexicans I'd leave them there
to starve.

Reed and Bartlett laughed.

—I understand completely said Reed. I fought in that
skirmish at Santa Clara last month. All we could see was
horses' asses heading for the hills.

Hull grinned and drew on his cigar.

—Look here Lieutenant he said. Put me down for fifty
dollars for the relief.

—Yes sir said Bartlett.

—And I'll see if my aides can't be coaxed to match that. They've got nothing else to spend their pay on except poxed *senoritas*.

The first relief worked through the night at Johnson's ranch spelling each other for sleep. Eddy gave out early and Ritchie sternly ordered him back to his cabin for rest. Guts piled up in the slaughtering shed through the night and the morning until Johnson turned his ranch Indians loose on them and then they quickly disappeared. The flour the Indians ground at their mortars went into sacks and the sacks were laced up in hides. Johnson contributed salt and the ladies of the settlement donated their entire store of coffee. The men staying behind would have to get used to tea.

Bartlett called the meeting at Yerba Buena at 7 P.M. He arrived a little early with Reed and the Reverend Dunleavy and found the saloon at the hotel crowded with men. It looked as if everyone in Yerba Buena was there. Bartlett guessed 200 men might be assembled in the room and made a mental note to encourage a large donation from the hotel for having provided its saloon with such a rousing business. He opened the meeting by reading his notice of assembly. He said that Governor Hull backed their efforts to the hilt and to emphasize that backing he read the petition from San Jose and repeated the Governor's words about petitions. The saloon erupted with laughter.

—Hell! someone shouted. We kin do a damned sight better than that!

—I hope so said the *alcalde*. I've never assembled you people before for a purpose like this. Now there's not much I can do officially. The Navy hasn't men or money for relief. What I'd like to do is turn this meeting over to you and let you organize it privately. I can't act as *alcalde* but I can certainly act as a private citizen along with you.

—Get a lawyer up there! someone called.

—Get old Frank Ward up there! He kin fix anything!

As soon as Ward took the chair he appointed a secretary

to keep the minutes and called on James Reed to describe the situation.

Reed had been prepared to speak but as he stood in front of the crowd he found unaccountably that he could not. His eyes filled with tears and in a choked voice he told them that his wife and children were starving and then apologized for his distracted state and sat down. He had already met many of the men in the room. They were shocked to silence by his emotion after the command he had shown them in the days before.

When Reed sat down Dunleavy leaned and whispered to him and then signaled the chair.

—Mr. Chairman he said to Ward. I've talked to Colonel Reed at length these past few days. I crossed from the States myself last summer. With your permission I would like to deliver the address that Colonel Reed's feelings in the matter prevent him from delivering himself.

—Come on up here said Ward.

Dunleavy came forward and Ward moved aside.

—Gentlemen said Dunleavy looking slowly around the room. Those of you who made the arduous journey from the States to this land of plenty know its dangers. Those of you who came to this excellent place by ship around the Horn may not be as familiar with the perils of the trail, though you too risked your lives on the storm-tossed sea and know the clutch of fear that attends all distant journeys. The trail is long. It passes across dusty prairies and treacherous rivers. Indians lie in wait and clicking fatal rattlesnakes. Disease sometimes stalks the wagons and along the trail appear the pitiful headstones of the graves of babes taken back to Heaven, hostages to hardship. Up the Platte and across to the Sweetwater and through the Rocky Mountains the trail passes and the mountains are cold. Colonel Reed remembers waking in July to find ice skimming the waterbuckets and he thinks now that ice was an omen of the tragedy yet to come. After the South Pass of the Rockies the trail enters the wilderness and the people become like the people of Moses wandering in an inhospitable land. And here the trail divides and here the Donner party made its fatal choice and took the Cut-off falsely recommended by Lansford Hastings, a Californian, my friends, a Californian who led these people astray. If all decent humanity and the spirit of Christ Himself did not cry out to us to relieve these sufferers, the simple fact that a Californian led them astray with false promises would compel every one of us who believes in the good name of this great new territory to rush to their aid.

Dunleavy paused and sipped a glass of water and the audience stirred.

—They crossed a salt desert in terrible heat he resumed quietly. They were five days crossing and the last three without water for man or beast. Colonel Reed himself was reduced to poverty by the loss of 18 of his best oxen. The season was late when they crossed the desert and now there was no turning back. Reduced in circumstance and embittered by Hastings' treachery they pushed on to Mary's River and followed its interminable dreary course. Food ran low and they sent two men forward to seek relief at Colonel Sutter's establishment on the Sacramento and in time that worthy gentleman sent relief back. Mr. Reed himself felt compelled at last to push forward to seek further relief. He left his lovely wife and four lovely children to be cared for by his faithful teamster Milford Elliott who cares for them still in the frozen fastness of the Sierra Nevada.

Dunleavy paused again.

—For there at last, my friends, is where they came, believing that they could still pass through to the Promised Land. But fate would not have it so. Snow fell early in the Sierra this year. Earlier than it has fallen, so I am told, for thirty years. For thirty years the Donner party might have passed through the mountains even at that late season but this year fate dealt otherwise with these courageous people and dropped upon them the terrible snow that bars their way as certainly as if a wall had been built at the gates of Paradise. They are up there now, my friends, without flour, without salt, without coffee, in tents or pitiful cabins that by now must be buried in the snow. They live off poor beef. Colonel Reed estimates they have enough to sustain them through the beginning of March, a scant four weeks hence. And then—and then—if relief does not come—if California does not rally to this cause—if petitions only are carried where strong men should ride—they will *starve.* Women and children and all. *They will starve.* And if that tragedy were to occur every one of us would carry the burden of conscience to our graves to be called forth by a just and unpitying God on the Day of Judgment.

Not a sound in the room. Dunleavy started low again.

—But men can be found. I know it. Here in this room. At Sutter's. At Sonoma and Napa and San Jose. They will require equipment. Horses. Beef dried and packed and flour. Wages. Wages for these men who will brave the perils of the Sierra Nevada to relieve the sufferers. You are proud of your great city, of Yerba Buena. Give to aid the suffering Donner party and history will record your name. Give to aid the suffering Donner party and you will fulfill the most profound words of the Psalmist. I imagine the people of the Donner party encamped miserably on the shores of Truckee Lake to the east of the pass. That is likely the place they came to when the snow fell. I imagine them encamped there, men and women and suffering children weakened with hunger and shivering with cold. Waiting as they have waited these terrible months for the sight of men working down from the pass that towers high above their encampment. I imagine them there and a mother perhaps, perhaps Mrs. James Frazier Reed, huddling before an insufficient fire with the Good Book opened in her lap, worried that her children are grown thin and wan, striving to think what might cheer them, and turning then to the words of the Psalmist. *I will lift up mine eyes unto the hills, from whence cometh my help.*

Dunleavy paused.

—My friends, *that help must come from you.*

Men surged forward yelling. Their fists were full of bills. Others crowded around Reed shaking his hand and slapping his back.

—Gentlemen! shouted the chairman. Gentlemen! Hold off please! Let's get organized before we leap! Sit down! Sit down please!

The crowd quieted and the chairman led them through the election of a solicitation committee and a committee to purchase supplies and a treasurer. Within minutes the solicitation committee had collected $700. Chairman Ward offered Reed the use of his launch *Dice mi Nana.* A big-bellied man named Selim Woodworth, a Passed-Midshipman in the U.S. Navy, offered his services to lead the expedition. His Navy training and the fact that he had trail experience carried weight. With the *alcalde*'s approval and the concurrence of the committees Woodworth was put in charge. Reed drank with him afterward and found him amiable if addicted to tooting his own horn. He told Reed he'd led a party to Oregon the summer before and then come on down to California to see the sights. He was on leave of absence from the Navy. Came across just for the hell of it he said. A great adventure.

—It is that said Reed shaking his head. It is that.

February 4

Pat Breen wrote Snowed hard all night & still continues with a strong S:W. wind.

Running a string of pack horses behind them the first relief rode out from Johnson's ranch in the early morning. It was raining hard and they were tired from 2 days and nights of slaughtering and packing but they figured to recruit themselves along the way. Eddy had urged them on. He told them every hour could mean a life.

The rain made the trail a quagmire. A pack horse stumbled in the mud and before the men could get to it it worked

[258]

itself free and bucked off its pack and hightailed down the trail. They strapped the pack onto Eddy's horse and sent him and George Tucker back for the runaway.

Pat Breen wrote until now not abated   looks as if it would snow all day

At Yerba Buena Reed oversaw the loading of the *Dice mi Nana*. Woodworth was up in town buying tents and gear. It looked as if he was outfitting a hunting camp for gentry. Smoked meats and a barrel of brandy came down to the wharf along with the beans and salt pork. Saddles. An American flag. Reed hoped to hell the Passed-Midshipman knew what he was doing. He figured to set up a base camp and work on from there. That would make sense if they could get enough men together to string out a line of caches to the mountains. Trust Navy men to put another Navy man in charge. Rank was thicker than water.

Pat Breen wrote snowed about 2 feet deep, now

The first relief's horses continued to mire but the men pushed on 10 miles before they camped for the night.

Eleanor Eddy couldn't hear her baby breathing. She asked Phillipine Keseberg to check it for her. Phillipine went to the bed and started to pick the baby up but stopped and came back shaking her head.

—She is dead she said.

Ellie moaned and tried to get up but Lavina Murphy came and took her in her arms.

—There ain't nothin for it honey Lavina said. Ain't nothin you can do. You just go on and cry yourself out now.

Eddy was right. Every hour could mean a life.

February 5

Pat Breen wrote snowed hard all yesteday untill 12 O'clock at night   wind still continud to blow hard from the S.W.   to day pretty clear a few clouds only   Peggy very uneasy for fear we shall all perrish with hunger we have but a little meat left & only part of 3 hides has to support Mrs. Reid   she has nothing left but one

hide & it is on Graves shanty. Milt is living there &
likely will keep that hide. Eddys child died last night.

Eddy and George Tucker started out again from Johnson's ranch about 10 in the morning. One of the ranch Indians had rounded up the runaway for them. Rain hit them
about noon. The hard snow in the mountains was a spate of
rain on the trail. They were trying to travel in 1 day what
the first relief had traveled in 2 and Tucker's horse couldn't
keep up. Eddy rode on shivering and wet. The rain was
cold.

About midafternoon the first relief gave up trying to
fight through the flood. They found a grove where 2 dead
pines lay crossed and build a fire at the junction. Water ran
ankle deep on the ground but they tore great sheets of pine
bark from the logs and cut branches and piled them over
the bark and succeeded in making a dry base for the packs.
They covered the packs with their saddles but they had no
cover for themselves and were forced to stand in the water
and shiver miserably in the rain. When Eddy rode into
camp that evening he found them all completely pissed.
George Tucker was still behind.

Reed was ready to board the *Dice mi Nana* to sail on the
evening tide when the *Sacramento* hailed the launch from
the harbor. Sinclair's letter went to Governor Hull but the
pilot filled Reed in on its contents. Reed followed him over
to the Governor's and after reading the letter Hull pledged
Reed $400 of Government funds to aid the relief. While
Reed was talking to Hull Caleb Greenwood burst into the
room pursued by one of Hull's aides. When things calmed
down he told Hull that the people of Sonoma and Napa had
pledged $500 to him and his men if they succeeded in re-
lieving the Donner party and he didn't bat an eye when he
heard Hull recite the contents of the letter. He said the
Stevens-Murphy party had been up the same creek in '44
and even camped at the same place. He'd helped build that
goddamned cabin up there and he'd helped those tenderfeet
get down the mountains.

Hull sent Sinclair's letter around to the hotels to be read in the drawing rooms and it caused a stir. At least they knew now that one relief was already started and they could concentrate on backing it up. It was likely to get some of the people out of the mountains. Hull authorized Reed to proceed with all possible dispatch overland with Greenwood and his men and not wait for Woodworth. Woodworth could transfer the supplies to the *Sacramento* and bring the launch on up and establish a base camp and then send more men forward. In the meantime Hull would see what he could do to collect donations from the sailors in harbor on the *Savannah* and the *Warren* and from the Marine garrison on shore.

Reed went out with Greenwood to see if they could scout more men and at one of the hotels he noticed what he had not noticed before, that Greenwood's eyes were yellow with pus and swollen almost shut. He wondered how the old mountain man thought he could lead an expedition over the California mountains in the dead of winter when he was certainly going blind.

February 6

Morning found the men of the first relief still standing in the rain. Their clothes were soaked. They steamed whenever they stood near the fire. George Tucker came into camp with a tale of wandering through the night in the rain without coat or shelter. He was so cold that when he took the chill off at the fire his arms and legs swelled up until he could hardly move. There was nothing to do but stand on and wait for the rain to end. Eddy thought of the beasts that bore the rain all their lives. They were different from men but no tougher. He might have felt like complaining but he remembered too well the Camp of Death. He didn't think he'd ever have anything to complain about again. Anyway Jot Curtis was doing enough complaining for them all. If they dried Curtis's complaints and packed them carefully they'd have a lifetime supply.

The sailors and Marines at Yerba Buena pledged $1300 to the relief. When he heard the news Reed was once again moved to tears. The *alcalde* applied to the captain of the *Savannah* in behalf of the supply committee and the *Savannah* sent in 200 rations, a 20 days' supply for 10 men. Yerba Buena was proving itself an extraordinary town. Reed had heard that the townspeople were fighting to keep their name. Some of the new emigrants wanted to call the place San Francisco.

Pat Breen wrote it snowed faster last night & to day than it has done this winter & still Continues without an intermission wind S.W. Murphys folks or Keysburgs say they cant eat hides I wish we had enough of them Mrs Eddy very weak

Death scratched at the cabins. A halfwit had given up first and the bachelors and an ailing old man. The babies died of lack of milk. But Eleanor Eddy's will was broken and other wills were cracking under the strain. Hope nourished better than hides but hope was fading. The snowshoers were almost 2 months gone. Ellie's baby was dead and she thought her husband must be dead too or he would have returned by now. Margaret Reed hadn't seen her husband since October but she knew without question that he was alive in California organizing relief. He would no more leave them to starve than he would allow himself to die before relieving them. Mr. Breen could pray all he liked. It wasn't God but men like Jim who would save them.

February 7

Sunday. About 7 in the morning the rain stopped and the clouds broke to warm sun. The men of the first relief felt about half alive but they turned immediately to building scaffolds and unpacking the beef and flour and laying both out to dry. The ground drained quickly and they built fires under the scaffolds to hurry the drying that the sun began. Once the scaffolds were up and the fires laid Glover sent the men off in shifts to sleep. Eddy wanted them to go on but Glover didn't see the benefit of pushing exhausted men. He told Eddy the men were working for wages and there was a limit to what a man would do even for $3 a day. Eddy saw the point and went off to get some sleep himself.

Reed and Greenwood departed Yerba Buena on the *Dice mi Nana*. They were crossing the bay to go to Sonoma to pick up Will McCutchen and Greenwood's men. Reed remembered one of McCutchen's tags. *Where there's a will there's a way.* So there was. He had $50 in his pocket for expenses and an order from the Governor for horses and Greenwood had what was left of the Government's $400 after purchasing supplies. Woodworth had the big money but Woodworth was the least of his worries at present.

Pat Breen wrote Ceased to snow last night after one of the most Severe Storms we experienced this winter the snow fell about 4 feet deep I had to shovel the snow off our shanty this morning it thawed so fast & thawed during the whole storm. to day it is quite pleasant wind S.W. Milt here to day says Mrs Reid has to get a hide from Mrs. Murphy & McCutchins child died 2nd of this month

Milt had used up the last of his hides at the Graves but he didn't tell Ma Reed that. He went on to the Murphy cabin in the hopes that he could scrounge enough there for himself and the Reeds. He hadn't eaten anything in 2 days. He was hardly able to make the crossing in the snow. He stumbled down into the cabin. The air stank of sickness. Everyone except Mrs. Murphy and young Bill Murphy was in bed. Milt could make out Keseberg's blanket-covered bulk over against the wall opposite the door. He realized then that he didn't have the strength to go back to the Graves. There wasn't any point to it anyway. He wouldn't find anything to eat there. He wouldn't find anything to eat here neither. What little they had would have to go to the women and children. There wasn't anyplace at the lake or at the Donners where he could find food unless he took it from women and children and he wasn't going to do that no matter what. The best he could do was to keep warm and hope relief would come. He didn't think it would come in time.

Eleanor Eddy knew she was dying. She called Lavina Murphy and the old woman came and sat with her and she made her promise to take care of Jimmy. Mrs. Murphy promised and Ellie asked her to bring the boy. Mrs. Murphy led Jimmy to his mother and Ellie weakly took his hand and squeezed it and then Mrs. Murphy led him away and put him to bed again. When she got back to Ellie she was gone. Milt had watched her die from his place by the fire. He wondered vaguely why they were being treated so badly. What they had done. Then he drifted off.

Gus Spitzer cried out at the Breen cabin in the middle of the night and woke the Breens and Margaret Reed. He was lying on the cot to the right of the fireplace with his feet near the door. Pat and Peggy stood over him and Margaret Reed heard him say that he was dying. He begged Peggy to put a piece of meat in his mouth so that he could die knowing it was there.

—Sure I won't waste good meat on a dyin man said Peggy.

She said it not coldly Margaret Reed thought but as matter-of-factly as she might say that they were short of wood.

February 8

Pat Breen wrote fine clear morning wind S.W. froze hard last night   Spitzer died last night about 3 o clock to day we will bury him in the snow

The first relief set out at dawn and made Steep Hollow creek early but the creek was flooded 20 feet deep with a swift current and ran 100 feet wide. The men were rested and dry now and not to be deterred. They scouted up a pine tall enough to bridge the creek and chopped it down and rigged guide ropes and carried the packs across on their backs. The horses were a harder case. The men frightened 2 of them into attempting to ford above the bridge and one made it across but the other was washed downstream and turned up upside down 20 yards below. The men ran across the bridge and down the bank and eventually hauled the half-drowned animal out of the water. After that they took it a horse at a time and stationed men on both banks with guy ropes and with enough pushing and pulling they finally got all the animals across and reloaded and rode out. By nightfall they had climbed above the snowline. They camped without grass for the horses.

February 9

Pat Breen wrote Mrs Eddy died on the night of the 7th Mrs Murphy here this morning pikes child all but dead Milt at Murphys not able to get out of bed Keyburg never gets up says he is not able. John went down to day to bury Mrs Eddy & child heard nothing from Graves for 2 or 3 days Mrs Murphy just now going to Graves fine morning

The first relief worked its horses through the snow and at noon made Mule Springs. Without grass the horses would soon be useless to them. Glover and Dan Tucker conferred with Eddy and decided to send the animals back. They detailed Eddy and Joe Varro to return the horses to Johnson's and as soon as the men had unpacked the supplies they led the animals back down the trail. Eddy was disheartened that he couldn't go on but he knew he couldn't hike a pack up to the lake in the snow. The others set to work building a brush tent for a cache. They cut forked saplings and planted them in the ground and laid poles across the forks and covered them with cedar brush. When the tent was finished they stored the supplies inside and began making up packs. Each man would carry about 50 lbs. of provisions on his back except for Curtis who insisted he could handle only half that much. Glover didn't argue. He wished he'd never let the old bastard come along in the first place and figured anything he carried in was that much extra.

After Eleanor Eddy died Milt had told Mrs. Murphy he needed the bed. She had wrapped the body in a blanket and helped him move it to the floor where John Breen found it when he came to perform its burial. Lying in a dead woman's bed unnerved Milt further but he found it easier and easier to slip back into memories of things that had gone before. He wasn't sure any more when he was sleeping and when he was awake. For a long time he went back to the buffalo days on the prairie when everywhere you looked there were buffalo and the smell of roasting meat filled the camp and he ate enough meat 3 times a day to keep him a little sleepy most of the time. Pretty Virginia would ride in and out of camp on her pony and Mr. Reed would thunder in like the wind with Glaucus loaded with his kill. Back of that were blank years when he was a boy alone without kin but even then there was fishing in the Sangamon and eating roasting ears out of the field in July. And then the factory work and Mr. Reed taking notice of him and the Reeds making him almost part of the family. He'd done right not to burden them and he wished now he'd given them their other hide instead of eating it himself. It wouldn't have mattered anyway to him since there wasn't any more. But once there had been buffalo so thick you could never get clear of their smell and the whole prairie as far as you could see for days and days of traveling was a big barnyard for buffalo as if the Lord kept a herd just to feed travelers and trim the grass down.

February 10

Pat Breen wrote beautiful morning Wind W: froze hard last night, to day thawing in the Sun

The first relief left George Tucker and Billy Coon to guard the cache and trudged out from Mule Springs bent beneath heavy packs. The snow had a crust but it wouldn't hold them. The first man in line broke trail and the others stepped in his footsteps. They tried to follow the Bear River, descending into its canyon from the ridge above, but by afternoon they realized they'd made a mistake. The canyons ahead were too narrow for them to pass. They made 6 miles and camped on the river near a grove of tall pines. The snow was too deep to scrape away. Tired as they were from breaking trail they had to build a platform of green logs as the Forlorn Hope had built before.

Pat Breen wrote Milt Elliot died last night at Murphys Shanty about 9 Oclock P:M: Mrs Reid went there this morning to see after his effects. J Denton trying to borrow meat from Graves had none to give they have nothing but hides all are entirely out of meat but a little we have our hides are nearly all eat up with Gods help spring will soon smile upon us

Bill Murphy brought the news of Milt's death to the Breen cabin and Margaret Reed went back with him. Lavina Murphy told her Milt hadn't eaten since he came over to stay. Hadn't even asked to eat and she hadn't enough to offer. Margaret understood that Milt had given his life for them. He had taken care of them all along and he was taking care of them now. She wanted to give Milt a decent burial but she couldn't move his body. When she got back she told Breen and he promised to send the boys along to help when there was time. He said with Milt gone the first order of business was to collect back whatever hides they might have left at the Graves. They couldn't do Milt any good but they could at least help themselves.

February 11

Pat Breen wrote fine morning wind W. froze hard last night some clouds lying in the E: looks like thaw John Denton here last night very delicate. John & Mrs Reid went to Graves this morning

The first relief attempted to climb back out of Bear River canyon but the snow was soft and deeper than it had been below and they were soon floundering. They stopped and spent the morning making snowshoes. When the work was done they set out again to climb to the ridge but the soft snow built up on the shoes in thick lumps like hard snow-balls. It pissed them considerably that they had wasted the morning but there was nothing for it but to throw the use-less snowshoes away and flounder on. They made the ridge by the end of the day and camped and built another plat-form on the snow. They had traveled only a few miles and no one was happy about it but Curtis was unbearable and finally Sept Mootry told him to shut up or he'd kick the shit out of him and the biggest mouth in the Sierra Nevada shut up.

Reed and Greenwood arrived at Sonoma where Green-wood collected his mountain men and Reed and McCutchen were reunited. Now McCutchen knew that his wife was safe at Johnson's but his baby still starving at the lake. The news hit him from both sides and for a time he couldn't decide whether to laugh or cry.

February 12

Pat Breen wrote A warm thawey morning   wind S.E. we hope with the assistance of Almighty God to be able to live to see the bare surface of the earth once more. O God of Mercy grant it if it be thy holy will *Amen* The first relief made Bear Valley in 10 feet of snow and Curtis led them to his wagon. The caches in the trees had been torn down by bears and when they dug to the wagon they found it also had been rifled and the flour was gone. As they set up camp it began to rain and sleet and they knew they were in for another miserable night.

February 13

Pat Breen wrote fine morning clouded up yesterday evening   snowed a little & continued cloudy all night. cleared off about day light.   wind about S:W   Mrs Reid has headacke   the rest in health The fire rug at the Breens was slowly getting smaller. Peggy began watching it to see why. It was a mouldy old hide. Peggy kept an eye on it as she went about her work.

Simon and Patty Reed were playing there and she noticed that Patty had a knife. The girl would cut little strips off the rug and singe the hairs off the strips and lay them near the coals with all the care of a blacksmith heating an iron. After awhile she would scrape the strips back from the coals and blow on them until they cooled and then she would nod her head like a fine lady and Simon would take one strip and she would take another and they would solemnly chew them up. Peggy thought there couldn't be much nourishment in the old rug but it likely didn't do them any harm.

The first relief spent the day drying out their packs after the rain. Once the supplies were dried they bundled about half of them up and hung them from the trees around the camp. Some of the men were talking about quitting. Glover hoped by lightening their packs to change their minds.

February 14

Pat Breen wrote fine morning but cold before the sun got up. now thawing in the sun   wind SE   Ellen Graves here this morning   John Denton not well   froze hard last night

Glover had a mutiny on his hands. Curtis had started grousing the minute he woke up. Digging out his wagon must have reminded him of his misery in Bear Valley before. He wasn't going one step farther without a horse to carry him. Ritchie and Greasy Jim soon took his side. Ritchie was righteous. He said he'd taken care of one poor sufferer back at his cabin and that had discharged his share of the responsibility for relief. Greasy Jim didn't make any excuses. He just wasn't going on through the snow. Some of the others were uneasy. They hadn't bargained for packing the provisions on their backs. $3 a day wasn't enough to pay a man for work like that. Glover thought to try browbeating but Dan Tucker soon pulled him aside. He said they couldn't grind the men into going. They ought to raise their pay. He was willing to go the extra expense. Glover asked him how much he would go and he said maybe $2 a day more. They turned back to the men and Tucker made the offer and the offer did the trick. Ritchie, Curtis and Greasy Jim said they wouldn't go for any amount of money but the others perked up. Sept Mootry looked straight at the mutineers and said he wasn't no coward. Ritchie didn't like that but he didn't do anything about it. The 3 went back and the 7 went on. Glover and Tucker. John and Dan Rhoads. Coffeemeyer, Sels, Sept Mootry. They were breaking new trail. The regular trail came down into Bear Valley through the gap to the east but that meant a hard climb over the valley wall. They decided to go up the valley to the low divide and over the divide to the Yuba River. They could follow its bed. The Yuba route wasn't any good for wagons but it might be good on foot. Save them climbing mountains with packs on their backs. They took turns breaking trail. With lighter packs the going was easier and they had the pride of not turning back to drive them on. When they got tired they could think of the 3 cowards crawling down to Johnson's with their tails between their legs.

Margaret Reed was determined to get Milt properly buried. The thought of the children in the Murphy cabin living with a corpse distressed her. Virginia wasn't strong but she insisted on helping. Breen loaned Margaret his 2 oldest sons. They brought along a shovel and a rope.

The stink in the Murphy cabin was past belief. After the fresh air outside Virginia almost fainted. She stayed near the door and stuck her head out when she couldn't stand it any more. The boys didn't seem to mind and she knew her mother wouldn't show it if she did. Her mother was talking to Mrs. Murphy. Mrs. Murphy was keeping everyone going. It looked like Keseberg just stayed in bed but someone must have been cutting wood for the fire. One of the Murphy boys. Milt was lying on the floor. They hadn't even covered him up. The other children were in bed. They stared at her like little owls and didn't say a word.

Margaret Reed knelt beside Milt's body. She touched the face. It was frozen solid.

—Bring the rope she said. Her voice sounded tired. We'll have to haul him out.

The Breen boys hesitated to touch the corpse and Margaret took the rope. She looped it around one of Milt's hands and the boys jerked it up the stiff arm. It pulled at the sleeve and then the sleeve gave way and the rope wedged around the arm at the shoulder. Margaret did the same thing for the other arm and the boys pulled the rope up again. She and Virginia took one end and the boys took the other and began turning the body into the door. Margaret's eyes filled. This was the boy who called her Ma. He hardly looked like himself any more. He looked like an old man.

They aimed the body into the door and pushed out onto the ramp and began dragging Milt up behind them. They kept slipping on the ramp and falling down. Virginia was crying but whether for her love of Milt or her weakness Margaret couldn't tell. The Breen boys worked in silence. Mr. Breen had trained them well. At the top of the ramp the body didn't bend. As they pulled it up onto the level it stuck above the snow. The head didn't loll. It was stiff as a board. Then they pulled it past the tilting point and it dropped to the level and the legs stuck straight out. The sun lighted Milt's face and his eyes shown. Virginia noticed them and cried more. She couldn't see into them. She remembered a time when Milt had taken a splinter from her hand with a needle. It wasn't easy to see the splinter and he had peered close and tried not to hurt her. When he'd opened the skin back from the splinter he'd looked and looked and then grinned and slid the needle flat across the opening and there lay the splinter clean from the wound and he hadn't even drawn any blood.

The boys dug a shallow grave. It was all snow. The sides were cut down through snow and the bottom was smooth snow. Standing in the grave they tramped the snow down and deepened the hole. They were ready to pull the body into the grave but Margaret insisted they remove the rope first. It was as hard to get off as it had been to get on. John Breen had to brace himself in the snow and hang onto Milt's head while the others pulled at the ends from below but finally the rope came free. Then the boys got into the grave again and pulled the body in.

—Heavenly Father Margaret prayed. Take this fine boy Milt Elliott unto Thyself. He died to help us live. She started to say ashes to ashes and caught herself. *Amen* she said.

The boys said Amen and crossed themselves and Virginia watched them and crossed herself too. She and her mother pushed snow into the grave and the boys shoveled. When the body was covered they took the shovel and the rope and stumbled back to the Breens.

Pat Breen wrote John & Edwd. burried Milt. this morning in the Snow

February 15

The Yuba River was frozen and bridged with snow and the men of the first relief had trouble following its course but in the morning they rounded the buttes along the river and could see they were heading straight toward the big mountains that extended north and south from the pass. The pass gave them a line and they pushed on. They had made only 3 miles when it began to snow. The new snow piled up powder that slowed them badly. Tucker's offer of extra pay had changed things. Without anyone saying anything he had taken charge. As the snow continued to fall he ordered a halt. They moved over from the river bed to the side of the valley and built a platform and a fire and began making snowshoes again. It was late in the day when they finished and after that they hiked through the swirling snow only 2 more miles. Then they had to build another platform for the fire. At least the grumbling was over. No one who stuck it before and heard the talk about the 3 who turned back dared to turn back now. He knew what the others would say. With the peaks in sight they were too close anyway. But they all worried about the snow. If it stormed hard they'd be in trouble.

Pat Breen wrote morning Cloudy until 9 Oclock then Cleared off warm & sunshine wind W. Mrs Graves refused to give Mrs Reid any hides put Suitors pack hides on her shanty would not let her have them says if I say it will thaw it then will not, she is a case

Mrs. Graves wasn't cruel. She had children to feed and she knew the Breens had meat left. Getting them to share it was Mrs. Reed's lookout.

February 16

Pat Breen wrote Commenced to rain yesterday Evening turned to Snow during the night & continud untill after daylight this morning it is now sun shine & light showers of hail at times wind N.W. by W. we all feel very weakly to day snow not geting much less in quantity

Margaret Reed had no more hides. The last piece had gone into the pot the day before. That was why she'd applied to Elizabeth Graves. Peggy turned adamant. There wasn't enough to feed her own. She'd spared all she could. They could only have the bones. It was chilling. She'd treated Gus Spitzer the same way. Margaret would have shared her food down to the last morsel. Now her children must watch the Breens eat while they starved. Peggy wouldn't even feed Virginia. She was a woman who could divide her heart. She knew her duty to her own but how could duty callous the soul. Jim had to be on his way. Somehow he would know their need. Down in the valley he would hear their need and find a way.

The Breens ate hunched over their plates. Pat and the boys took care not to look at the Reeds and by some impulse of embarrassment Margaret kept her children away from the hearth. She made them stay in bed and keep warm. But Peggy glared at her defiantly whenever she caught her eye.

With the end of the snow the first relief pushed on. Their snowshoes carried them over the new powder but the going was hard. Tucker called a halt in midafternoon. The long effort was sapping their strength. They were done in and they'd only made 5 miles.

February 17

Pat Breen wrote froze hard last night with heavy clouds runing from the N.W. & light showers of hail at times To day same kind of Weather   wind N.W. very cold & Cloudy   no sign of much thaw

Peggy didn't give the bones left over from the cooking to Margaret Reed but left them on the hearth to be taken. Margaret took them and boiled them continuously in her pot. They added flavor and not much else to the water but she discovered that bones she had boiled for a day or two crumbled apart. She could pound them into a grainy material like corn meal and put them back in the pot liquor and feed her children that way. The children ate willingly except Virginia who wouldn't eat at all. Margaret didn't know how much good her bone soup was but it was better than nothing. Virginia babbled for hours about California. She talked of the sun there and the good food. She said she saw her Pappy riding down the valley through fields of corn. He was coming for them any day. Riding over the mountains on Glaucus swift as the wind.

The trees in the summit valley were buried under the snow. Tucker guessed the snow must be 30 feet deep. By the end of the day the first relief had made the east end of the valley where the snow sloped abruptly up to the pass. They were about to give out. Tucker decided to lighten the packs again and after they had built the platform and the fire they set to work sorting out provisions and digging a cache. Every man contributed from his load. They'd have to count

on getting back to the cache before the varmints beat them
to it.

February 18

Pat Breen wrote Froze hard last night to day clear
& warm in the sun cold in the shanty or in the shade
wind S.E. all in good health Thanks be to Almighty
God *Amen*

The first relief began the climb to the pass. Even with
lighter packs they had hard going through the soft snow.
Glover fell and couldn't get up. He called out. The men got
him out of his pack and helped him up. It was clear he
couldn't climb with the extra weight. They began taking
turns going forward and dropping their packs and coming
back for Glover's. The climbing was hell. Dan Rhoads gave
out not long after Glover. He and Glover began working
together through the snow while the others took turns cart-
ing their packs. No one complained. No one had the breath
to complain. They were high in the mountains and the air
was thin.

They reached the pass at noon. Tucker was the first one
across the flat to the ledge on the other side. He scanned the
valley for signs of life but saw only the level glaring snow.
Eddy had said the cabins were built about half a mile below the lake. Tucker couldn't see any smoke. If anyone was
alive there ought to be smoke. The men came up with him.
Glover was chewing on a piece of beef. He looked a little
fresher. If the party had all died they'd made the trip for
nothing. But the glare was so bad it might be they just
couldn't see through it. They rested and ate and pushed on
downhill. No point in going back without taking a look.

Peggy Breen was watching Virginia Reed. The girl had
tossed and turned for 2 days but now she was still. For the
first time Peggy's resolution failed. She went to Virginia
and shook her but the girl wouldn't wake. She was almost
gone. It wouldn't be too late if they could get some meat
into her. Peggy went back to the fire and laid a log on. It

would be a sin to let someone die with food in the shanty. But if she fed Virginia they'd expect her to feed the others. That she couldn't do if she was to save her own. She'd have to make that clear to Margaret.

—Margaret she said. Come out with me. I've got to talk to yi.

—What about Peggy?

—Never yi mind just come on out.

The women pulled on their coats and started out the door. They heard a shout and looked at each other and scrambled up the steps cut in the snow. The glare blinded them and they turned around wildly trying to see where the voice had come from.

Tucker saw black scarecrows staggering on the snow.

—Hello! he called. Over here! Over here!

Through the glare the women saw the men coming into the clearing. Their hearts were pounding. They couldn't believe their eyes.

—Here! Margaret Reed yelled. Over here!

Breen heard the shouting inside the cabin. He yipped and jumped to his feet and started out the door. His boys followed behind him.

Tucker came up to Peggy Breen. She grabbed his coat and stared into his face.

—Be yi men from California or do yi come from Heaven?

She was babbling. He gently pulled her free and stood her aside. He moved her as easily as he would move a child. Then she caught herself and remembered why she had left the cabin.

—Her child's dyin man. She shook Margaret Reed. Yir girl's dyin. Get some food down to her quick.

Tucker signaled Mootry and he took Margaret Reed's arm and led her toward the cabin. Breen popped up shouting among his boys. Even close upon the cabins after he had seen the smoke Tucker hadn't been able to figure out where the people were. It didn't occur to him until he saw the scarecrow women come up that they were buried under the snow. They looked like death warmed over and they sounded a little crazy but thank god they were still alive. If they could run around the way they were running around right now they could make it down the mountains. But Jesus they looked terrible.

Glover asked after Mrs. Graves and Breen directed him toward the cabin. Glover had known Graves back in the States. He wanted to help the widow. The children were swarming around the men. They said *what did you bring us* and the men gave them biscuits they'd made along the way. Patty Reed thought they were the finest whitest biscuits she'd ever seen and she took hers aside to eat it as slowly as she could. There might not be any more.

Tucker and John Rhoads hiked to the Murphy cabin to look into conditions there. The cabin was cold and gloomy and instead of the children clamoring for food they lay in bed indifferent. Tucker found one of the hides Mrs. Murphy had been cutting up for cooking. The flesh side was purplish and soft. He shuddered when he realized they'd been eating it and clamped his jaw to keep his stomach down. It made him mad. They were living like filthy animals. Then he caught sight of Keseberg glaring at him.

—What's the matter with you mister?

—Why have you taken so long to come? asked Keseberg coldly. Could you not face a little snow?

—Why you son-of-a-bitch said Tucker we come as fast as we could once we got the news.

—*Ja* said Keseberg and where is the food?

—You'll have food when I've fed these babies. How come you didn't take care of them?

—I am sick said Keseberg.

—You wasn't too sick to keep a fire going.

—The boy kept the fire going said Keseberg.

Tucker spat and turned to the hearth where Rhoads was putting meat on to boil and mixing biscuit dough. As the smell of the meat rose from the pot the children left their beds one by one and crawled over to watch. Tucker saw them coming and his eyes filled and he bolted for the door and went out.

At the Breen cabin Virginia Reed rallied to the broth her mother spooned between her lips. Virginia would live and somehow Jim had heard their need but Mr. Mootry had no recent word of him. He had been at Sutter's and then unaccountably had gone south to fight a war.

February 19

Pat Breen wrote froze hard last night   7 men arrived from California yesterday evening with some provisions but left the greater part on the way   to day clear & warm for this region   some of the men are gone to day to Donnos Camp   will start back on monday

Tucker, Mootry and John Rhoads left at dawn for the Donners. They arrived soon after the sun was well up and found no one stirring but their shouts soon brought Tamsen Donner out onto the snow. She greeted them with reserve. Tucker thought she hadn't changed at all. She was always tiny and thin.

It was different with George Donner. In the tent under the snow he lay restless on his cot. The infected arm was grotesquely swollen as if it alone hadn't lost weight from hunger. Donner's eyes wandered feverishly from face to face and he seemed hardly to know they were there. The girls were little scarecrows. They pulled away from the big men as if they hadn't seen such giants before. They would have hidden in the corners of the tent but Mrs. Donner called them out to do their hellos. John got to work cooking and Sept Mootry went over to the other tent to see after Mrs. Jacob Donner. Noah James was still with her.

—We're so grateful that you came said Tamsen to Tucker.

—We got going just as fast as we heard said Tucker.

—Who brought you word?

—Will Eddy and them other people. They finally come through.

—Thank God said Tamsen.

—Look here. The first thing you ought to do is eat.

Tamsen shook her head.

—We must feed the children first.

She went to the fire and laid out bowls. When Rhoads had the stew ready he ladled it out and Tamsen called the children one by one. They took their bowls and scurried back to their corners. Then she carried a bowl to her husband and began feeding him. Tucker watched in amazement. She was some lady.

Rhoads ladled out a bowl for Tamsen and left for the Jacob Donners carrying the pot. Tamsen finished feeding her husband and began to eat. She took small bites as if she didn't want to show her hunger.

—How bad was it? asked Tucker gently.

—We got along Mr. Tucker said Tamsen.

—On hides?

—On hides. Tamsen sipped the broth and then set the bowl down and looked at Tucker. We had only one hide left this morning.

—What would you of done?

—Jean Baptiste has been looking for the cattle we lost in the snow. He has a prod with a nail on the end that he pokes down into the snow.

—That would be a help said Tucker.

—Yes said Tamsen. That would be a help.

The men worked through the day cutting wood. Mootry had returned from the Jacob Donner tent with word that Noah and 2 of the older children were strong enough to travel. Aunt Betsy would stay with the younger children. Tamsen would send her 2 oldest girls but the little ones couldn't go. Nor would she agree to go so long as her husband wasn't fit to travel. Tucker could see that George Donner wouldn't survive his wound but so could Mrs. Donner. It was her business if she wanted to stay. The only trouble they had was with Jean Baptiste. He wanted to go so bad he could taste it. He knew how much food the relief had brought and he could calculate as well as the next man how long it'd last. They told him he'd have to stay and help out. He threatened to follow them anyway and they told him harshly they'd shoot him if they saw his greasy face anywhere along the way. Then Tucker felt ashamed for his harshness and promised Jean Baptiste there'd be another relief along soon. He didn't know for sure but he figured the word had gotten down to Reed and help was on its way.

February 20

Saturday. *Pat Breen wrote* pleasant weather

There wasn't much else for Breen to say. The men were getting ready to leave on Monday. Breen wouldn't go nor any of his family. They still had meat and why risk the terrible crossing with spring so near? Another relief would be along any time and with a pack of the others going there'd be more for all. All the Reed people were going. That would ease things right there.

Reed and McCutchen had spent the night with Greenwood and his men at Sutter's Fort. The second relief had 12 men all told and 40 horses and mules. They figured to see Woodworth arrive on the *Sacramento* in the morning but they rode down to the river and found no one there. Reed half expected it. Woodworth was one of those loud-mouthed sons of bitches who claimed all the credit but never get the job done.

—Shit said Greenwood. I never did trust them soldier boys none. Got to have their tents an mules or they ain't worth a bucket of warm spit.

The brown river rushed by swollen with rain.

—We need to get across Mr. Greenwood said Reed. Woodworth was supposed to be here with the launch. Reed sat Glaucus on the bank above the river.

—That ain't no sweat said Greenwood. We kin whop up some bullboats right quick.

—How quick's that? asked McCutchen.

—Kill us some elk for hides. Take maybe a day or two.

Reed looked at McCutchen and back at Greenwood.

—We haven't got a day or two.

Greenwood squinted his rheumy eyes.

—You kin always swim he said casually.

Greenwood dispatched 5 of his men to hunt elk. They wouldn't have far to travel. The elk came down into the foothills in the winter to avoid the snow.

Mary Murphy felt better than she had felt in weeks. The meat was so good it almost made her sick. The men had cut wood for them and they had a fire all day. Crossing the cabin she noticed the baby. Her niece Catherine Pike. Its thin arms were twisted in its blanket. Its mouth with the one tooth hung open and its eyes stared.

—Ma! Mary called with fright.

Lavina Murphy came over. She looked at the baby shaking her head and then untangled its arms and pulled the blanket over its face.

—The poor thing's passed on said Lavina Murphy. It's better off that way. She went back to the hearth.

Mary smoothed the blanket. The body hardly made a lump except the head.

February 21

Sunday *Pat Breen wrote* thawey warm day

Reed and McCutchen had their passage. Early in the morning a small schooner had come sailing down the river and put in at the landing below the fort. It was Perry Mc-Coon, one of Sutter's men. He agreed to ferry the 2 men across but said he couldn't take on 40 horses. Reed sought out Greenwood.

—We've got our boat. He's willing to carry us over but you'll have to go ahead with your boatmaking. We'll go on up to Johnson's and get started on the provisions.

Greenwood studied the boat.

[281]

—You need any cash? he asked Reed.

—I've got plenty to get started on. Johnson'll wait to be paid.

—We'll shag ass up there fast as we can. Greenwood grinned. Didn't mean to rile you none tother day. Get on with what you got to do and we'll be there afore you know it.

They shook hands and Reed and McCutchen rode to the water.

Tamsen Donner saw the party off from the Donner camp. Elitha and Leanna were going and Solomon and Will Hook. Noah James. Mrs. Wolfinger. Tamsen told the girls to say they were the children of Mr. and Mrs. George Donner. That would see them through until she could come down.

—You're sure relief is on its way? she asked Tucker.

—It's got to be ma'am. The word went right out from Johnson's.

—Because the provisions you left won't last long.

—I know that.

Tamsen held his eye.

—And when they're gone we'll have to find other means of sustenance.

Tucker paled.

—They're coming Mrs. Donner. Never you worry.

Reed and McCutchen arrived at Johnson's before noon. In the same yard where the first relief had dried its meat they shot down 5 steers and began the work of butchering. Johnson loaned his Indians again for grinding wheat.

Saturday at the lake camp Billy Graves had begged his mother to let him go out with the first relief. She told him she needed him to cut wood for her but after he worked on her long enough she relented. She said if he could cut 2 cords of wood before the men left then he could go. She didn't think he could do it but he cut 1 cord that day and now in the late afternoon he finished up the second. He ate some meat and biscuits and fell into bed before sundown.

Leanna Donner almost collapsed on the crossing from the

Donner camp. Tucker put her up with the Graves for the night. He met with the men and they planned their return. It seemed to him the Murphy cabin was the worst hit. With Mrs. Keseberg and her girl going there was only Keseberg and Mrs. Murphy to take care of the others including the Foster and Eddy boys. Keseberg wasn't worth a damn. John Rhoads had seen the dead baby. He'd fed it the first day they arrived and it grieved him that it had died. He said he'd carry the other little Pike girl Naomi. He knew the baby's mother from Johnson's. That would take some of the burden off Mrs. Murphy. She was in poor shape herself. No one thought all the sufferers would get through but they might as well make the try. There wasn't much to stay for. The meat and flour the men were leaving wouldn't last a week.

February 22

Pat Breen wrote the Californians started this morning 24 in number some in a very weak state   fine morning wind S.W. for the last 3 days   Mrs Keyburg started & left Keysburg here unable to go   I burried pikes Child this morning in the snow   it died 2 days ago.

By the time Greenwood and his men arrived at Johnson's, Reed and McCutchen had 200 lbs. of beef dried and bagged. Greenwood had brought flour from Sutter's and with the flour the Johnson Indians had ground it added up to 700 lbs. The second relief started out as soon as they could get the packs onto the horses. Reed rode at the head with Greenwood and set a fast pace but the valley was a swamp from the rains.

Breen had miscounted. There were 23 going with the first relief and 17 of those were children. They followed the trail the men had made coming in but the children couldn't step from one footprint to the next. They had to climb and crawl. John Denton was weak and so was Leanna Donner. Tucker didn't know what else to do but to push on.

Then Tommy Reed gave out. He was heaving and crying and Margaret Reed knew he couldn't make it. Glover studied the situation and saw the inevitable.

—He'll have to go back ma'am.

Margaret held the boy in her arms.

—There's nothing back there but misery.

—We can't slow down Mrs. Reed said Glover. We got to get across before another storm comes.

—My god said Margaret what am I going to do?

—I'll take him back ma'am.

She shook her head.

—Who would look after him? We've no people back there.

Glover shuffled his feet in the snow.

—One of your girls could go.

—And what will become of them?

—I'll come back for them.

She looked him over.

—Are you a Mason by any chance?

Glover started.

—Why yes ma'am I am.

—Let's get moving! Tucker called back from the front of the line. Ain't no time to waste!

Margaret Reed took Glover's arm.

—Then I want you to promise me on your word as a Mason that when you reach the valley you'll come back and bring my children out.

Glover nodded.

—Yes ma'am. I promise you that. Only providing your husband don't come up first.

—All right. Patty was at her side and she turned to her. Patty darling. Someone must take care of Tommy. Your sister's not strong enough.

—I know Ma. I'll go on back with Tommy.

Glover signaled to Mootry. They'd have to carry them both back. Mootry came over and heard Glover's explanation and picked up Patty. The girl looked down at her mother.

—If you never see me again Ma said Patty do the best you can.

But back at the cabin Peggy Breen wouldn't let the Reed children in.

—I've got enough to care for meself she raged at the men. There isn't food for them two. Yi can just take them back.

—Hush up woman said Glover. There's relief on the way. These two can't go on.

Pat stood behind his wife shaking his head. Mootry caught the gesture.

—By god you people is going to take these two kids. They got more spunk than you do. He put Patty down and jammed himself close to Peggy. You take these kids woman or you'll deal with me.

Peggy fell back.

—We'll take them she said but yi'd better leave food for them. There's nothing here. I'll not feed them at the expense of me own.

Reed's second relief made 10 miles and camped in grass in the foothills of the mountains. At least they were out of the mud.

Glover and Mootry found their party camped at the head of the lake. They had made 3 miles that day over the snow. They dined on a strip of beef and a spoonful of flour each.

Pat Breen wrote Paddy Reid & Thos. came back with Messrs Grover & Mutry.

Pat didn't mention how he had greeted the children and Mootry and Glover kept the story from Mrs. Reed as they had kept the story of the Forlorn Hope from all the sufferers. None of them knew how many had died.

February 23

Pat Breen wrote froze had last night   to day fine & thawey has the appearance of spring all but the deep snow   wind S:S.E.

The last food was gone from the Donner camp. Jean Baptiste had had no luck looking for the cattle buried un-

der the snow. Tamsen had carefull saved the tallow from
the beef the men had left. She cut it into squares and fed
her children. They treasured the squares. Nibbled at the
edges and savored the fat. They ate it so slowly they made
it last for hours but now it too was gone. The children were
hungry and her husband was weakening. They still had
part of a hide left but after tasting beef and flour again
they could no longer eat it. She called Jean Baptiste and
the little man came to her side. She led him out onto the
snow. Silence and sun filled the valley. It was a beautiful
day.

—The children are hungry she said.

—I know this said Jean Baptiste.

She looked away to the white hills.

—Then you know what you must do. Jean Baptiste nodded
but she didn't see. I said you know what you must do.

—Yes said Jean Baptiste. It is a bad thing.

—It's necessary said Tamsen. Go and do it. I'll speak to
Mrs. Donner.

Jean Baptiste hiked to the clearing where they had
buried their dead and began to dig. His hands struck something hard and he brushed the snow back from Reinhardt's
face. The eyes stared up at him flecked with snow. He
flinched and began to shake but he kept on digging in the
snow until the body was clear and then he realized he would
need something more than a knife to cut the frozen body
and he jumped up and stumbled back to the tent. The body
would thaw in the sun. In the meantime there was the head.
He got a saw and returned. Pulling on the head as he might
pull on the end of a log he dragged the body out onto the
snow. He was sweating. He knelt beside the head and
clamped one hand over the face to steady it and to cover
the eyes and with the head wedged between hand and knee
he set to work sawing off the top of the skull.

When Ned Coffeemeyer woke in the morning at the camp
above the lake he discovered that the lacings were gone
from his snowshoes. They'd been cut free and he wondered

who the hell would mess up his snowshoes like that and then he understood.

—Why goddamn it he said someone done et the lacings. He carried the frames to Tucker at the fire. Look here Dan. Someone et my lacings.

Tucker studied him levelly.

—There's worse things could happen.

—Well what the hell am I supposed to do for snowshoes.

—You can trade off with one of the others said Tucker. These people seen things you can't believe.

—Yeah said Coffeemeyer. Well, I ain't never seen nothing like this. Suppose I ought to set a guard on my boots at night.

—Wouldn't be a bad idea Ned said Tucker. I'd keep my fingers pretty well covered too if I was you.

Coffeemeyer burst our laughing.

After a scant breakfast Tucker's party began the climb to the pass. They were almost out of provisions. Even with the men helping the sufferers along the line stretched out far down the slope. Halfway up to the pass Phillipine Keseberg fell to the snow. She could no longer carry Ada and she screamed for help. Joe Sels came back to her and spoke to her in German and she calmed down. She offered him a gold watch and $25 to carry her girl and he accepted readily and slung the blanket from his shoulder and climbed on with Phillipine trying to follow. Behind them came Margaret Reed and Virginia stumbling up the slope pulling Jimmy between them. He could hardly walk.

Tucker crossed the flat at the top of the pass and looked down into the summit valley. The sight paralyzed him. The snow was disturbed around the cache and the packhides scattered. Something had torn up the cache. He waited for his men and when they caught up with him he told them their only hope was to send forward to the next cache. He picked Mootry, Coffeemeyer, Glover and Dan Rhoads to go on and they started immediately down the slope into the valley.

Reed's party rode forward through the foothills. They stopped before they reached the snow. They wanted to push the horses as far into the mountains as they could get them and this was their last chance for grass.

After halting to camp in the summit valley Tucker looked over the cache. He found the tracks of a panther and a fisher and some kind of animal he didn't know. At least they'd left the hides. There'd be some meals in that. He thought about Coffeemeyer's snowshoes and decided to sleep on his own. If he didn't need them for the snow he could save them for food. The thought of eating rawhide turned his stomach. Back at the fire someone said John Denton was missing. Tucker asked if anyone had seen him but they'd all been too intent on their own efforts to notice. He sent John Rhoads to hunt for the Englishman. Rhoads dragged Denton into camp hours later. He said he'd passed out in the snow. Took an hour just to rouse him. Denton looked about half alive. He lay so close to the fire his coat was steaming. It was a sheepskin and Tucker wondered if someone would try to eat that. Everything depended on the 4 men. They had crossed the valley and disappeared from sight down the river canyon. It was 2 days to the next cache and 2 more days back. If another relief didn't come up before then they'd have more trouble on their hands than he dared to think about.

Pat Breen wrote shot Towser to day & dressed his flesh Mrs Graves came here this morning to borrow meat dog or ox they think I have meat to spare but I know to the Contrary they have plenty hides I live principally on the same

The gunfire fetched Mrs. Graves. After tasting fat beef from the packs of the first relief she couldn't stomach hides. They all felt that way except the Breens. The Breens alternated eating hides and meat. The Breens could live on granite and pine chips if they had to. Towser was sacrificed to strengthen the children, including Patty and Tommy Reed.

February 24

Pat Breen wrote froze hard last night   to day Cloudy
looks like a storm   wind blows hard from the W.   Commenced thawing   there has not any more returned from
those who started to cross the Mts.

The children were no longer hungry at the Donner camp.
Georgia and Eliza couldn't understand where the food had
come from but their older sister Frances knew. They were
cheerful and she was frightened. Her mother saw her mood
and told her it was all right. She said the Good Lord had
provided them with food and it was their duty to eat it. It
wasn't sinful she said. Frances knew that it was wrong but
she couldn't help herself. It was all there was. Jean Baptiste ate like he'd never stop. He ate and ate and went out
for more until her mother stopped him and then he went
out and didn't come back for a long time and her mother
said he must be over at Aunt Betsy's. So they were eating
it there too. Now when the wind howled she heard voices.
The people that were dead were crying. Her mother told
them not to go out. She didn't want to go out anyway and
see the things in the snow. Georgia and Eliza were playing
dolls again. The only game they ever played any more was
pretending to feed the dolls. It was a good thing they were
too young to know.

A mile out of the camp in the summit valley John Denton
failed. He told Tucker he was snowblind and said they
ought to go on and save themselves.

—Only send back relief if you can said Denton.

—As soon as we can said Tucker. He was moved by the
Englishman's calm and he gave him his tobacco pouch and
pulled his quilt off his pack and exchanged it for Denton's
thin blanket. He gave Denton the little food they had left
too. Denton waved them goodbye. Jimmy Reed told his ma
he wanted to stay with Mr. Denton. He looked so comfortable and warm. The boy cried when his ma made him
go on.

Reed's party reached Mule Springs early in the evening

and began repacking the horses for the snow. The men hung
their saddles in the trees and sent their mounts back down
the trail. From there on they would go on foot and lead the
pack animals. The boys were boisterous. They acted as if
they were out on a bear hunt. They clowned and swore and
played but they got the job done. Greenwood wasn't so
lighthearted. His eyes bothered him worse than ever and
he decided not to attempt the snow. He said his son Brit
could stand in for him. Brit said him and 2 other pukes and
Greenwood growled and gave him a shove.

The first relief made 8 miles. They were well out of the
summit valley but they had nothing to eat. People were
dazed and there wasn't much talk. Tucker had the fire built
high for Glover and his men in case they were anywhere
near. There wasn't much chance of that.

Ada Keseberg had been unconscious when Joe Sels
opened the sling at the end of the march. Phillipine held
her in her arms through the evening. She died without waking. Phillipine began shrieking again. She didn't want to
let go. They had to pull the dead girl away. Margaret Reed
sat with the woman trying to calm her and the men buried
the body in the snow. The death dazed them more. They
were camped on a mountain of snow. Suspended between
Heaven and Hell.

February 25

Pat Breen wrote froze hard last night   fine & sun-
shiny day   wind W.

The first relief made a breakfast of rawhide but they
were slow in starting with the wind in their faces. Tucker
led the way and looked back to see a line of skeletons stringing behind him. Their coats and hats made the people look
thick but their faces reminded Tucker of the face of Death.
They were better off moving than sitting still. At least the
exercise kept them warm. They had a good crust of snow
to walk on in the morning. It was proving to be the best
time of day. The snow was dazzling and Tucker remem-

bered a time when it had seemed to him as pure as anything he knew. Now it seemed evil and he thought he knew the hatred the starved people behind him must feel for it. They would never go back to the mountains. If they got down to the valley they would look up at the mountains and shiver in the heat of summer. Sometimes he wondered what he was doing up there. He owed nothing to no one and now his belly ached with sour rawhide and bile burned his throat. Who was to say what a man owed. The debt was being paid. He was buying his life just like a man would buy a turn of corn. Paying a share to the miller and taking the rest home. You came home with less than you had when you left but what you had was ground fine and you could use it to perk your children and make your wife smile. What was behind him almost crawling over the snow was people with nothing but the bare life left. And what was back at the cabins was something less than that. Except for the Breens. Glover had told him how they greeted the Reed kids. They were made out of flint. Flint hid in chalk and when the water washed the chalk away the flint tumbled out in balls the size of pears. The water didn't wear it at all. It washed down into creeks and lay there and there wasn't nothing you could do with it. Crack it open and it was the same inside as outside. Hard. So these walking lives dragged along behind him with their mouths open sucking in the empty air. He wondered what was wrong with the air and then it hit him that the air had no dust in it. Not one speck of dust. It was air no one had ever breathed before. That was why it burned the lungs. It was raw. It'd never carried a shout or the smell of sweat before. He didn't know if he'd ever come back to the mountains again either. It didn't seem likely.

Lavina Murphy showed up at the Breens. Peggy unbent enough to offer her a cup of broth and after she had gulped it down she started crying.

—It's just a nightmare she said. Just a nightmare. There ain't nothin over there but a few old hides.

—We've got nothing better said Breen nervously.

Lavina glanced from side to side.

—Keseberg is talkin crazy she said. He's talkin about eatin the dead. Milt is lying out there in the snow froze just like a beef.

—Tis a sin to think that! said Peggy sharply.

—The wolves howl around up there at night said Lavina. It's gonna be them or us. If we don't get them bodies they will.

—Yir talking nonsense said Pat. The California men said there'd be more coming. The hides'll last through.

—The babies don't take to the hides said Lavina. The babies is dying afore my eyes. They ain't got their mas no more. It just about tears me apart.

—Tis a hellish thing to molest the dead said Peggy. Her voice was cold. Tis a thing to burn in Hell for.

Lavina's eyes flashed.

—You kin talk Missus High-an-Mighty. You got beef and you got your man to keep the fire.

—Much good he does said Peggy.

—But them babies is dyin over there. I got to feed them. Their mas left them to me. She looked around again and her hand clawed the air. You think others ain't already done it? The Donners done it.

—And how do you know that? asked Pat.

—The California men was talkin. That's what Mis Donner told them. They was lookin for their oxen that was buried in the snow but if they didn't find them they was goin to have to do something worse. She held Peggy's eye. It ain't no sin Miz Breen. Sin is letting babies die when there's food to eat.

—I hear the Divil talking said Peggy looking away.

Lavina grinned.

—I don't notice you offerin to share your portion. You ain't got no cause to pass judgment. You ain't no more than a hypocrite. Shakily she stood up. I guess I done wore out my welcome. I thank you folks for the broth. She grinned again. You folks want a feast here soon you just come on over. The latch string's always out.

After Lavina left Breen shrugged.

—She's daft he said.

—Aye said Peggy with contempt. Something o' that.

Lavina passed Keseberg digging in the snow. His back was turned. She didn't want him to see her and she moved on quickly to the ramp and descended to the cabin. When her eyes adjusted to the darkness she went to the hearth and began building up the fire.

7 miles away over the snow Betsy Donner pushed back the flap of George Donner's tent and stepped in. Tamsen looked up from bathing her husband's hand and saw her sister-in-law's face and paled.

—What do you think I cooked this morning? asked Betsy Donner and then she answered her own question. Shoemaker's arm. It wasn't no different from a ox leg Tamsen. Her voice broke. Oh God what's to become of us?

Tamsen was at her side.

—Hush she said. There's no help for it.

Tucker's party made 8 miles. The men cut pines and built a platform on the snow. By afternoon the crust had softened enough to make hard going for the grownups but the children at least had been able to stay on top. Some of them gave out even so and had to be carried. Margaret Reed and Virginia kept Jimmy moving with promises of a horse when they got to California. They whispered he'd never have to walk again. Virginia said Hail Marys to herself. The prayers made a rhythm for walking. If she got down from the mountains she was going to convert for sure. That was a promise to God she meant to keep.

The Reed party had started late after lightening the packs on the horses and mules. With packs that averaged only 80 lbs. the chances were better the animals could work farther in. 2 miles out from camp one of the mules failed and they left it where it was stuck and hauled on. They made 6 miles and halted when the horses showed signs of giving out. They'd had their last grass that morning.

Pat Breen wrote Mrs Murphy says the wolves are about to dig up the dead bodies at her shanty, the nights are too cold to watch them, we hear them howl.

Breen had no sooner written the lines when he realized that the men from California could tell the difference between the marks of wolves and the marks of knives. Instead of trying to cover up for the old woman he'd be better off making clear that his own family wasn't involved. He couldn't erase what he'd written and he decided to make a proper record tomorrow.

February 26

Pat Breen wrote froze hard last night to day clear & warm   Wind S:W: blowing briskly Paddys jaw swelled with the toothache: hungry times in camp, plenty hides but the folks will not eat them we eat them with a tolerable good apetite. Thanks be to Almighty God. *Amen* Mrs Murphy said here yesterday that thought she would Commence on Milt. & eat him I dont know that she has done so yet, it is distressing The Donnos told the California folks that they would commence to eat the dead people 4 days ago, if they did not succeed that day or the next in finding their cattle then under ten or twelve feet of snow & did not know the spot or near it, I suppose they have done so ere this time

It was the longest entry Breen had written since his summary the first day. It made him uncomfortable and he showed it to Peggy. She read it with satisfaction.

Milt Elliott's body lay on the snow. One leg was missing. Keseberg had sawed it off cleanly at the hip but now as the body thawed the stump oozed and a pink stain spread out below it. The belly was swelling in the sun. When Keseberg appeared at midmorning it strained against the shirt that confined it. Keseberg felt a wild craving that meat didn't assuage. Looking furtively around him he unbuttoned the shirt and raised his knife and plunged it into the belly. The liver was still half-frozen and he had to pry it from its place below the ribs. Then he cut it free. It was slippery and to hold it he cupped it in both hands. The craving made his head pound. He ran back to the cabin. From a great distance he saw himself running with a man's liver in his hands.

Reed's party made a late start. Even though they were lightly packed the horses had trouble with the snow. 200 yards from camp Reed called a halt and told the men they'd have to pack the rest of the way in on foot. That stopped their clowning for a time. They unloaded the horses and remade the packs. In an hour they were ready and got into line and hiked on.

Tucker's party was strung out more than a mile over the snow in the valley of the Yuba. No one said much any more. It was an effort to put one foot in front of the other. They dragged on through the sun and the snow. By dusk they had made the buttes above Yuba bottoms. Bear Valley wasn't more than a day away. The men built a fire and the half-dead survivors huddled close. Then 2 men appeared out of the gloom and a cheer went up. It was Mootry and Coffeemeyer. Their packs were full and as soon as they could they passed out beef and the people settled into silence again. They chewed and grinned at each other and chewed and grinned some more. Mootry told Tucker they'd made Bear Valley but hadn't seen hide nor hair of another relief. Glover and Dan Rhoads had decided to go on to Mule Springs where they'd left the big cache with Tucker's boy and Billy Coon. They figured by the time Tucker got to Bear Valley they could be back with provisions from the Springs. After that it ought to be easier. Tucker wondered where the hell the other relief parties could be. If he got all the way down into California without any help he'd damn well know the reason why.

Glover and Rhoads met the Reed relief 3 miles below the

Bear Valley cache. It was too late to overtake Mootry and Coffeemeyer but Reed figured the provisions the 2 men carried would last the people through the night. Reed's men had made 15 miles that day through the snow and couldn't go farther without rest. Glover was surprised they hadn't found George Tucker and Billy Coon at Mule Springs. Apparently they'd left the cache and gone on down the trail.

While the men rested Reed stayed up late baking sweet bread.

February 27

Pat Breen wrote beautiful morning sun shineing brilliantly, wind about S.W. the snow has fell in debth about 5 feet but no thaw but in the sun in day time, it freezing hard every night heard some geese fly over last night saw none

Reed sent 2 of his men back to the previous camp for the provisions they had cached when they unpacked the horses. He rushed the rest of the men as much as he dared. Glover had told him his wife and son and older daughter were among Tucker's party and he wanted to reach them. He knew even as he hurried that he would have only moments with them before he went on to the lake where Patty and Tommy had been returned. Glover had told a grisly tale of death. Reed left a man in camp to keep the fire up and bake more bread. 4 miles out they met the first of Tucker's party in Yuba bottoms. Reed had moved fast but big John Turner had distanced him. Turner was looking for Mrs. Reed. He saw Tucker first.

—Is Mrs. Reed with you? Tell her Mr. Reed is here!

Margaret Reed heard the call. After all the months since Jim had been exiled on the river the news was more than she could bear. She tried to run but the snow darkened before her and she collapsed.

Virginia ran on. She saw her father ahead.

—Pappy! Pappy!

Reed ran through the snow. They came together and she fell against him. He took her arms and lifted her up.

—Your mother, girl! Your mother! Where is *she?*

Virginia pointed behind her and he let her go. She slumped to her knees as he ran on by. There was Margaret. She saw him coming and shakily stood up and then he reached her and held her in his arms.

—Margaret! She was light as a feather. She was hardly alive but she was crying and smiling at him and he was crying too and there was Jimmy behind her.

The others were calling for bread. *Bread* they said *bread.*

—Oh Jim Margaret said. I thought I'd never see you again it's so good to see you again.

Reed was pulling off his pack. He shoved his hand inside and pulled out a sweet biscuit and put it in his wife's hands and then Jimmy was beside him and some of the others and he handed out the bread all around.

—*Jim* said his wife when she could speak again. Patty and Tommy are still at the camp. You've got to go for them right away. There's nothing to eat up there but hides.

—I know said Reed. I'm going right on. These men will take care of you. Our camp's just a little ways down the trail.

—Go on Jim said Margaret go on and get Patty and Tommy.

Reed gathered his men. He left Tucker and the others of the first relief to help the survivors into the Bear Valley camp.

Pat Breen was out cutting wood when a motion caught his eye. He looked up and saw an Indian standing a distance away on the snow. The Indian had a pack on his back. He wore a cloak woven out of some kind of fur. Breen kept his ax at ready in front of him. The Indian was shaking his head. Breen started to close the distance between them but the Indian held up his hand. Breen stopped and watched the strange figure lay something in the snow. Then still holding up his hand the Indian backed away into the trees to the west and turned around and loped off. Breen went forward. He found a little pile of roots on the snow. He picked them up and sniffed them. They appeared to be some kind of bulbs. He stuffed them into his shirt and went back to his woodcutting. Would wonders never cease.

The snow had gone soft by midday and Reed and his men found themselves plunging in up to their waists. They weren't getting anywhere and finally Reed felt compelled to call a halt. He discussed the situation with Turner who recommended night travel when the cold had frozen the crust. It seemed to Reed a sensible idea but he chafed at the delay. Their packs weren't helping much either and they decided to lighten them. They'd need the cache on the way out from the lake.

Billy Graves was the first of Tucker's charges to make it into the Bear Valley camp. Everyone was in by night. The man Reed had left to keep the camp tried to watch the food supply but Will Hook managed to eat too much and got sick. The guard made the boy swallow tobacco juice until he threw up and then laid him down beside the fire. Some of the other complained that they were still hungry but the guard kept them away from the food. He told them too much food could kill them.

February 28

Reed and his men left at midnight and struggled on for 2 hours but the snow was still not frozen hard enough to support them. They camped again and at intervals checked the crust and by 4 in the morning it was solid. They made 14 miles by noon. The summit valley was just ahead of them. Reed called together the 3 youngest men in his party and asked them if they would be willing to go on and see if they could get over to the camp. Their names were Clark, Cady and Stone. They said they'd give it a try after they'd had a rest. They left about 5 and Reed watched them fighting forward through the snow until they disappeared from sight. It amazed Reed how much difference a few years of age made in a man's stamina. Healthy as he knew he was he gave out sooner than the younger men.

That morning in Bear Valley the guard had noticed Will Hook on his hands and knees swaying in the snow beyond the campfire. The others had already left for Mule Springs. Billy Graves was still in camp because his feet were frostbitten and he didn't want to walk. He crawled out to see what was wrong with Will but when he got to him Will suddenly keeled over and died without making a sound. His belly was swollen and his pockets were stuffed with food and Billy guessed he'd eaten himself to death. The guard came out and they emptied Will's pockets. The death was enough to urge them on despite the fire and Billy's frostbite and as soon as they had buried Will Hook they set out.

Pat Breen wrote froze hard last night to day fair & sunshine wind S.E. 1 Solitary Indian passed by yesterday come from the lake had a heavy pack on his back gave me 5 or 6 roots resembleing Onions in shape taste some like a sweet potatoe, all full of tough little fibers

Before midnight Reed's 3 scouts had reached the head of the lake. They would have gone on but they saw a line of Indians crossing the lake on the open snow. They counted 10 of them. The men had no weapons. They decided to lie low and hid out for the rest of the night without fire in a grove of pines.

March 1

Pat Breen wrote to day fine & pleasant froze hard last night

The snow had settled so much in the past few days that when Clark, Cady and Stone rounded the lake they could see Breen's cabin. They headed for it and heard there of the condition of the Donners. Clark and Cady went on to the Donner camp. Breen directed Stone to the Murphy cabin.

Reed, McCutchen, John Turner, Hiram Miller and the remaining 2 men Jondro and Dofar came in late in the morning. Patty sat on a corner of Breen's roof waiting for her father. When she saw him she tried to run but fell in the snow. He hurried to pick her up. She was babbling of the wonder of Masons. Mr. Glover had promised to relieve them on the word of a Mason and here was her Pa. Reed asked her if Tommy was dead and she shook her head and pointed to the cabin door and he carried her with him below. He nodded shortly to the Breens and turned to Tommy lying in bed. The boy hardly knew him. He asked Patty if this was his Pa and she told him yes but he asked her over and over as if he wasn't sure.

Breen prepared Reed for the Murphys but when he and McCutchen got there it was worse than he expected. He passed Milt Elliott's mutilated body on the way over. Down in the cabin Stone was washing out the children's clothes. His face was twisted with disgust. Georgie Foster and Jimmy Eddy lay abed smeared with their own filth. They were crying and stretching out their arms for food. They were smeared with their wastes and blotched with the bites of vermin. The cabin stank past belief. The bones of Milt's leg lay on the floor beside the hearth. Keseberg wasn't much cleaner than the 2 boys and his bites were as bad as theirs. His hair was filthy and tangled and there was dried blood on his face.

—Have you fed these boys? Reed barked at Stone.

—I gave them as much as I dared said Stone. They ain't et much.

—They're still hungry said Reed. He pulled biscuits from his pockets and gave them one each and they stuffed them into their mouths. When they had swallowed the first he gave them another and another and then caught himself and stopped but they still stretched out their arms. His eyes filled and he turned to McCutchen. We've got to wash these tykes he said. The lice've eaten them alive.

—Jesus Christ Almighty said McCutchen. I ain't seen nothing like it in all my life.

—There weren't nothin for it said Lavina Murphy weakly from her bed. I tried to take care of them but I just couldn't keep it up. She was crying. I tried to take care of them the best way I knew.

—It's all right Mrs. Murphy said Reed. He barely recognized her.

—They been in those beds for two weeks she said. There weren't nothin for it.

—You just rest there said Reed. We'll take care of it. You just turn away there and we'll strip down and get to work.

Lavina turned over and faced the wall and Reed and McCutchen stripped to their drawers and carried their clothes outside. They didn't need a dose of vermin to complicate their work. They heated water and made a soap solution and then they washed the 2 boys. Both had swollen bellies. Their bodies were red and raw. Reed set his face to keep from weeping. He wasn't a man to have regrets but he would almost have given his life not to have made the decisions he made back on the trail. People had died because they'd decided to go for Hastings' Cut-off and some of the people who lived might be wishing they were dead by now. The evidence of how they'd lived was all over the floor of the cabin and there was likely more of the same at the Donners. It was a hard case, a hard hard case.

The warm soapy water soothed the boys nearly to sleep. McCutchen got tallow from his pack and they oiled them down. They dug out some fresh flannel and wrapped the boys and put clean blankets on their beds and laid them down.

The other children were in better shape and Reed went next to Keseberg's bed.

—We'll need to wash you too said Reed.

—That cannot be said Keseberg hoarsely. I am the man who would hang you. Why do you help me now?

[301]

—It's just common decency Keseberg. I'd do the same for man or beast.

—Let the other man do it then said Keseberg. I cannot bear that you should do it.

Reed bent over and pulled back the blanket. He began unbuttoning Keseberg's shirt and the German pulled at his hands and Reed firmly pushed them aside. McCutchen got Keseberg's pants off and his drawers and together they began washing him just as they had washed the children. Keseberg held himself stiff throughout the ordeal and sometimes he whimpered. They found clean clothes for him in one of the trunks. Reed wondered why he hadn't kept himself clean. Why he hadn't kept the children clean. There was something wrong with this big German. He didn't have feelings like other men. His body wasn't fat but it wasn't starved either and the boys were. Reed finished the work quickly and with mounting disgust.

—What about the woman? asked McCutchen.

Reed blushed and shook his head.

—We'll have to leave her the soap. Maybe one of the other women could come over and help her. I'll speak to Mrs. Breen.

Peggy Breen refused to have anything to do with the Murphy cabin or Lavina Murphy. Reed saw that it was futile to argue with her. Mrs. Murphy would have to get on alone. Turner and Brit Greenwood were down at the Graves cabin. Stone was still at the Murphys' and Cady and Clark had gone over to the Donners'. Reed thought he should go too but the day was nearly done and he'd seen as much as he could stand. He thought if he saw more suffering he'd be likely to want to kill somebody. Probably Keseberg. He asked Jondro and Dofar to set up camp on the snow. He couldn't bear to sleep in the ghastly cabins. He fed Patty and Tommy with him at the campfire but let them sleep inside. They weren't recovered enough to bear the cold.

Pat Breen wrote there has 10 men arrived this morn-

ing from bear valley with provisions   we are to start
in two or three days & Cash our goods here   there is
amongst them some old mountaniers   they say the
snow will be here until June

That information finally decided Breen to go. His hides
were used up but he still had meat. He'd thought spring
would end the storms and melt the snow enough to let him
take his goods out. Now he knew otherwise. He'd take his
family over the mountains with Reed's party. Having made
up his mind to go he closed his diary for the last time and
went to bed.

March 2

McCutchen went down to the Graves cabin to help out.
He already knew that his baby was dead but he wanted to
see the grave. Reed took the other 3 men and set out for the
Donners. Hiram Miller was eager to see them again. He'd
left them months before and made California by way of
Fort Hall with Edwin Bryant and Owl Russell.

They met Cady on the trail. He took them aside to pre-
pare them.

—We come into camp said Cady and found that fella John
Baptist carrying a leg. Old Donner'd sent him over to borrow it from Miz Donner an it was her husband's leg Mr.
Reed. Jesus Christ it was just sickening. John Baptist saw
us comin and threw the leg in a hole an when we got to the
hole there was this head starin up at us. They'd cut off
the head and then they'd taken the arms and legs offen the
body and cut it open and cleaned out the lights. We got on
then. Three little girls was sitting on a log eatin a half-
cooked liver and a heart. Oh and there was some other
bodies in some other holes around there. What was left of
em.

Reed nodded and went on to the Jacob Donner tent. Like
the cabins at the lake it was now partly clear of snow. Betsy
Donner was prostrate inside. She had eaten the dead just
as her children had but she drew the line at using the flesh

of her husband. Reed had the men clear a space in the snow down to the ground and then they relocated the tent. They carried Betsy Donner in her bed to the new location and made her comfortable and Jondro built a fire and began cooking beef. They were sickened by what they had seen and decided to go over to a pine grove to rest and collect their wits but their path took them by the open graves and Reed saw a familiar face staring up at him and stopped short. It was Uncle Jacob's head. The body looked like what was left when you'd trimmed out a beef but the head lay there severed at the neck staring up. It looked almost alive. The gray eyes were open and the grizzled beard clean and the jaw set. Reed shuddered. He wondered what tales the head would tell if it could talk. An old man who had seen prosperity and honor but who wanted more and who ended up a severed head lying in a snowpit in the middle of the ungodly mountains. McCutchen would have a Shakespearian saying or two if he were here but he wasn't and Reed could think only of waste. He thought as he had thought before that it seemed to be only the men who died and he wondered what fatal weakness lay at men's hearts that women didn't seem to suffer. They were supposed to be the weaker sex but there was his wife coming over the snow and here were the women presiding over this orgy of life. They had their roots down somewhere out of sight deep in the earth. The proof of it was that the men were always the ones who wanted to move on. Margaret would have been happy to stay in Illinois and so would the Donner women. So here was Jacob's head as a warning to stay put. People said of someone who got fool notions that they lost their heads. They'd all lost their heads. The women picked up the pieces. Reed didn't see how he could fault them for eating the dead. Maybe at the lake where there were still hides and where the Breens still had meat to eat but were too selfish to share it but not here. Folks couldn't live on snow.

They moved on then to the grove and after they'd had

time to recover they went to the George Donner tent. Tamsen was alive and strong as Reed had expected but he didn't expect to find George Donner so wasted. He could see from the condition of the arm that his friend wasn't going to live. While the others prepared meat and bread he sat with George and talked. The older man seemed obsessed with explaining what had happened to them. He kept apologizing for what they had done until Tamsen finally stopped him. She looked squarely at Reed with open eyes.

—We did what we had to do Mr. Reed.

He nodded.

—I know you did Mrs. Donner. No man can say otherwise.

But Reed couldn't persuade Tamsen to leave with them when they prepared their departure in the late afternoon. He explained to her that Woodworth was supposed to be coming but couldn't be counted on. She insisted on staying with her husband even though Reed was leaving Cady and Clark to take care of those who were forced by weakness to remain behind. Solomon Hook and Mary and Isaac Donner would go. Tamsen's girls weren't strong enough to go alone. Jean Baptiste was willing to stay since Woodworth was coming. That would leave 3 men to help Tamsen out with George and Betsy and the girls. Young Sammy Donner would be left behind too.

With that it was time to return to the lake. Reed said his goodbyes solemnly. He knew he'd never see George Donner again.

The survivors with the first relief got into Woodworth's camp at Mule Springs at the end of the day. They could hardly credit what they saw. There were horses and trees and green grass. Tents everywhere and hard, healthy men. The organizer of it all sat in a camp chair outside the largest tent. He had a man rubbing his feet. It made Margaret Reed furious. People were starving up in the mountains and here was this man Woodworth who was supposed to relieve them sitting having his feet rubbed to stave off frostbite. There was whiskey in camp too. She told Virginia it looked like they ought to turn things around and take care of *him* but Virginia was too distracted to take much notice. One of the men at the camp had proposed to her the minute he laid eyes on her and he'd been following her around ever since. Every time he did something for her he repeated his proposal. She didn't flatly turn him down. The attention made her feel alive again. She thought she'd string him along. But it was funny. She was just skin and bones and she wasn't even 14 yet.

March 3

Reed prepared to leave at noon. He asked Stone to stay behind to take care of the people at the lake. The Graves were going and all the Breens. Patty and Tommy. Keseberg said he wasn't well enough to go. Reed thought otherwise but he didn't care if Keseberg went or not. Mrs. Murphy had to stay. She was too weak to travel and the children at her cabin needed care.

The traveling was slow. Some of the children had to be carried. No one seemed to be in any hurry and Reed's prodding didn't faze them. Reed had hoped to make the head of the lake where they would be poised to cross the pass the next day but by dusk they had only progressed a mile or 2 and were forced to camp on the lake's north shore. Elizabeth Graves had brought along Jay Fosdick's violin. She thought Jay was still alive. Pat Breen played the violin for the camp that night to celebrate his freedom from the prison of the cabins.

March 4

The day before the men helped Elizabeth Graves retrieve $500 in coin from its hiding place in a cleat nailed to the bed of her family wagon. During breakfast Turner and Brit Greenwood got to kidding about it. Greenwood proposed a game of euchre with the money as the prize. Elizabeth overheard the joke and it threw her into a panic. When the party set out she stayed behind and buried her money. She wasn't far behind. The people were dawdling again.

Stone didn't like the duty at the lake camp. On the way up he and Cady and Clark had talked over the Donner party. The one thing they knew for sure was that the Donners were rich. People said they'd brought out wagons of store goods and plenty of money. And he was at the lake and his partners were at the Donners. As soon as he could he packed up and lit out.

Stone arrived at the Donner camp and found Cady. Clark was off hunting bear. Cady said Mrs. Donner had seen the tracks the day before. He said they didn't need Clark anyway and after he and Stone had talked they went to the George Donner tent.

Tamsen welcomed them warily. She didn't like the look in their eyes.

—What is it gentlemen?

—We're going to go on out of here Mrs. Donner said Cady. You got enough help here without us staying around eating up the food.

—I suppose that's right said Tamsen. But what about Mr. Clark?

—He'll stay. He's a good tracker. He'll do you right.

—Looky here Mrs. Donner said Stone you ought to let us carry some of your stuff out. If it just sits up here the Indians is likely to rob you.

Tamsen studied her hands. She preferred Indian robbers to robbers of her own race.

—My most precious possessions are my children she said. You should think about them before you think about material things. She stared at the 2 men and they shifted uncomfortably. I would make it worth your while to carry my girls to Colonel Sutter's.

The men looked at each other.

—Such as what? said Stone.

—Whatever you think fair said Tamsen. Perhaps three hundred dollars.

—That don't hardly seem enough said Stone. It's a long way from here to Sutter's. We'd be riskin our lives to take three little toddlers over them mountains.

—But a hundred dollars for each child is a great deal of money said Tamsen.

Cady grinned.

—If we was of a mind to we could take it all. Ma'am.

—Shut up said Stone. We ain't thieves. Mrs. Donner you give us five hundred dollars and we'll consider the matter settled. We'll get them kids to safety as fast as we can.

It was better than robbery. A compromise between her need and their greed.

—All right gentlemen Tamsen said. If you'll wait outside I'll get the girls ready. Cady and Stone left and she got the money from its hiding place. She dressed the girls in their best and warmest clothes. Dresses of linsey and quilted petticoats and thick wool stockings. Georgia and Eliza wore hooded red cloaks. Frances wore a heavy shawl and a blue hood. I may never see you again Tamsen said to the girls when they were dressed. But God will take care of you. When you get to the fort I want you to find your sisters and stay with them. Now tell me what I taught you to say.

—We are the children of Mr. and Mrs. George Donner. The girls recited the litany together and then Tamsen led them to their father to say goodbye. He hardly understood what was happening. They smelled the sickness in his arm as they kissed him goodbye. Then Tamsen called the men and gave them the money and the children. She pointed to a pile of family silver she had laid out on a trunk.

—You gentlemen may take that too if you can carry it. It will serve for the children's needs at the fort until my husband and I can arrive there.

Cady and Stone loaded the silver into their packs. Stone picked up Eliza and carried her out and Cady took Frances's and Georgia's hands and followed. Tamsen came up onto the snow to watch them. Not far from the tent Cady realized that Georgia would also have to be carried and picked her up. Tamsen smiled. She was taking a risk

but it was a risk she would just have to take. If all was as
Mr. Reed had said then the men wouldn't get far before
meeting Mr. Woodworth's party. She prayed he would
come. Mr. Donner's life was no longer in question but her
children's were and so was Betsy's. Her own was less important. In the mountains she was fine but how could she
ever face civilized people again? By now the story of what
the men of the relief party had found here must have been
passing down the mountains. She'd wanted to open a school
for young ladies in California. Who would send her daughters to such a school now? She'd told Mr. Reed that they
did what they had to do but she also knew that the thing
they had done had consequences. She would not live with
ridicule nor would she live with other people's pity. But
what would come remained to be seen. Right now it was
good that the girls would be relieved. If worst came to
worst Elitha and Leanna were old enough to raise them.

Out of sight of the tents Cady and Stone stopped and put
the children down. Stone spread out a blanket for them
to sit on and took Cady aside. Frances watched them. She
knew what they were talking about. They wanted to leave
them there and go on. Steal Mamma's money and just leave
them in the snow.

—Don't worry she whispered to Georgia and Eliza. If they
leave us here I'll get us back. I know the trail.

—I know the trail too said Georgia. I can do it too.

But the men returned and picked the younger girls up
again and set out for the lake with Frances following them.

By the time they arrived late in the afternoon Cady and
Stone had repented of their sentiment. They were sick of
carrying children and silver too. Sick of Frances telling
them to slow down. They took the girls to the Murphy cabin
and carried them inside.

—We're goin to leave these little girls here Stone told
Mrs. Murphy.

—You cain't do that said Lavina Murphy. We ain't got
enough food as it is.

—There'll be another relief along here any day now said

Stone. We got to go meet them and bring back food for you folks.

Keseberg rose up angrily.

—They do not stay! he told the men. There is nothing for them here!

—You goddamned German said Cady. You got your nerve. You don't tell nobody *nothin* after the things you done.

—What have I done? said Keseberg. I have done nothing. I have done no wrong. I have kept people alive.

—Shit said Cady shut your filthy mouth. He shoved Keseberg down onto the bed.

The girls stayed and the men hiked to the Breen cabin to spend the night.

Reed had succeeded in herding his party no farther than the foot of the pass. He'd left most of the provisions with the Donners and the people at the lake. The packs held only another day and a half's worth of food. Pat Breen's fiddling that night was more an irritation than a pleasure. The wind was shifting to the west and the night was cold.

March 5

Reed was worried. Woodworth might be coming but he hadn't shown up yet and Reed decided he'd better sent some of the men on to the next cache to bring back food. It was a calculated risk since he needed the men to carry children if he was to make much progress. He picked John Turner, Jondro and Dofar as the strongest he had and told them to push on to the first cache. If it wasn't disturbed one of them was to bring back provisions while the other 2 went on to the second cache. If they met another relief they were to hurry them up. They were willing. They knew how little food was left. Their bellies urged them on.

They had already climbed to the pass and disappeared when Reed got his people well started. He told them they had to get over the pass and down the other side by the end of the day if they expected to avoid the terrible cold in the heights. For the first time they seemed to understand the urgency but their best efforts were feeble. Parents and children alike slipped down and had to be helped up and Reed had only 3 men left to help. He was grateful for his nearly empty pack to the extent that it left him free to carry Tommy slung in a blanket on his back. Somehow Patty got along with no more help than his willing hand. She was a wonder. It seemed to Reed she had a stronger spirit than any man there.

The Donner girls were terrified. The cabin was dark and cold. The woman was nice to them but the big bearded man wouldn't let them out of bed. When they cried he yelled at them.

—Be quiet you crying children he said or I shoot you!

Even Eliza stopped crying when she heard that. They lay together in bed and shivered.

Reed's party made the summit valley late in the afternoon and camped where the 2 reliefs had camped before. The camp was out in the open at the edge of the valley but it gave them the advantage of firewood already cut. The men felled green trees to make a platform for the fire and cut pine boughs the people could spread their blankets on. Even the men had begun to fail. They'd been living on daily rations of a pint and a half of sizing made by cooking up flour with water.

Clouds closed over them with the darkness and the wind began to blow. It looked like a storm was coming and Reed feared for their lives. Turner at least should have gotten back from the nearest cache. It wasn't more than 5 miles away from the camp. If Turner hadn't made it back big as he was then the cache must have been robbed and it would be days before the men could get to the next one and return. A storm would pin them as fast as it would pin Reed's people. He saw death coming with the storm if they couldn't get provisions. They were all but out of food. The children were already moaning about the cold. It was a dreadful cold so high up in the mountains but Reed felt colder still with the possibility of losing everything after having come so far. He had thought the effort of relief would redeem him from the guilt of his past judgments and now he may have brought these people to one more grief. They'd be better off back at their cabins than up on a mountaintop. But they could no more go back than they could go forward in the teeth of a storm. It was like the Wahsatch and the salt desert. Every time they went forward the land closed in treacherously behind. The land was hunting them down. There was nothing between Laramie and California but deadly wilderness. It was a wonder America had ever been settled at all. It was like a wild beast that kept itself quiet until you troubled it passing by and then it roared up out of its cave. Men hadn't made much headway with it. They crept in from the ocean shores and put up their cabins and their towns and the land lay quiet but it hated what they did to it and when it had the chance it ate them alive.

The storm broke over them in the darkness in a rage of snow and wind. The wind bit like a pack of mad dogs and set the children to crying and their parents at their prayers. McCutchen was swearing but Miller and Brit Greenwood lost their courage and huddled down to pray with the rest. It was a fight to keep the fire going. The snow blew so hard that sometimes a man standing a few feet from the flames couldn't even see them before his eyes. He might as well have been blind. They relaid the fire on its platform but the heat began melting a hole below the platform in the snow. When the logs of the platform shifted over the hole they threatened to dump the fire into the pool of snow-water and put it out. The men worked off and on all night to keep it alive.

March 6

The storm blew on unabated. Daylight improved the visibility but still they couldn't see more than 20 feet. The women cooked up the last of the provisions. A spoonful of gruel each was all that was left. Reed and McCutchen worked cutting pine boughs against the wind and the cold.

They chose long thick branches and as fast as they cut them they stuck them upright in the snow to make a windbreak. The other men threw snow against the boughs to pile up a drift. Slowly they built it up until it blocked the wind but the fire was still in danger. After the windbreak was secure the men took turns cutting a supply of wood from the dead trees around the camp. The children cried that they were hungry and the women cried that they were cold. The men had to come back to the campfire 5 or 6 times every hour to get warm. The wind sliced through their heavy clothes as sharply as their axes sliced through the trees. A foot of snow had piled up around them and the storm blew worse than ever. Reed dreaded the coming night.

Cady and Stone were holed up comfortably at the Breen cabin with ample provisions in their packs but there was no food left at the Murphy cabin. When night fell Keseberg got out of bed long enough to piss in the corner and then went and stood over the bed where Georgie Foster and Jimmy Eddy lay. Georgie was nearer the outside and Keseberg picked him up and carried him to his own bed.

—What're you doin? Lavina Murphy called to him. Where you takin that boy?

—The boy looks cold said Keseberg. I will keep him warm. He laid Georgie on his bed and crawled in beside him and pulled up the covers.

Reed had the first watch at the camp in the summit valley. He didn't dare sit still but worked to build the windbreak higher and wider behind the people sleeping huddled around the fire. He took the full force of the storm in his face. The blowing snow nearly blinded him. His beard was caked with ice and he felt his clothes freezing on his body but still he kept on building the break and feeding the fire. After awhile he no longer felt cold. His hands stopped doing what he demanded of them and his mind darkened. He struggled with the thing that was taking him but finally it was no use and he slipped down into the snow. With no one to feed it the fire burned lower and lower until only a few coals glowed red in the wind. Night and darkness covered the sleepers and Reed lay insensible in the snow.

Peggy Breen woke shivering. She saw that the fire was out and threw back her blanket and stumbled to the first sleeping man she found and tried to kick him awake. It was Will McCutchen and he jumped up in a blast of curses and looked wildly around him. Everyone was awake now and some were screaming. The fire was out. They would all perish with cold. McCutchen grabbed Hiram Miller and propelled him toward the woodpile.

—Get us some kindling! he shouted. The fire's gone out!

McCutchen set to work feeding pine needles into the coals as he blew on them. Miller grabbed an ax at the woodpile and pain shot up his arm and he felt that his hands had split open. He cut kindling anyway wincing with pain and carried the chips back to McCutchen a handful at a time. Mrs. Breen still railed at McCutchen and finally he shoved her back onto the snow and told her to leave him the hell alone and she shut up.

The fire burned again. Miller had stumbled over Reed on one of his trips to the woodpile and now he and McCutchen fought to wake the man. They hauled him to the fire and worked him over but it took what seemed like hours before he opened his eyes. When he was sensible again they told him what had happened but he already knew from the voices of the children around the fire. They said *Thank god for the fire. How good it is. I'm glad, I'm glad we got a fire. Oh how good it feels. It's good the fire didn't go out.*

March 7

Still the storm blew but by now the men had built the windbreak high and piled up a bonfire and warmth and hunger dulled the people at the camp enough to quiet them. McCutchen had gotten so cold the night before he'd burned through 4 shirts to the skin before he realized he had his back too close to the fire. Relief was struck down by the storm as certainly as they were. They knew they'd have to wait it out and they did as little as possible. They lay by the fire and huddled together and slept.

When Keseberg got out of bed Lavina Murphy looked over and saw that Georgie Foster was dead. Keseberg noticed her staring and nodded.

—*Ja* he said. The boy died during the night. I found him that way now. It is just as well. At least he died warm. Lavina's face screwed up with fear. He died of hunger said Keseberg. You have seen that before. Why do you look like that? The boy died of hunger! Keseberg saw the children watching now. He turned and picked up Georgie's body by the shirt and the head lolled. Look you children! he shouted. You see he died of hunger! Eliza and Georgia began to cry and Frances shushed them. Here said Keseberg I put him up for all to see! He carried Georgie's body to a stob of pine that stuck out from one of the logs on the wall and hung it up by its shirt collar in plain view and the face stared at them until later in the day when Keseberg took the body down and laid it by the hearth and began to cut it up.

Early in the morning Will Eddy and Bill Foster left Johnson's ranch on horseback and despite the drenching rain rode 50 miles to Mule Springs. They expected to find Woodworth's camp but instead they found a note Woodworth had posted saying he'd moved the camp forward to Bear Valley.

March 8

With dawn Reed saw signs that the storm was slackening. The wind would entirely cease for minutes at a time and then it would blow again as bad as before. There was little hope now of relief. When the storm ended they'd have to push forward to the nearest cache. Those who couldn't go would have to wait where they were and pray for a miracle. If the miracle was named Woodworth it'd be a miracle for sure.

Patty called her father and he went to her side. Mary

Donner was crying and beside her one of her brothers lay dead. Reed thought she was crying over her dead brother but then he saw she had pulled off her shoes and was rubbing her feet. He knelt to examine them. One of them was white with frostbite and the other was burned. The burn looked ugly. She must have stuck the foot into the fire in her sleep. The boy had died so quietly at night that neither of the girls could say when it happened. They woke in the morning and he was dead. Reed surveyed the others huddled on the rim of the deep hole the fire had melted in the snow. He feared the first death wouldn't be the last.

Clark had waited out the storm at the Jacob Donner tent. He was strong enough to keep himself warm wrapped in blankets but it was otherwise with the Donner children and just before the storm ended at noon 3-year-old Lewis Donner died. Betsy was beside herself. She was losing her family one by one. They were all dying. The children who went over the mountains with Colonel Reed might have died too. She took up her dead boy and staggered to the other tent and laid the body in Tamsen's lap and collapsed crying before her.

Reed was ready to go. He was furious with the Breens. They had decided to stay behind. Hiram Miller was carrying Tommy. Patty insisted she could walk. Solomon Hook was going and even Mary Donner with her burned foot. Elizabeth Graves was hardly alive and she and her children would have to stay but the Breens had the strength to go. —By damn Pat said Reed you're crazy if you think anyone's going to come along here and find you. If they were coming they'd of been here by now storm or no storm.

Breen stared up vaguely at Reed from the shelter of the windbreak. He was warm and comfortable and couldn't imagine what the fuss was all about. Peggy could do the talking. She was good at it.

—Sure you tend to your own knitting James Reed said Peggy from the other end of the line of Breens. The Lord and the Vargin will watch over us. We've no strength to go on over the snow and all of us days now without a mouthful of food.

Reed struggled with his anger. It wouldn't do any good. The Breens had always stuck fast wherever they were set down like toads wedged into rocks. That was the best they could think to do and if their bellies didn't prove to them it was time to move on why would he expect he could?

—Mac! Hiram! Reed signaled the men to come over. I want you as witnesses that these people refuse to go on with us. They're taking their own lives in their hands and that's their business but the blood of their children will be on their heads if they insist on staying.

—All right said Mac and Hiram nodded.

—You know that Woodworth can't be relied on Reed called to Peggy Breen. Relying on Woodworth is like leaning on a broken stick. I don't expect he's gotten much beyond Bear Valley if even that far.

—By the saints said Peggy Breen leave us alone.

Reed turned away to examine the preparations the others had made and found the wood piled and the men and children ready to go.

Clark and Jean Baptiste buried the dead Donner boy in the snow with Tamsen watching. The burial hit home with Clark and he saw he'd have to get to work if he wanted to survive. He took up an ax and set out to cut wood but at the edge of the grove of tamaracks he found the tracks of a bear cub. Just before the storm began he had stalked a she-bear and her cub and fired on the she-bear and hit her but then lost her trail in the blowing snow. Here was the cub back again without its ma. He ran to the tent and got Jacob Donner's gun and set out following the tracks. He must have killed the she-bear. He tracked the cub over the new snow for more than an hour. The trail led up the hill west of the camp. He felt himself going light-headed from the climb. He was starving just as sure as the Donner people were starving. He stopped to rest and then climbed on. The trail turned under a shelf of rocks and disappeared. Clark

examined it carefully and saw that it led to a cave and sat
down disgusted. He might just as well stay there and freeze.
There was nothing left to eat at the camp and no one in his
right mind went chasing into caves after bears. The old
she-bear might be holed up in there just waiting for him
to crawl in so she could take her revenge. He sniffed at
the entrance but no smell came out and he couldn't hear
a sound. He'd been living with scarecrows until he felt
like a scarecrow himself. He stared down into the hole
but he couldn't see anything. It was pitch black inside.
He had to get the cub or give up. Then he remembered
his gun. Maybe he could scare the cub out. He got powder
and ball ready to reload and stuck the barrel as far down
into the cave as he could reach and fired and pulled back
from the hole and reloaded. When the smoke cleared he
crept carefully forward and listened at the hole. There
wasn't a sound. Disgusted he crawled back out from under
the cliff and stood up. The cub's tracks weren't very big.
It would have to be a new cub just whelped this winter.
If it was kill or die he'd be better off trying to kill. He laid
down his gun and took out his knife. He might as well fight
it out. He crawled back to the hole and started to slide his
feet in when the snow gave way. He fell into blackness. His
arm hit a rock and bounced up and his knife flew past his
face and then he was sitting half-wedged at the bottom of
the cave. He reached wildly around for support to push
himself up and his hand touched fur and he jerked his arm
back and yelled and tried to scramble up and felt the fur
again and realized it wasn't moving. He grabbed the fur
and pulled and slid the cub toward him. He must have hit
it with his shot. It was deader than a doornail. He'd shot
it by god. He gave himself time to catch his breath and then
set to work climbing out of the cave with his prize.

Reed's party hadn't gone far from camp when they saw
that Mary Donner wasn't up to the journey. She couldn't
walk on her burned foot. She was terrified of being left but
Reed promised to send relief as soon as he could and Brit

Greenwood carried her back. They waited for Greenwood and when he returned they moved on. By midafternoon they had crossed the summit valley and entered the canyon of the Yuba. They were all slowing down. Their hunger was telling on them and the bitter cold that had followed the storm.

—Pa! called Patty Reed. I see the stars! Pa I see the stars and the angels! She was stumbling in the snow. I never knew I'd see the angels. Oh they're so beautiful.

Reed was beside her and McCutchen too. She was blue with cold.

—She's dying said McCutchen. She's gone daft.

—Rub her said Reed. I've got some crumbs I saved from the packs. He pulled a mitten from his pocket and worked the crumbs from the thumb where he had stored them into his mouth. When they were softened he put his mouth to his daughter's and forced the crumbs between her lips with his tongue. Her mouth worked and she swallowed them. He took more crumbs and repeated the process while McCutchen warmed her arms and her back. She stirred.

—Oh they're going away she said. Oh Pa don't take my angels away.

—It's all right honey Reed said softly. It's all right. I'm going to put you up on my back now and carry you. He slung a blanket and took up his daughter and they all moved on.

At the Donner camp Clark dressed out the bear cub. He packed the quarters in the snow and took the innards inside George Donner's tent wrapped in the pelt. Tamsen set to work cooking. She had 2 invalids now. Betsy Donner's collapse was complete. Like Mr. Donner she would have to be fed. Jean Baptiste would care for Betsy's children.

Eddy and Foster came up to Woodworth's camp in Bear Valley just as the sun set over the western wall. They knew from Mrs. Reed that their sons were still at the lake camp and they expected to find Woodworth gone forward but here was the bastard warm in his tent with half a dozen men guarding the camp as if the Indians might attack them any hour. And a man to cook and a man to carry water when Reed's relief must be stuck somewhere between the lake and the valley in the storm. Without even stopping at the fire they descended on Woodworth in his tent.

—By God gentlemen said Woodworth as they came in. It's good to see you.

—What the hell are you doing here? said Eddy. Why ain't you gone on after those folks up there? Eddy stood braced before Woodworth and Foster glared from beside him.

Woodworth sat at a camp desk. He didn't even have his boots on. The question flustered him and he pushed his chair back to stand and then thought better of it.

—Why the guides have gone on he said. They went over with Colonel Reed.

—You don't need no guides said Eddy. You had the god-damned trail them others made until the storm come up.

—Ah but that's just it Mr. Eddy said Woodworth. We only just arrived here at Bear Valley when the storm closed us in. We've been waiting for this weather.

—Shit said Foster you left Johnson's days ago. You got all them bastards sittin on their asses out there when there's folks up in them mountains dyin.

Woodworth frowned.

—There's no need for cursing Mr. Foster. We know our job here. The Governor and the *alcalde* put me in charge. He pointed a finger at Foster. And I'd advise you not to attempt those mountains.

Eddy and Foster looked at one another and back at the fat man beyond the desk.

—We been over them mountains before said Foster. We know all about them mountains.

—Look here Woodworth said Eddy. We intend to go on and if you give a damn about your name you better come on with us. My boy's up at the lake and Reed's out there somewhere in the snow. Their blood'll be on your head if you don't shake loose and come on.

—Surely you don't intend to go on tonight? said Woodworth nervously.

—Nope said Eddy but you better be ready to move out at
dawn tomorrow or I'll report to the Governor about you
personally.

—Well that's fine Mr. Eddy said Woodworth. That's ex-
actly what I had in mind in any case.

—Sure you did said Foster. You was just about to put your
boots on when we come in. Let's go Will. Leave this son-of-
a-bitch to hisself. I can't stand to look at him no more.

—Tomorrow morning gentlemen said Woodworth and Foster spat on the floor and held open the tent flap and then
followed Eddy out.

Cady and Stone had wasted no time getting started when
the storm ended at noon. They packed the money and the
silver Tamsen had given them and struck out over the snow.
They'd never intended to drag the 3 little girls with them
and they didn't bother now to tell them they were going.
By midafternoon they had crossed the pass and skirted the
camp in the summit valley and by nightfall they caught up
with Reed. He had an idea what they were up to but he was
too tired to argue about it. It was enough that they carried
a little beef and flour and were willing to share it with his
men and the children. Patty had come completely back to
life. Toward the end of the day when the men were getting
discouraged and had begun to talk about giving up she'd
even encouraged them to go on. *God didn't bring us this far
just to let us perish* she told them and it shamed them all.
McCutchen had called her an angel. An angel she was.
When they made camp Reed realized that his feet were
numb. He pulled off his boots and found his toes white with
cold. The others were complaining too and he told them to
stick their feet in the snow. After they got a fire going their
feet agonized them. It would be that much harder to get on.
Reed slept that night rolled up in his blankets with Tommy
on one side and Patty on the other. They kept each other
warm. With the children alive beside him he felt like a con-

victed man who had won a reprieve. How long the reprieve would last he didn't know. There must be relief somewhere beyond the snow but where was Woodworth and his boat-load of supplies?

Peggy Breen was mistress of the camp in the summit valley. She had her family laid out along the windbreak with their feet near the fire. It was melting down a deepening hole in the snow and across the hole she could see Mrs. Graves and her baby and her other children lying much the same way as her own. Peggy had no milk for her baby. Her milk was 3 days gone. But she had a trick or two left for all that. Half a sugarloaf in one pocket of her cloak and a paper full of seeds in the other. She'd saved the seeds all winter thinking she could carry them down to California. The baby had a sugartit and from time to time she took the kerchief away and tied up a fresh corner with a lump of sugar from the loaf. The sugar kept the little thing alive and quiet too.

Late at night Peggy heard one of the Graves girls call to her mother to cover her up. She called 3 times before Mrs. Graves responded. The mother said she was tired from caring for the baby and needed her rest. Cover yourself she said. Then Peggy heard her talking in a strange voice and she woke her husband.

—Pat said Peggy get up now and go see after Mrs. Graves. She don't sound right.

Pat did as he was told and found the woman unwakeable. He picked up her baby and brushed the snow off the woman and covered her with her blanket. He woke Nancy Graves and gave her the baby and she took it in her arms. Pat returned to his place on the other side of the fire.

Peggy still wondered what was happening and watched Elizabeth Graves carefully. She saw the woman throw one arm over her face and then lie still. She waited for a time but saw no more movement and she got up and went over. The body was already cold. Peggy shook her head and crossed herself and went back to her blanket and wrapped

it around her. Death had visited them again. She saw the
star of morning in the sky. It reminded her of the Heart of
Mary and with her eyes full she began to pray. She was
consistent even in that. She prayed not for the soul of
Elizabeth Graves but for the children's lives and Pat's and
her own.

March 9

Eddy and Foster had their breakfasts on Woodworth before dawn and saw to it that the Lord High Commander
was on his way with them by first light with 5 of his men.
They had just crossed over into Yuba bottoms when they
saw 3 men ahead and hurried forward to meet them. They
were Dofar, Jondro and Turner. Turner the mountain man
had given out in the storm and the other 2 weren't much
better off. They told Eddy that after the storm they'd gone
on to the second cache and found the food there. The first
cache had been clawed down and eaten. Reed and his party
couldn't be far behind. Dofar said he'd carried part of the
second cache back and hung it in a tree for them and to
protect it from varmints he'd cut off the lower branches of
the tree as he came back down. Eddy told the men there
was food and fire in Bear Valley and saw them started on
down and pushed on.

Brit Greenwood found the cache Dofar had left. He and
Hiram Miller were working ahead of the rest of Reed's
party. They cut down the tree and helped themselves to
dried beef and Greenwood called back to Reed. He signaled
the finding of the cache and Reed yelled that he understood
and waved the men on.

Peggy Breen found another body on the Graves' side of
the campfire in the morning. Little Franklin Graves Jr.
must have died soon after his mother. The fire had burned
so far down through the snow that it hardly gave them
warmth any more but when Peggy went to the edge of the
hole to look at it she saw a patch of brown at the bottom.
She wondered what it could be and only then realized it

must be the ground. The fire had melted all the way to the ground. She hadn't seen the ground outside her cabin since long before Christmas. She went to John Breen and shook him and he opened his eyes.

—John she said. The fire's burnt to the ground. Yi must climb down and see if we can camp there. The boy blinked at her. Are yi listening to me John? Get up and go down to the fire.

He seemed to understand then and threw aside his blanket and stood up

—What is it Mither?

—Bejesus John the *fire*. Go down and see to the *fire*.

She pulled a tree limb to the edge of the snowhole and swung it over. The cut end stuck up to make a ladder. John climbed carefully down. He patted the ground with his hands.

—It's dry Mither! he called up. Dry and warm! Come down!

Peggy roused the others and saw her family down with the 2 babies and then the Graves children and Mary Donner. She pulled firewood off the pile and dragged it to the edge and slid it over the side where John stopped it and stacked it below and then she herself went down. The sun was shining into the snowhole and with the fire it made a comfortable shelter.

Woodworth gave out in the middle of the afternoon. He insisted they stop and camp. Eddy argued with him but he paid no attention. He ordered his men to halt and since he was paying them they did.

—What's his trouble? asked Foster when Eddy came back.

—He's tired of carrying his blanket said Eddy. We might as well hold up. We can't go it alone.

Sitting around the Woodworth campfire as the sun set the men heard a noise from up the trail. Woodworth said it sounded like a wild animal but the others knew better. Eddy and Foster jumped up and ran forward shouting. The shouting was soon returned and the 2 parties closed on

each other. Miller and Greenwood came in ahead. Woodworth was all action now. He hiked on and found Reed and
McCutchen and the children. They were saved for sure.
Woodworth's men relieved the relief men of the children
and carried them back to camp. The men of the relief
walked on bloody feet. Like Eddy in the final days of the
Forlorn Hope they had left a trail of blood behind them on
the snow.

Betsy Donner died peacefully at sunset. Clark's bear
meat had not come soon enough to save her. Tamsen wondered if it had come soon enough to save any of them and
she wondered if it mattered after all.

March 10

The look of the 3 mountain men and the men of Reed's
party inspired no confidence in Woodworth's men. Reed
had told Woodworth of the 14 people he left behind at the
camp in the summit valley and argued for their immediate
relief but Woodworth hadn't committed himself to the task.
In the morning Eddy and Foster brought the matter up
again. No one looked keen on it and they offered to pay
anything anyone would ask in wages to go on with them.
Someone said that was easy to do when they were dead
broke. Reed and Miller added their reputations to the offer
but the same man said they were as bad off as the other 2.

—I can't believe you boys would let those people starve to
death up there said Reed. It'd be on your conscience for the
rest of your lives.

—It wouldn't be on my conscience said one of Woodworth's
men coldly. You said yourself they had a chance to come on
and didn't take it.

—Not all of them said Reed. Mrs. Graves and her children
were too weak to travel.

Another of Woodworth's men stood up. He towered
above the campfire. He was well over 6 feet tall.

—By God it'd be on my conscience he said. Mr. Eddy, I'll
go with you whether these others go or not.

—I don't think that would be wise said Woodworth.

—Why not said the man.

—How much do you weigh John?

—Bout two-twenty.

—I doubt that the crust would hold you. Another 50 pounds of provisions on your back and you'd probably break right through.

—What's your name friend? asked Eddy.

—John Starks said the big man.

—I thank you for your offer said Eddy but I guess Woodworth's right.

Eddy and Foster wanted to go on without help. Reed argued against it. 2 men would put themselves in danger and they couldn't bring people out by themselves. There were too many children that needed carrying now. Reed said if Eddy and Foster came on back to Bear Valley with him he'd try his damndest to talk Woodworth into taking charge of a relief or at least agreeing to pay the men for going on. Reed thought his knowing the circumstances of the relief effort would carry its weight with Woodworth. It was only a day's delay in any case and if Eddy and Foster still wanted to go on they wouldn't have lost that much time. Reluctantly they agreed.

Lying in a stupor in the morning sun Pat Breen found himself thinking of the last entries in his diary. Mrs. Murphy had turned to eat Milt and the Donners had eaten the dead and the dead lay waiting now at the top of the snow-hole to ease their starvation. It was the only chance they had to live. They hadn't eaten in a week and some of them were hardly alive any more. Peggy had gone frantic with fear and every few minutes she moved from one child to the next checking it for the breath of life. Once she had come to him crying that James was dying and he had barked at her to let him die. His fury shocked him. He'd never stood up to her that way before and now when she forbade him to talk of saving themselves as the others had done he wondered if she was right. If lives belonged to Almighty God then the saving of them was His too and why would He be putting flesh within their reach if He didn't mean them to use it? Why would He be sending them so near to safety if He meant to let them die along the way?

He told her harshly what he intended to do and she was too weak to hold him back. He climbed from the snowhole. The climb exhausted him and he dropped to his knees like a penitent and crawled to Elizabeth Graves' body lying stiff on the snow. His eyes blurred. How could he be doing what he was doing. Baring the woman's body seemed worse to him than the act that would follow. She was a stranger to him. He had to bare her body or cut her face and he could not cut her face. His hands shook when he unbuttoned her dress and he fumbled at the buttons. He was crying now. Terrible, terrible. The nearest flesh before his eyes was her breasts. Because of the baby they hadn't wasted away. He took one in his hand. It was cold and firm and the lack of warmth eased the horror he felt and with his knife he sawed the breast free and laid it aside and went to work sawing the other one. With the first cut the work had become easier and before he was through he had cut open the belly and hacked out the liver and the heart.

Climbing back into the snowhole he could hear his wife moaning below him. He looked over his shoulder. She was covering her face. Pretending not to see what he had done. She frightened him and for a moment he thought of taking the loathsome things he carried in his coattails back to the body and somehow fixing them back on but hunger surged in him the more desperately for his nearness to the fire and he climbed on down and soon he had the flesh roasting on a spit. The children crowded round him and he rationed them each a portion. He fed the Graves children too and Mary Donner. The Graves children were eating of their own mother. Breen was a man who had lived on hides when there was meat to eat and it seemed to him Mrs. Graves would have approved the use of her body. She had given them birth from her body and now they were sustained by it once more.

Peggy Breen avoided the food for as long as she could but by afternoon she too had come forward to the fire. It seemed to Pat that she cared more for the opinion of others than for the providence of God. He realized then that it was her condemnation of Mrs. Murphy that had put him off back at the lake camp. What evil was there in eating the dead? If men ate the flesh of animals what was the evil then in extremity in eating the flesh of men? The evil was in dying or letting others die without accepting the bounty of Almighty God. That was stiff-necked pride sure.

Back in the comfort of Bear Valley Woodworth allowed himself to be convinced of the need for relief and offered to pay the men $3 a day to go on with Eddy and Foster and $50 each for carrying out a child. He put a little twist on the $50 by insisting he would pay it only if the child was not a man's own. The 2 fathers snorted at that. It was about Woodworth's style. Foster said they should have licked his boots the minutes they came into his tent. John Starks wouldn't be put off by Woodworth's natural science. He said if he broke through the snow he'd just have to swim his way on over. That tickled McCutchen who had taken a liking to his fellow giant right away. Starks on his side hadn't heard McCutchen talk about the *Anthropophagi* more than twice when he settled in next to the man and asked him where that mouthful came from and McCutchen spent the rest of the evening filling Starks in on *Othello* and practicing him until he could toss off the word like a trooper. *And of the cannibals* he intoned *that did each other eat, the Anthropophagi, and men whose heads do grow beneath their shoulders* and on the last phrase he pointed to Woodworth and Starks roared against the silence of the snow.

As soon as she was safely in camp and thoroughly warm Patty Reed had turned aside to count her treasures. All through the days and nights crossing the mountains she had kept them hidden inside her dress for fear the men would take them away. She had Penelope who'd suffered as much as she from hunger and had seen the angels too. She had a lock of Gramma Keyes' gray hair tied with a scrap of blue-flowered lawn and she had a glass salt-cellar with a silver lid. It was so small that she could hide it in her hand by covering it with her thumb. Now at last there was salt in camp and she carefully filled the little cellar from the sack and sat with Penelope by the fire shaking salt into her hand and slowly licking it off. It tasted better than anything she had tasted ever in her life.

March 11

Stone was going back with Eddy and Foster. Hiram Miller to see after the Donners. John Starks and 2 of Woodworth's other men, Oakley and Thompson. Woodworth wouldn't go. Reed and McCutchen were in no shape to travel but Woodworth was playing the General again. Foster was pissed but Eddy didn't care. He had his men. They were fresh enough to push through. They set out at dawn with Eddy in the lead.

Tamsen had feared for her girls since the beginning of the last storm. She had worked on Clark and Jean Baptiste every day to convince them to cross to the lake camp to see if there was news. Clark was curious about Cady and Stone and finally agreed to go. He made the lake camp by noon and descended into the Murphy cabin. The litter of bodies around the entrance told him most of what he wanted to know. Inside the filthy cabin he took in the bones and wads of hair that lay scattered on the floor. The girls were there looking like wild animals but worst of all he surprised Keseberg cutting up the body of a dead child. Keseberg didn't even acknowledge his presence but went on with his grisly work while Mrs. Murphy whispered her fears to the visitor. She told Clark she suspected Keseberg of murdering her grandson in his bed. The body Keseberg was butchering was Jimmy Eddy's. The boy had died during the night but as far as she knew he had died naturally in his own bed while Keseberg was sleeping. Clark left as fast as he could for the Donners. It was going to be his last errand. Obviously Cady and Stone had lit out as soon as the storm was over and left the girls behind. The bear meat was gone and no one could make him stay where people were crazy enough to eat the dead. The snow was settling fast. He and Jean Baptiste ought to be able to get over the mountains. He'd have a pack of goods from the Donner wagons too for his help. They owed him as much as he could carry out. His bear had kept them alive.

March 12

Driving on from their camp on the Yuba Eddy's party crossed into the summit valley. A little ways up the valley they reached the place where John Denton had been left behind. Others had passed the body without stopping but Eddy remembered Denton well and paused to pay his respects. He was surprised to find a pencil still clutched in Denton's frozen hand and poking from the snow a leather daybook. He shook it free of snow and opened it. There were notes through the days. The last entry was a poem. Eddy hiked on and caught up with the others. Denton must have written the poem sitting in the snow waiting to freeze to death. It was smudged and the edges were wet but it was still readable.

> O after many roving years,
> How sweet it is to come
> Back to the dwelling-place of youth,
> Our first and dearest home;
> To turn away our wearied eyes
> From proud ambition's towers,
> And wander in those summer fields,
> The scenes of boyhood's hours.

But I am changed since last I gazed
Upon that tranquil scene,
And sat beneath the old witch elm
That shades the village green;
And watched my boat upon the brook—
It was a regal galley—
And sighed not for a joy on earth,
Beyond the happy valley.

I wish I could once more recall
That bright and blissful joy,
And summon to my weary heart
The feelings of a boy;
But now on scenes of past delight
I look, and feel no pleasure,
As misers on the bed of death
Gaze coldly on their treasure.

The Englishman had turned back to England. Eddy shook
his head and put the daybook away. It amazed him how
people were willing to die. Maybe if he had a village green
to remember he'd be willing too. But he had a wife and a
baby to remember and a son who might still be alive. And
staying alive was worth almost anything you had to do.
That was a fact threaded right through his bones. Denton
had written poetry when he ought to have been crawling
west to the sunset. The least animal would have done as
much. Would have tried to crawl on and gnawed its leg off
too if something held it back.

Tamsen Donner left for the lake camp on Clark's snowshoes. She asked to borrow them the night before when
Clark came back with his frightening news. He didn't want
to loan them but he also didn't want her to know he was
taking off and leaving her people behind. Her going was the
best thing that could happen. It would give him and Jean
Baptiste time to search the wagons and get away.

She had never seen the lake camp before. As she worked

her way slowly along the trail Clark had made back and
forth over the hills she wondered at her lack of curiosity.
Certainly she'd had enough to do taking care of her husband and the children. Yet the suffering of the people at the
lake camp had never touched her much. She cared for them
as she cared for all sufferers but she cared fiercely for her
own. If she was strong and her kin were weak then she was
responsible for their very lives. Nothing less could justify
the things she had done to preserve them from death. She
had seen too much of death in her life. It was the lot of
women. Birth and sickness and death. She had made her
way into the world of men and books but she had seen what
men seldom saw. The worm in the apple and the apple in
the worm. It took all curiosity away. It left the one last
thing. It left duty but she was capable no longer of any but
formal duty. There was one other need. The babies she had
pushed from her body into the world must be spared. When
that was certain the rest would be acceptable.

The litter around the cabin didn't surprise her. She had
learned to live with the dead. But inside was something
else. Her girls rushed to her dazed and cried against her
body and over their heads she took it in. The bones and hair
and filth that covered the floor. The old woman lying abed
with her last remaining child, a boy whose name or age
Tamsen could not calculate from his old-man's face and
half-bald head. The monstrous man with dirty hair and wild
eyes and a beard ropy with grease. The smell of the place, a
smell she knew and a smell that would never again leave her
memory. The smell of filth and sickness but above that the
smell of a meat they never knew until they came to the
mountains, a smell like gamy pork. The girls were weak.
Clearly they couldn't go back with her. There was nothing
else for her to do but stay and hope that the men would
care for her husband and the child and that he would understand. Clark was nervous with her before she left. She
wondered if it was the sight of this awful cabin or the discovery that his companions had left the girls and gone. It

might have given him an idea of his own. Nor could Jean Baptiste be trusted. But Mr. Reed had said relief was on its way. She talked to the girls until she calmed them and with Keseberg watching her cooly from the stool against the wall where he sat smoking his carved white pipe that curved around like a question mark she took up a bucket and went out to get water. The girls needed a bath.

Eddy and Foster expected the scene they found at the starved camp but the other men hardly knew where to rest their eyes. Down in the pit Pat and Peggy Breen lay sunning themselves beside the fire. A pot steamed from a spit and nearby lay the mutilated remains of Elizabeth Graves. The Breens had stripped the dead arms and legs down to the bone and gutted the trunk and against the stick-figure of its mother the baby Elizabeth Jr. lay crying. Peggy Breen started up guiltily when she saw the men looking down but she was trapped and could do no more than hide her face in her hands as she had hidden it before.

The men descended into the pit on steps someone had cut. Eddy took up the Graves baby remembering his own and rocked it until it stopped crying while one of the men pulled the pot from the fire and dumped it into the snow and refilled it and started it heating again. They needed soup but he would make a soup that men could eat.

Thompson and Hiram Miller were going on to the lake with Eddy and Foster. Miller hoped to carry out the Donner children. Oakley and Stone were ready to leave the Breens to their own devices. They hadn't thought to find so many left alive and the way the Breens had chosen to preserve their lives disgusted them. Eddy argued with them and so did John Starks but they wouldn't change their minds and finally they demanded a vote. Oakley said aye and Stone said aye and both men turned to Starks. His face was red.

—What's your vote? said Stone. You kin see you're licked.

Starks kicked the snow and tossed his head.

—Why by God I won't leave these people. You do what you got to do. I'll see them out of here or die trying.

—You kin die then said Stone. I'm carryin this here baby out and none more.

—I'll take the Donner girl said Oakley. That leaves you this other boy Starks. He's your lookout whatever you do about the Breens.

—I'll handle it said Stark. I'll handle it all and you bastards can belly on back to Woodworth and collect your pay.

March 13

Eddy's party left at dawn and reached the lake camp by 10 in the morning. It was incredible to Eddy how much the camp had changed. The cabins still half-buried in the snow and the litter of dead scattered around the clearings made him fear the worst and out of some instinct of self-protection he shouted ahead of their coming before they arrived at the cabin by the big rock. Tamsen Donner heard the shout and popped up into the sunlight and shouted back to them. Hiram Miller ran up to her and she gave him a hug of welcome but when she saw Foster and Eddy her face fell. Keseberg met them at the door. He saw Eddy first.

—I ate your boy he blurted and Eddy advanced on him and he backed away. He was dead! shouted Keseberg.

Eddy looked around for a club but Foster was also looking around and Georgie Foster was nowhere to be seen. He knew the worst then and he reached out to Eddy and stayed his hand.

—The son-of-a-bitch's gone crazy Will said Foster. He don't know what he's sayin.

Keseberg collapsed on the bed sobbing and Eddy stood looking down at him. His clothes hung loose on his body and a smell of rot came off of him more powerful than the smell of the cabin floor. This thing had lived among the dead until it wasn't worth even looking at any more and it was still alive like something that crawled out of a graveyard in the dark of the night. All the time Eddy had taken and all the suffering he'd been through led right to this cabin and his dead son. This was the whole thing squeezed into one small place.

—Keseberg! said Eddy. Look at me!

The German looked up from red eyes buried in black sockets and Eddy caught the eyes and held them with his own.

—If you make it to California I swear I'll hunt you down and kill you. Do you understand me?

Keseberg's eyes narrowed.

—*Ja* he said. I understand. You want me to stay here and die. I am not fit to live among you civilized men any more.

—You're already dead said Eddy. You died the first time you had a chance to get out of here and decided it was easier to stay.

—I could not walk said Keseberg. His voice was strangled now. I wounded my foot.

Foster summoned all his contempt.

—*Horseshit* Keseberg he said.

Thompson came in then from exploring the other cabins.

—Would you believe there's beef over at that other cabin? Must be two quarters stacked outside the door still frozen solid.

Eddy turned back to Keseberg.

—Why didn't you eat the beef Keseberg?

—It was buried in the snow. I didn't know it was there.

—You knowed it was there said Foster.

Keseberg glared at the men.

—There is more strength in human flesh than in beef and it is not so dry. I did not eat for pleasure. I ate to save my life. I fed these *kinder* too. And the woman.

Tamsen Donner had waited for Eddy outside. Knowing what he would find in the cabin she feared his reaction and when he climbed to the snow she immediately took his arm.

—I'm so very sorry what happened to your son she said. Eddy nodded but didn't speak and Tamsen feared his mood more than before. Mr. Eddy she said I have fifteen hundred dollars in silver and you may take it all if you—

—I wouldn't take a dollar of your silver Mrs. Donner he interrupted. I came here to relieve those as were left and that's what I mean to do. We'll carry your children out.

—Oh thank God said Tamsen thank God.

—You ought to go with us Mrs. Donner.

She shook her head.

—My duty is with my husband.

Eddy started. He had imagined George Donner was dead.

—Has his arm healed then?

—No Mr. Eddy. Mr. Donner hasn't long to live.

—Who's over there with him?

—Little Sammy Donner said Tamsen. Uncle Jacob's boy. And Jean Baptiste and Mr. Clark.

—Couldn't they see your husband through?

Tamsen started to say no when Thompson and Hiram Miller brought her girls up from the cabin. They had their coats on and their red and blue hoods and suddenly she wanted more than anything to go with them.

—If you could wait she said to Eddy. If I could only go back long enough to be sure of my husband's comfort.

It was Eddy's turn to look away.

—We can't wait. he said We've got to get back before another storm. We'd risk everything if we waited.

Tamsen dropped her hand from his arm and composed herself.

—I understand she said. You have suffered enough.

—It ain't that said Eddy.

—Whatever it is I understand the need. Take my girls and go and I will see what comes. With the men over there we ought to be able to work something out. But save my children.

Eddy left at noon carrying Georgia Donner. Hiram Miller had Eliza and Thompson carried Frances. If he couldn't bring his son Foster could at least bring his wife's little brother Simon. Before he left Foster talked to his mother-in-law. She seemed relieved that they were going. She told Foster that she had wanted to die many times but had hung on to see the children through. He tried to give her some jerky but she turned her face to the wall. He left the meat on her bed and told her goodbye and went out with the others. Keseberg stayed stubbornly behind.

Oakley and Stone had quickly moved ahead of John Starks and his 9 charges but losing their company didn't weaken Starks' resolve at all. He would carry 2 children forward half a mile on his back and then return for 2 more. He said they were so light he'd carry them all at once if there were room on his back. The Breens dragged the others on as best they could. They had a reason now. They knew that if they could reach Bear Valley before another storm their ordeal would be over. Over forever and to be forgotten as quickly as they could.

Eddy's party found Clark and Jean Baptiste camped at the head of the lake when they arrived there at the end of the day. He knew then what Mrs. Donner must also have discovered that afternoon. That George Donner was still alive and Sammy Donner with him and that she had signed her death warrant when she chose to go back to the camp by the creek. There was nothing for it. He had done all a man could do. She chose her fate.

Clark leaned against a pack of goods but unlike Eddy's men he carried a gun. Jean Baptiste had one too. Eddy felt like cursing them but he saw no reason why they shouldn't have tried to save their lives. Except that Clark could have carried Sammy Donner out as easily as he carried the pack of goods.

March 14

At the top of the pass Eddy stopped for the last time to look back. He could see a column of smoke rising from the Murphy cabin. Keseberg was still going about his business. Eddy wondered if the big German didn't have more strength than any of them. Even in his madness he was hanging on. Mrs. Murphy wouldn't last long. Nor George Donner nor the boy. The big question was Mrs. Donner. She was strong and healthy. She was even a little fat. Eddy wondered what she would do. Georgia stirred at his back and he felt the wind blowing through the pass and gave up wondering and turned and went on. He turned back once more as he was descending the slope on the other side but he'd gone too far. He could no longer see the white frozen lake or the screen of trees or the single line of smoke from the cabin but only the seamless blue sky.

Eddy's party caught up with Starks and the Breens in Yuba bottoms and within an hour of their meeting a new relief party arrived from the west. Woodworth was its reluctant leader. Glover, Coffeemeyer and Mootry had found him at Mule Springs and argued him into going for the Breens. Woodworth proceeded to make a point of telling Mrs. Breen that she could thank him for her safety. Peggy was her old self again. She spat at Woodworth's feet.

—Thank *you* she said wiping her mouth against her sleeve. I thank nobody but God and Starks and the Vargin Mary.

That was enough to collapse Woodworth. He heard Eddy's list of those remaining at the camps with impatience and refused to relieve them. He said he couldn't be responsible for those who chose to remain behind. No one argued with him. The snow had wrung them dry.

FOUR
VICTIMS

March 15

Keseberg was not yet alone. The old woman lay always on her bed and gave him no help. Her eyes followed him about the cabin in reproach. Even outside the cabin on the snow where he went to escape them they followed him. She watched him from the eyes of the dead that were opening now as the sun melted away the gravecover. She was dying and she reached over to the dead and animated them to keep vigil. Wherever eyes stared at him he approached stealthily and kicked snow over them to blind them again.

March 16

No man dare judge him. It was a thousand to one any other man would perish. A constitution of steel alone could endure what he endured. He was the most miserable of men, deserted, forsaken, hopeless. His misery should have sounded across the mountains and called forth a mighty expedition.

Responding to a craving he sawed off the top of Milt Elliott's head and scooped out the brains. They made good soup.

March 17

At night sometimes the old woman moaned. She reminded him of his mother who had been a consumptive. She had disapproved of his marriage. It was one reason he left Westphalia. She coughed blood but the coughing was not so terrible as the fitful way she breathed. The breathing was regular and then it was gasping even when the blood did not come. At any moment when she was gasping it had seemed to him his mother might die. He heard the gasping across the years and felt his own chest contract in time.

Eddy and Reed. Reed bathing him and Eddy threatening his life. The women knew him better. They bent away from him in fear and respect. *Der Aasgeier. Der Aasjäger.* Carrion-vulture and hunter of corpses. He had read once of a captain from Boston who met with an accident at sea. The captain from Boston saved his life by eating his dead comrades. He had shared their tragedies and hardships. He ate his comrades and shared their tragedies and hardships again. And passed them through and delivered them again to the sea. So the clock returns to 12 and again returns to 12. The captain from Boston suffered no loss of reputation and lived on peacefully in his captain's house by the sea. Men regarded him with a certain respect and women with a certain fascination. Americans were no better than other peoples. They jingled their huge land in their pockets but in the end it bought no more than other gold. These things scattered on the snow like nine-pins.

March 18

As he did each morning Keseberg went out to cut wood. The stumps of the trees the men at the lake camp had cut during the winter now stuck out high above the snow. Keseberg noticed a tree that someone had been too weak to cut down. It bore a hundred shallow wounds. He felled a small pine and began to chop it into logs but his ax glanced off and hacked his heel. He cursed and dropped the ax and collapsed on the wet snow. He worked off his moccasin.

The heel hung by a flap. It was a miracle he had not cut an artery. The wound was deep and the pain deep and dull. Dark blood welled over the flap and stained the snow. Holding his foot he wondered if he should bother to staunch the flow. His wife and his little girl Ada depended on him if they were still alive. They could not all have survived the crossing of the mountains. The very silence of the men who came over assured him of that. He worked the flap doubtfully and then pressed it back in place and set his heel into the snow. Blood soaked the snow and enlarged a circle of red around the heel but after a time the circle steadied. He took off his shirt and tore it into strips and tied up his foot. Then he stood and retrieved the ax and cut himself a crutch from the pine.

March 19

The old woman was unconscious. She had not eaten since the foreigners came. When she died he would be alone. He sat beside her waiting for the moment when the ghost would leave her body but after an hour when she showed no sign of going he got up and went out and limped to the Breen cabin. It was the best of the cabins. He would make it his home after the old woman died. It had beds and a real fireplace. He noticed the beef beside the door and made a face. He would never eat poor beef again. He cut wood and stacked it near the hearth and then dug in the trunks the Breens had left behind for goods to make up a bed.

March 20

He dreamed his mother's dying and woke in a sweat to the sound of the old woman's rattle. The cabin was dark except for the glow of the coals on the hearth. He hobbled there and blew the coals alive and lit a pine split and carried it to the old woman's bed. Her mouth opened and closed fitfully like a beached fish and then her body convulsed and her limbs shook as he had seen an epileptic shake once in the street and she went limp. A smell came up from the bed and he realized with disgust that in death she had befouled herself. He backed away and took up his crutch and left the cabin. A faint blue light glowed above the hills to the east. The air was still and cold and around him was absolute silence. Trees cut black lines into the sky where a few stars still stuck against the blued gray of the false dawn. He smelled the pungent smell of pine.

He returned inside and leaned his crutch against the door and moved to the old woman and threw off her quilt. He had eaten enough of carrion. He took her feet and backing up dragged the body off the bed onto the floor and then turned and put himself in harnass between her legs and panting heavily hauled her out the door and up onto the snow. The sky to the east was pink now and overhead the palest blue. He descended into the cabin again and found his saw and retrieved his crutch and climbed back out. Kneeling beside the body he broke the band that held the underdrawers and worked them off the hips and down and backed up and pulled them off the feet and dropped them in the snow. They were only slightly stained. Kneeling again he cut around the thigh of one leg to the bone. As he cut blood rushed from the wound and he leaned away to let it run out into the snow. It melted a hole in the snow and to avoid it he hauled on the feet and turned the body aside. When the blood had drained he kneeled again and finished cutting around the thigh. The grizzled sex hung beside his hand. He opened it with the point of his knife but the gesture made him shudder and he withdrew the knife and wiped it on the old woman's dress and put it away. Then he took up the saw and sawed through the bone until the leg was free. He dropped the saw beside the body and stood and picked up his crutch. He bent and grasped the severed leg by the ankle and straightened and set his crutch under his shoulder and limped off toward the Breen cabin dragging the leg.

When the water was hot he washed the leg. The old woman had a mole on the inside of her thigh and a birthmark at the back. The skin hung loose on the leg where the flesh below had wasted away. It was still better than carrion and with the leg washed he peeled back the skin and severed out the long muscle of the thigh and sliced it across and set it to boiling in the pot. It occurred to him that he should have caught the blood. It would have added salt. While the pot boiled he cleaned and charged his pipe. It was a meerschaum carved with the cheerful ruddy face of a *Bürgermeister*.

March 21

He awoke at night to the sound of scratching on the roof over his head and waited in terror. The scratching came again and he thought for a long moment that the dead were scratching at the cabin and then he understood that there were wolves outside. They were trying to get in to eat him and eat the dead bodies. He bolted out of bed and shouting and stumbling in the darkness he dragged a trunk in front of the door. The scratching ceased and he decided he had scared the wolves away but back in bed he slept no more. When it was light he loaded one of his guns and stealthily went out. He found the corpse of Gus Spitzer with the belly torn away.

March 22

The flesh of the dead would not support him forever. Starvation had taken the strength from it and eating it was like feeding straw to horses. Spring would bring back the birds and the wild game and perhaps he could improve himself to cross the mountains. The Californians would not return for him. They reviled him for his loathsome diet but left him no other choice. He ate what he must eat to live. If he died they would be respectful of him. In death they would say he was a brave man but in life his suffering reproached them for their indifference to his fate. Eddy would shoot him! Then let Eddy shoot! The man might as well shoot the Donner girls. They ate of Eddy's child as certainly and as willingly as he. The girl Eddy had carried out of the camp lived because she had eaten Eddy's child. *Der allmächtige Gott* had provided only the one horrible way to survive. It was on His shoulders that the burden fell.

March 23

A letter from Sheriff McKinstry, Selim Woodworth's superior on the committees of relief, arrived by courier at Johnson's ranch. McKinstry demanded that Woodworth outfit another expedition. Grudgingly Woodworth complied. He hired Bill Foster and young Bill Graves, John Starks, John Rhoads, Ned Coffeemeyer, John Sels and Dan Tucker. Bill Graves hoped to find the money his mother had buried at the head of the lake before she crossed the pass to her death. The relief rode out near the end of the day with a string of pack horses.

Tamsen Donner nursed her husband and Sammy Donner at the tent by the creek. Sammy was hardly alive and she cared for him as she might care for a baby. Her husband was as patient with death as he had been patient with life. The infection consumed his arm to the shoulder but during the hours when he was lucid they talked of their years together and of their children and Tamsen read to him from the Bible. She agreed that when his ordeal was ended she would attempt to reach California. To him it was a magic word. Living off the dead Tamsen discovered that she was gaining weight. Her dresses no longer fit and to clothe herself she found Aunt Betsy's dresses and cut them down.

March 24

Woodworth's relief made Bear Valley. It was nearly free of snow but beyond the valley the snow was still too soft and deep for horses. Woodworth had no stomach for packing and none of the others proposed to pack in unsalaried and alone. George Donner and the boy were surely dead by now. Mrs. Donner had chosen her fate when she turned aside from the last relief. Keseberg could have brought himself out long ago if he had a mind to. There was always the possibility of another storm. The men camped for the night and prepared to return to the settlements in the morning.

March 25

Life was a burden. Minute succeeded to minute without sound and hour succeeded to hour without speech. Against the silence Keseberg organized his day. Upon arising in the morning he built up the fire. When he was warm he steeled himself to go out among the corpses and collect from them his breakfast. He favored the internal organs that seemed to contain some special strength. With breakfast done he smoked his pipe and then limped to the grove of pines beyond the cabin to cut his daily supply of wood. The work occupied the morning and at noon he returned to the cabin and ate from the breakfast pot. Afternoons he slept or searched among the other cabins or the wagons. He cut his supper from the limbs of the dead and made a stew. Through the evening he brooded by the fire and went early to bed. But it was impossible to keep his schedule. Cutting wood he would find the ax faltering and lean against a tree and stare at the axhead until his eyes blurred. No thoughts came at such times but only a blankness. His sleep in the afternoons and at night was troubled and sometimes he would wake in terror so intense that only by drawing himself together with his arms around his knees could he contain it. He felt in the midst of his terror that he had done something for which he could never atone. The mark was on him and it would follow him down all the years of his life. There was an instinct in human nature that revolted at the thought of touching, much less eating, a corpse. He had violated that instinct. It was the burden he would forever bear. Keseberg the cannibal. Christ Himself suffered no more.

March 26

Faust was such a man as he, freighted with unspeakable knowledge. To know another human being, to know his country and his name. To hear his opinions gravely spoken across a fire after a good supper. To see him at work and measure his skill with his hands or with his mind. But to find him sprawled in death in the snow. To disassemble him like an ox or a pig. To uncork his head and remove the very stuff of his soul! In the blackened pot boiled thoughts and memories. Names of children never to be born. Congealed desires. Speeches and proverbs and the intimate sense within each man of the body itself. Of its metamorphoses from infancy to manhood. It was knowledge such as only the Devil could use.

March 27

Among the dead he could select the qualities of life. The Murphy woman was good with children. She had lived until the last child was gone from her and then had turned off her life as an innkeeper might turn off the spigot on a barrel of nourishing beer. The Reeds' idiot herdsman had a way with cattle and could see at night. Eddy's wife was young and *schön* with a wide pelvis that could comfort a man and a gentle narrow back. Spitzer was only a brute but brutality was an essence too. The babies had their innocence that they wore as a maiden wears pearls. A stew of each would strengthen the King of the Forgotten Dead. *Der König des vergessenen Toten.*

March 28

He brought the muzzle of his pistol to his mouth and crooked his finger on the trigger but the faces of his wife and child rose up before him and stayed his hand. They were penniless and friendless in a strange land and without him how would they live?

March 29

When he pissed he pissed the discontinued lives of the dead and when he shat he shat the discontinued lives of the dead. He would carry them with him down to the end of his own life. Secretly he would live for them and when he was reviled they would be reviled also. Men hated the dead and those who had truck with the dead. The dead were *momento mori* that flung their hopes back in their faces. That was why they sent no relief to him. That was why the mountains bent to close him in.

March 30

He cracked a marrowbone and spooned the buttery marrow with a baby spoon the Breens had left behind.

March 31

He was born under an evil star. Among all men on the face of the earth the Almighty God had singled him out to show how much misery a man might bear. He dreamed of trolls and saw in the most monstrous of them the delineation of his own features.

April 1

Chopping wood and chopping wood. The Master of Axes could choose among 5. He kept them in the cabin standing in a row and sharpened them with a whetstone on which were carved the initials J.F.R. The Master of Watches had 3 laid out on the table by the hearth. He set them together but they had schemes of their own and stealthily slipped apart. They lied about time. Time was inexorable. On the bed opposite his own the King of the Forgotten Dead laid out chinaware flowered in red and blue and purple. Glass tumblers and vials. Arrowheads. A bridle bit. A cooper's inshave and a row of metal buttons. But the King was poor. He found no gold. In his pot swam loathsome things that made his belly groan.

[349]

April 2

If men loved him they would come and kill him. He had gone up at night to the wolves but they fled before him on the snow.

April 3

The *Dreck* grew into trees and into men and when they had fulfilled themselves or even before they rotted down into *Dreck* again. He would welcome honest rot. The snow preserved the dead as if they were alive. They gazed at him through glazed and staring eyes and never blinked. Men said the Devil winked at you. It was God who stared. He covered their heads with snow but the snow melted away in the sun. Frantically he went from corpse to corpse turning them over. Let them stare into the earth and see where they would go!

April 4

He had foreseen the danger that first time they halted before the pass. Had he been well and able to push ahead he would have led them to safety. Later he had given Reed's children a portion of the flour Stanton had brought over from Sutter's Fort. His care saved the lives of his wife and daughter and the wood he cut spared the Donner girls. They owed him much. He should claim a reasonable recompense for his work. They could never repay his suffering. They should have come for him long ago. They had come for women and babies and he was an educated man who had much to offer California. He was conversant with 4 different languages and spoke and wrote them with equal fluency. He knew German and Spanish and English and French. He could ride a horse as well as a riding master and keep books better than any clerk. He understood the principles of frugal management and of effective correspondence. He was a master of men. Under his direction they produced the finest work.

April 5

He was growing stronger and with his strength his manhood stirred. Phillipine had breasts like melons. They were deep and full. Her body had challenged him. It was one of the reasons he had married her despite her Catholicism. Her passion had weakened when the children began to come. She was cowardly before the pain of childbirth. He had beaten her for her refusal to submit and after awhile she refused no more. The Devil coupled with beasts and with the dead. He selected them for their silence. They were mute and could tell no one of the unspeakable things He did. But the beasts were terrified and the dead were cold. It was evil to think of such things. The living for the living and the dead for the dead. But what for the King who dwells between?

April 6

The grim consumptive arms surrounded him and the dead breath blew. He would have his revenge. He would have his revenge. The man in the mirror had a madman's eyes. The man in the mirror put a pistol to his mouth and sucked it like a teat. *Lewis! Lewis! Verlasst mich nicht! Lass mich nicht allein! Ich liebe dich!*

April 7

Kings do not murder themselves for self-murder destroys the body of the State and the body of Nature which are in their Kingship reflected. The history of nations was no more than the sum of the histories of noble men. The laws men made were parsings of the decisions of heroes. Fate was large and overbearing but there was room in her corners for heroic motions of freedom. A man could put his left foot before his right or his right before his left. He could turn a little this way or a little that. The shift of his weight shifted ever so slightly the motion of the earth and communicated his decision out to the Firmament. The boy

Baylis's organs were reversed as in a mirror. His heart was on his right side and his liver on his left. Who could imagine such a miracle? *Der Aasgeier* could imagine it. He was in charge of such miracles. They fell within his province just as in some provinces grapes are grown and in other provinces barley. If a man would put his foot down the whole earth would shake. But the stamping of feet would only settle the grains of earth and raise the mountains higher. There was a crack in everything God had made and it drained off compassion as water drains into a hole.

April 8

In the tent by the creek Sammy Donner died and Tamsen returned from burying the shrouded body in the snow to find her husband weeping.

April 9

One death led to another. It was a truth Tamsen had known since she met Death in North Carolina long ago. Her husband was restless in the morning. She sat with him. The arm stank but she was used to the smell of the arm. He told her again to go to the children and called her Mother. He looked into her eyes with the eyes of a frightened child and she met his look with calm and his awareness went away. He was unconscious through the afternoon and died at sunset without waking. His strong body was weakened but it had not withered away. With warm water she washed her husband. From the family chest she took her best linen and worked it beneath his body so that the lines from opposite corners would form a cross that sprang from his heart. One corner she brought over and tucked beneath his body and the other she brought over and folded under and pinned above his chest. The corner above his head she folded over his face and pinned with the same pin and then she brought the lower corner over his feet and pinned it at his shins. It was finished then and she thought that it had not been an ordeal. It had released her and she could go. She made up a small pack and a blanket roll and put on her coat and scattered the fire and left.

—Mr. Keseberg! Mr. Keseberg!

Keseberg started up.

—*Ja* who is that?

—It's Tamsen Donner!

He rushed to the door and threw back the flap and she stumbled into the cabin. He grabbed her to hold her up. Her clothes were wet. She was cold as ice.

—I fell into the creek coming over. Can you build me a fire?

—*Ja* I build a fire said Keseberg. I build a fire. He turned and blew up the coals while she collapsed onto the hearth.

—Oh thank God she said. I didn't know if I would find you alive.

—I am alive said Keseberg. The King lives. He looked at her. You must remove those wet clothes. There are more here. You will freeze to death. The fire flared up. Here said Keseberg I get you a blanket.

He pulled one of the blankets off his bed and held it up to her as she took off her coat. She was shivering but he saw that the body beneath the dress was not starved. So she had fed herself well just as he had done. She was strong like him in that. With her coat off she wrapped the blanket around her shoulders. He sat on the hearth and busied himself at the fire and she undressed beneath the blanket.

—Where are the clothes? she asked.

—Here I get them for you. He went to the trunk and opened it and pulled out a dress. Here is something.

She took it and turned away from him and stepped into the dress. It was much too large for her and she easily pulled it up and buttoned it. She kept the blanket over her shoulders and sat on the hearth. Her feet were bare and Keseberg noticed her fine small ankles.

—It is so good to hear a human voice said Keseberg.

She searched his face.

—My husband died today Mr. Keseberg.

—I am sorry.

—He suffered so long that I think it was a relief to him to go.

—*Ja.* I heard about his hand. So there are two of us now. It will be good to have company. I have been lonely here among the dead.

—I must go to my children.

—You will not stay and wait with me for relief? It is madness to go over the mountains alone.

—I *must* see my children. said Tamsen fiercely. They are all I have left in the world.

—But Mrs. Donner if strong men cannot cross the mountains to relieve us you should not think of crossing alone. There have been wolves at night.

—I must see my children.

—Very well then said Keseberg you must see your children.

—I know I may not survive.

—And you know you may not survive.

She looked at him curiously.

—Please do not repeat my words Mr. Keseberg. Listen to me now. I have a good deal of money at my tent. Far too much for me to carry. I would like you to take it to my children when you leave here.

—*Ja* said Keseberg and where will I find this money?

—It is hidden in the bottom of the trunk at the head of my husband's bed.

—I am to be your hero then.

—I don't understand.

—You wish me to carry over your money.

—Yes. And give it to me. Or in case I don't survive the crossing to my oldest daughter Elitha. Of course you must keep some portion for yourself.

—Of course said Keseberg. But that is not necessary. I have money of my own. And when do you propose to leave me?

—I'm terribly tired said Tamsen. Would I impose on you if I stayed here for the rest of the night?

Keseberg grinned.

—Not at all Mrs. Donner. May I offer you some food?

Tamsen's eyes widened.

—Have you—?

—No Mrs. Donner I have only what we all have had.

—Then I want nothing.

—You are too good to eat the dead?

—I am not too good. I have eaten what I must eat but the snow uncovered some of our beef and I have lived on that these past few days. There is some in my pack. It will suffice me.

—*Ja* said Keseberg. Then shall we go to bed? He stood up. Please take my bed. I will sleep beside the fire.

—That isn't necessary said Tamsen. I'd be glad to sleep in any of the beds.

—They are lousy. Mine is clean.

—All right said Tamsen. I'm sure you know how much I appreciate your kindness.

—*Ja* said Keseberg. You are a fine woman.

Tamsen got into bed and Keseberg pulled his quilt and blankets over her and returned to the fire. He stared into the flames. They ate away at the logs as if they were seeking some corruption and the smoke blackened the stones at the back of the chimney. After awhile the woman's breathing became regular. She had fallen asleep. She had come to him not to bear him company but only to use his house and go on. The girls had no need of her. They were among crowds of people at the fort across the mountains and he was alone. His urgency stirred him and he got up and moved to the bed and stood above the woman. Her fine face was composed in sleep. He had never seen anyone more beautiful.

Abruptly he threw back the covers and fell on her and she woke up screaming.

—Oh my God! Oh my God!

He tore her dress away. The flesh was warm but she was screaming at him!

—*Halt's Maul!* he shouted. *Halt's Maul!* Shut up! Shut up! She kept on screaming and he lashed his fist across her face and rammed his knee into her belly and she moaned and stopped struggling and he ripped open his trousers and forced her legs apart and pushed himself into her and all that had locked within him broke apart with a shattering of ice broken against rock. She would not leave him alone! She would not leave him alone! He lurched from the bed and grabbed the single-headed ax from its place by the door and turned and she was screaming and he raised the ax high and her body flashed before him and he swung the hammer of the ax down and she stopped screaming and lay still. He dropped the ax and fell on her again and he was weeping and she was warm. He pulled the covers up over their heads. The shape of the hammer was on her forehead. The King's anointment. He ran his hands over her body and after awhile still weeping he lay over her and took her again.

April 10
Mein Gott Mein Gott Mein Gott Mein Gott Mein Gott Mein Gott Mein Gott Mein Gott Mein Gott Mein Gott Mein Gott Mein Gott Mein Gott Mein Gott lass mich nicht allein!

April 11
He filled 2 kettles with her blood and from her belly he extracted a thick layer of fat. He cut off her head and looking carefully around him across the snow he carried it to the Graves cabin and dug up the cabin floor and buried it there. Her flesh was succulent. It was the best he had tasted in months. She had left him her gold and silver and the body of her husband would not be old as the bodies of the dead around him were. She should have welcomed him instead of threatening to leave him alone as if she too reviled him. No one could revile him when he carried the unfinished lives of the dead within his body as a woman carries a child. He was heavy with the weight of their lives. He had a sacred duty as certainly as any knight. He would live for them. They would never tell.

[356]

He had held her womb in his hand. It was shaped like a pear and it contained his seed. He had buried it also in a secret place. When the world was old and the races of men had perished of corruption it would sprout and grow. It would make such a race as no man had dared to dream of.

April 12

She hissed at him to go. She was one of the dead he carried within him now. He dressed to go and passing the spring on the hillside he saw green grass. He was most of the day crossing to the Donner camp. Wild geese sometimes flew by high overhead. A few patches of sodden ground were clear of snow. He would not forever be locked into the fastness of the mountains.

At George Donner's tent he found the body and unwrapping the shroud he looked upon the face of the man who had given his name to their journey west. Indecision and cowardice came to this. A face of wax above a mutilated arm. 3 ox legs lay across the arms of a chair near the door of the tent. The woman had cut a chunk of meat off one of them. He built a fire on the hearth but instead of the beef he turned to the corpse. He had tasted the wife and now he would taste the husband. He found a saw. It had seen such duty before. The evidence lay scattered about the camp. He sawed off the top of the skull with satisfaction.

April 13

A new expedition left Johnson's ranch early in the evening. Its captain was a man named Thomas Fallon. He was an Irishman and a mountain man and he carried in his pocket a letter from the *alcalde* authorizing his party to salvage such goods as they could find and keep a portion of the receipts. With him rode Coffeemeyer, Sels, Dan Tucker, John Rhoads, Bill Foster, a settler from Johnson's named Keyser and 2 Indians. Captain Fallon was a worthy leader for a buzzard's expedition. Men called him Le Gros. He fought with Fremont but before and after that commission he fought with whoever crossed him. His expedition proceeded easily along the Bear. Only Keseberg and Mrs. Donner might still survive at the mountain camp.

April 14

Keseberg found the silver in the trunk but suspected there might be more. He worked through the day digging among the goods the Donners had hauled in their wagons. Some of the packs had been spread out on fallen trees by an earlier relief but much had been left in the wagons. Bales and bundles of dry-goods. Tobacco and shoes and powder. Silks, calicos, delaines. The woman's journal! Keseberg read it avidly but the last entry directed her to his cabin and he carried it to the fire and page by page burned the record away.

April 15

Fallon's expedition arrived on horseback in Bear Valley. The snow had retreated to the head of the valley. The party camped there and sent the horses back by the Indians. They would pack into the mountains over the firm snow.

April 16

Hidden in one of the wagons Keseberg found another $200 in gold and a box of jewelry and a brace of fine pistols. He could not carry out so much coin. He circled the Donner tent and noticed a pine and near it another pine with a branch pointing to the base of the first. He got a shovel and the silver from the tent and dug a hole at the place where the branch pointed and buried the silver there. He wrapped the jewelry in a bolt of silk and discarded the box. The bolt would make a pack. He stuffed the gold into his waistcoat and the pistols into his belt. If he carried out all the goods left at the camp it would not be sufficient recompense.

April 17

Fallon's party reached the lake cabins and even Le Gros, sweating from the exertion of the hike, was struck dumb.

He had seen massacres of Indians and of white men but he had never seen such mutilation. A young woman's body with the limbs sawed off and an ax slash across the head. An old woman missing a leg, a saw lying beside the body in the snow. The bodies of babies with the livers and lights drawn out. The men in the earlier reliefs had come upon the dead unexpectedly and couldn't compass what they saw. Fallon and his men were ready for horror and took its full measure.

A shout and they raced from the cabins to see 3 Indians running away. They must have hidden themselves when the men came up. They left behind their bows and arrows.

The men searched the cabins for 2 hours looking for goods and finding only the mutilated dead and then they left for the Donner camp. Halfway there they found the trail of a man wearing shoes. It led them to the Donner tent where they found a fresh trail heading back to the lake. In the tent they discovered George Donner's hacked body and a kettle of his flesh and the ox legs almost untouched. They made camp and began examining the Donners' goods.

Keseberg had left the Donner camp early in the afternoon with his pack of silks and jewelry. He missed the trail and wandered lost until after dark when he broke through a snowbridge into a creek. The cold night air froze his clothes to his body and it was late when he staggered into the lake camp and found the Breen cabin. In the darkness he flopped into bed and rolled himself in his quilts. Slowly he warmed and finally slept.

April 18

Someone had visited the cabins. His goods were thrown everywhere. Phillipine's jewelry, his cloak, his pistol and ammunition were missing. It must have been the Indians. He loaded and primed George Donner's pistols and stuck them into his belt before going out to search among the corpses.

Fallon's men gathered the most valuable Donner property and spread it to dry in the sun. The fresh trail toward the lake camp intrigued them. Had the man deliberately avoided them? It didn't make sense unless it was a stranger come to loot.

April 19

Dan Tucker, John Rhoads and Bill Foster made up light packs and set out for the lake following the trail but lost it in the melting snow and struck directly for the cabins.

Keseberg lay brooding on his bed among the bones. He started up when the men came into the cabin. He hadn't heard them coming. They saw a pan beside the hearth with a liver in it. He'd been at work even as they camped at the Donners.

—*Ach* said Keseberg. You have come for me at last.

Foster grimaced.

—Was you the only one left alive?

—Where's Mrs. Donner? said Tucker.

—Dead said Keseberg they are all dead.

—Well how's come Mrs. Donner is dead? said Foster. She looked right well when I saw her last.

Keseberg's eyes darted from face to face.

—It is a long story he said. She died here in this cabin.

—I just bet she did said Tucker.

—When Herr Donner died she crossed over to here. She was wet and cold. I think she got into the creek in coming. She was wild, crazy. She kept saying *My children I must see my children*. She lay down and in the morning she was dead. It was hunger or the suffering of her mind or the chill she took in the creek. It killed her.

—Where's her body? said Rhoads.

Keseberg looked away.

—I eat it. He turned back to them and his face was twisted. It was the best I ever taste! I took four pounds of fat from it!

—Jesus H. Christ said Foster.

Rhoads noticed then the kettles of blood. The blood had clotted to a drying purple mass.

—Where'd you get that blood? he asked Keseberg.

Keseberg studied the kettles.

—There is blood in dead bodies he said.

Tucker spoke softly.

—And what'd you do with the Donners' money?

Keseberg stood up then and faced them. So that was why they had come. Not for him but for the money and the goods. They were scavengers.

—I haven't the money.

—But you was over to the Donners day before yesterday said Tucker.

—*Ja* said Keseberg hurriedly. I look for it. She made me promise sacredly that I would get the money and take it to her children if she didn't live. I look for it. She must have hidden it before she left.

Foster had walked past Keseberg as he talked. He found the pack with the bolt of silk and flung it open.

—What's that then you son-of-a-bitch? What's that god-damned silk? Look here! There's jewelry too!

Rhoads and Tucker rushed Keseberg. They had him by the arms before he knew what was going on.

—Leave me alone! he shouted.

—Shut up! barked Tucker. He pulled the pistols from Keseberg's belt. Rhoads patted Keseberg's waistcoat and felt the gold and dug into the pockets and pulled a handful out.

—You didn't find it did you said Foster. Jesus what a filthy lying bastard you are. Where's the rest of it.

—I have no *rest of it* said Keseberg. That is money that belongs to my wife. The silk and jewelry also.

Foster pushed him onto the bed.

—Listen you bastard he said. We're helpin you out. We don't do no more than talk sense. There's people over at the other camp that wouldn't think a damned thing of hangin you up on one of those pines out there. They'd just as soon see you dead as look at you.

—I have no other money said Keseberg.

—Shit said Foster. He winked at Rhoads. You're a good man John he said. You tell this bastard how things are.

—Keseberg said Rhoads. If you'll tell us the truth we'll do our best to keep Fallon Le Gros away from you. He's killed a lot of men in his time. He'd kill you and not even spit. He don't much like what you been doin up here.

—I have no other money said Keseberg. I swear before God I am innocent.

Foster shook his head.

—You sure don't give a goddamned about your neck do you.

Tucker looked disgusted.

—Let's get out of here. We know what we need to know. He turned to Keseberg. We're going to leave our packs right here and we expect to find them here when we get back.

—I am no thief said Keseberg sullenly. Whatever you think.

Foster roared.

—Hell no you ain't no thief. You're a goddamned angel of mercy.

April 20

With 100-pound packs on their backs Fallon and his men left the Donner camp for the lake. Before he left Foster wrapped George Donner's body into its shroud. They made no attempt to bury the other remains. The last thing they noticed as they left the camp was the body of a horse that had emerged from the snow. Keseberg must have seen it too and passed it by. Fallon hated the man before he even met him. How could anyone eat the dead when there was animal flesh nearby? It was foul and monstrous.

They neared the Breen cabin and Fallon called a halt. Keseberg must have heard them coming. He could sit in the cabin and fret while they cooked up some breakfast. Fallon would just as soon settle his belly before he had to look at the things scattered on the snow.

After breakfast they left their packs beside their campfire and Fallon led the way into the cabin. He was a huge man. Swarthy with a full black beard and hair down to his shoulders like an Indian. Keseberg sat at the table eating from a pot. He followed Fallon with his eyes until the man stood over him.

—You ready to tell us where the money's hid?

Keseberg paled.

—I have no money. You have taken my money.

—Why goddamn you Keseberg you know where Donner's money is and by god you'll tell me! I ain't goin to multiply words with you. Here. Foster. Bring me that rope.

Keseberg pushed up from the table and backed toward the hearth.

—I have no money he said. Those things belong to people in California. The silk and the jewelry and the gold.

Fallon advanced on him with the rope in his hands.

—You tell me *now* where the money's hid or I'll have your filthy neck.

—*Nein!* yelled Keseberg.

Fallon was on him and bent the rope around his neck. Keseberg struggled to pull it off but Fallon threw him to the floor and began choking him. His face turned red.

—I tell! I tell!

Fallon dropped the rope and stood back. Keseberg climbed to his feet rubbing his neck.

—The money! shouted Fallon.

Keseberg stared at him sullenly until he made a move to pick up the rope.

—*Ja* said Keseberg. The money. It is buried under a tree.

—Where? said Fallon.

—At the Donner camp. It belongs to the Donner children.

—Shit said Fallon I know who it belongs to. It sure as shit don't belong to you. Dan, John, take this bastard over to Donners and dig up that cash. We'll wait for you here.

Tucker and Rhoads set out with Keseberg. Fallon and the others moved the packs up the trail to the lake and came back to the camp outside the cabin and settled in for the day. Foster went to the Murphy cabin to collect a few family effects and found John Landrum's body freshly opened and the liver taken out. He had stood in the cabin and watched Keseberg eating his wife's little brother. The thought made him sick.

Tucker and Rhoads brought Keseberg back to the lake camp in the afternoon with $273 in silver. They had been curious about the horse and the ox legs. They asked Keseberg why he didn't eat them and told Fallon what he answered.

—I couldn't believe it Tucker said. He looked at us like we was crazy. He said it was too dry eating. He said human liver and lights was a deal better and the brains made good soup.

Keseberg ate his meal in the cabin before the men came for him. They stood in the door while he packed his few belongings and then he gathered the bones of the dead into a box and blessed them. He had a duty to them that no scavenger would ever know.

—God will forgive me for what I have done he said. I could not help what I have done. I shall go to Heaven yet.

Tucker turned away. Finally he felt pity for the man. He'd wondered when it would come. After the days he'd spent with Fallon he'd feared it wouldn't come at all.

Fallon moved his party up the lake for the night with Keseberg following behind.

April 21

The last relief started for Bear Valley. The men paid no attention to Keseberg. He could get along as best he might. Most of them wouldn't have been sorry if he died along the way. He was too weak to keep up with them but by nightfall he found his way into camp. They would have distanced him but the heavy packs slowed them down. There were more packs than men and they progressed by carrying one pack forward and returning for the next. They still managed to hike well into the summit valley.

April 22

Alone on the snow Keseberg stopped at an old campfire. The bluffs of Yuba bottoms rose up to the south. Logs lay charred on the snow. The day was sunny and cloudless and blue. Tucker had given him some coffee and he built a fire over the old campfire and scooped up snow in his coffeepot. Waiting for the water to heat he studied the bluffs. The snow still covered them. They faced away from the sun and he imagined they were white with snow even in summer. Even when the grass grew up in the valleys and bottoms the snow still clung to the rocks of the mountains. He would always know the snow for a warning. Snow would always remind him of the mountain camp and the days and nights of horror he had lived there. No one on earth had ever suffered more than he. It was best now to forget. It was best to bury that part of his life. He had come to California to begin a new life. Now he must begin that life with a vengeance. He noticed a piece of calico sticking from the snow. It lay within reach of his hand and waiting for the water to boil in his coffeepot he began to play with it. It could not be a kerchief. He gave it a tug and the snow loosened around it. It was larger than he had thought. He saw the pattern of the calico then and something broke loose in him and he stood and with both hands jerked on the calico and the frozen body of his daughter Ada sprang forth from the snow into his arms.

FIVE

AFTERWARD

Edwin Bryant wrote When the return party of Gen. Kearny reached the scene of these horrible and tragical occurences, on the 22d of June, 1847, a halt was ordered, for the purpose of collecting and interring the remains. Near the principal cabins, I saw two bodies, entire with the exception that the abdomens had been cut open and the entrails extracted. Their flesh had been either wasted by famine or evaporated by exposure to the dry atmosphere, and they presented the appearance of mummies. Strewn around the cabins were dislocated and broken bones—skulls, (in some instances sawed asunder with care for the purpose of extracting the brains,)—human skeletons, in short, in every variety of mutilation. A more revolting and appalling spectacle I never witnessed. The remains were, by order of Gen. Kearny, collected and buried under the superintendence of Major Swords. They were interred in a pit which had been dug in the center of one of the cabins for a *cache*. These melancholy duties to the dead being performed, the cabins, by order of Major Swords, were fired, and with every thing surrounding them connected with this horrid and melancholy tragedy, were consumed. The body of George Donner was found at his

[369]

camp, about eight or ten miles distant, wrapped in a sheet. He was buried by a party of men detailed for that purpose.

From a ranch in the Napa Valley Virginia Reed wrote We are all very well pleased with Callifornia particulary with the climate let it be ever so hot a day thare is allwais cool nights it is a beautiful Country it is mostley in vallies it aut to be a beautiful Country to pay us for our trubel geting there

Lake of the Forest
April 1970–September 1972